THE COMPLETE
ENCYCLOPEDIA OF
ROSES

THE COMPLETE
ENCYCLOPEDIA OF
ROSES

Informative text with over 1,000 color photographs

NICO VERMEULEN

REBO
PUBLISHERS

© 1998 Rebo International b.v., Lisse, The Netherlands

This 2nd edition reprinted 2004

Text: Nico Vermeulen
Production: TextCase, Groningen, The Netherlands
Redaction: Renate Hagenouw (for TextCase)
Cover design: Minkowsky Graphics, Enkhuizen, The Netherlands
Graphics: Studio Imago, Amersfoort, The Netherlands

ISBN 90 366 1513 5

Contents

Foreword

Every book on roses can only really be regarded as a snapshot in time. The wide assortment of roses changes so rapidly that by the time an author has completed his or her book, new varieties of roses have already appeared on the market. Generally speaking, we can say that half of the roses that figure in the average book of fifteen years ago are no longer available. Better roses have replaced them. What's more, such books were compiled from texts placed alongside archive photos that are therefore older than the descriptions given.

The basic principle behind the Illustrated Encyclopedia of Roses was therefore to be as up to date as possible with the roses that were to be included. And we have succeeded in this. First of all, there are the roses that have proven their worth throughout the years and that are still very much in demand. Secondly, the book features newer roses that have been tested and approved in numerous rose gardens. And finally, leading rose breeders have helped us with information regarding their newest and most promising introductions.

A second principle was that as many as possible roses included in this encyclopedia should also actually be available. Particularly because of the international character of the Illustrated Encyclopedia of Roses, not all the roses included in this book will be available in every country where the book is sold. However, we have tried to come as close as possible to our ideal, namely an encyclopedia you can leaf through and read to find the most suitable roses for your garden.

The over one thousand color photos first give you an idea of their beauty, after which you can read the descriptions to determine whether the particular rose bush is suitable for the purpose you have in mind. As this encyclopedia is intended for the average plant enthusiast, we have kept technical terms to a minimum. However, when such terms do appear, if necessary you can refer to the Explanation of terms on page 15.

The Illustrated Encyclopedia of Roses is, in brief, a very practical reference book for anyone who wants to know more about the 'queen of flowers' and how to get the most of it in the garden.

Nico Vermeulen

1 Explanation of symbols

In this encyclopedia we have placed various symbols below the descriptions of each rose. These give a clear and immediate overview of all the important characteristics.

But what do these symbols actually mean? And what about the names and figures above each description? An example is given below.

Rosa Bingo Meidiland®

(MEIpotal) Meilland (1994)

This rose has a striking combination of brightly colored buds and soft pink flowers. The buds open to reveal single flowers with a white heart and yellow stamens. The shrub branches profusely to about chest height. The dark green, glossy foliage remains attractive the whole summer, as Bingo Meidiland® is very resistant to black spot and mildew.

@ 80h ♀♀♀ ∽ ✚ ADR TOP

Each description begins with the trade name (in the above example, Bingo Meidiland®), followed by the patent name (here MEIpotal), the name of the breeder (Meilland) and the year of introduction, respectively.

TRADE NAME

This is the name used by the suppliers. In this encyclopedia we have tried as much as possible to use the name originally given by the breeder. Different countries often use other names for the same rose. These have been included as synonyms and refer to the original name.

PATENT NAME

The patent name is the name by which a rose is officially registered. This name can be important, also for private gardeners, as different roses may sometimes be on the market with the same trade name. The first three letters usually refer to the person who bred the rose. An official cultivar name should start and end with single quotation marks. We have not done this in this encyclopedia, as it is not always clear what the official name is. Sometimes it is the trade name, in other cases the patent name. If instead of a patent name there is a dash, this means that there is no patent name or that the patent name is the same as the trade name.

BREEDER

This is the name of the breeder. It can also be a company name as sometimes there are more people responsible for cultivating new roses.

INTRODUCTION YEAR

The year given is the year in which the rose was introduced on the market. The Illustrated Encyclopedia of Roses has used information provided by the companies as much as possible. If not available, the year of registration was used (which is nearly always close to the year of introduction).

Below the description example we see the symbols @ 80h ♀♀♀ ∽ ✚ ADR TOP. You should read this as rose group (@), height (80h), flowering period (♀♀♀), fragrance (∽), resistance (✚), ADR- award and top rose (TOP), respectively.

ROSE GROUP

The first symbol refers to the group to which the rose belongs. Those who are familiar with the groups will know roughly what the rose should look like. And the rose enthusiast would then also know how the rose should be pruned. You can read more about this in the chapter Rose Care. See also later in this chapter Detailed explanation of the symbols and their meaning.

HEIGHT

This figure gives the average height in inches. Various factors affect the final height of a rose, such as type of soil, nutritional condition of the soil, protection from wind and pruning method.

FLOWERING PERIOD

This symbol indicates the flowering period. Some roses produce a single flush of blooms per year, some in intervals (repeat or remontant varieties) while others bloom throughout the summer. See also Detailed explanation of the symbols and their meaning.

FRAGRANCE

Evaluating the fragrance is quite difficult. For a start people's ability to smell varies. What's more, the fragrance of roses changes throughout the day and the intensity varies according to the weather. Even the composition of the components can change, so that the impression of the perfume can differ from one moment to the next. See also Detailed explanation of the symbols and their meaning.

RESISTANCE

This symbol indicates that the rose is not very susceptible to fungal diseases such as mildew, rust and black spot. This symbol is only given if the rose is shown to be and remain healthy during tests. As the information concerning resistance is by no means complete, this does not mean that a rose without this symbol will easily succumb to these diseases.

ADR

The ADR award is granted by the German Allgemeine Deutsche Rosenneuheitenprüfung. In view of its strict requirements, great value is attached to this award. The roses are tested at a minimum of ten locations in Germany without the use of chemical pesticides. ADR roses are therefore nearly always healthy. Not all companies, however, submit their roses to testing.

TOP ROSE

Top roses are the most highly valued roses from tests in the Netherlands. Test locations where no chemical pesticides are used have recently been included in the tests, making some top roses appear more susceptible to disease.

Explanation of the symbols

⊛	= botanical rose/wild rose
◉	= old rose
✿	= large-flowered rose / Hybrid Tea
✿✿	= floribunda /cluster-flowered rose
⚘GB	= English rose
▣	= patio rose, including miniature rose
⊕	= park or shrub rose
↔	= ground cover rose
⌇	= climber
_h	= figure in INCHES representing the average height
⚘	= once-flowering
⚘⚘	= repeat / remontant
⚘⚘⚘	= continuous-flowering
⌒	= no fragrance or hardly noticeable
⌒⌒	= slightly fragrant
⌒⌒⌒	= fragrant
⌒⌒⌒⌒	= very fragrant
✛	= resistant rose
ADR	= rose that has received the German ADR award
TOP	= rose that has received the Dutch top rose award

Detailed explanation of the symbols and their meaning

Symbol ⊛: botanical roses. A botanical or wild rose exists as a wild plant in nature. The wild roses form the basis of all cultivated roses.

Rosa glauca, a botanical rose

Rosa canina (dog rose), a botanical rose

Rosa Primaballerina®, a large-flowered rose

Symbol ◉: old roses. An old rose or historical rose is one of the oldest groups of cultivated roses. They flower once or twice per season. During their development the continuous bloomers of China had not yet been involved. See also 'modern roses' in the Explanation of terms.

Rosa Ghislaine de Féligonde, an old rose

Rosa Rouge Meidiland®, a large-flowered rose

Symbol ✿: large-flowered roses. The large-flowered roses used to be called Hybrid Teas. They are derived from crossing the continuous-flowering Chinese tea roses with other groups. Originally there was usually a single large, well-formed flower on each stem. These days, as crosses have been made with roses from a diverse variety of groups, the typical characteristics have slowly been lost, and the large-flowered roses seem to increasingly bloom in trusses (clusters).

Symbool ✿✿: floribunda. Floribunda roses derive from crossings between polyantha roses and large-flowered roses. The first floribunda rose, Rosa Rödhätte, was introduced by Dines Poulsen in 1912. The bush carries clusters with flowers at the end of the stalks.

Symbol ♥GB: English roses. The English breeder David Austin crossed old roses with modern roses to produce a group he called English roses, but

11

Rosa Milrose, a floribunda rose

which are also known as Austin roses. They have
the flower form and wonderful fragrance of old

Rosa The Pilgrim, an English rose

roses and bloom the whole summer, just like
modern roses.

Symbol ▣: patio roses. Patio roses and miniature
roses are grouped here into one category. They are
particularly suitable for smaller gardens and flower
boxes, tubs and pots. They grow less profusely than
ground cover roses and usually grow no taller than
twenty inches.

Symbool ◉ : park or shrub roses. The group park or
shrub roses has increased in popularity over the last

Rosa Lovely Fairy, a patio rose

Miniature roses in Kasteeltuinen Arcen, the Netherlands

Rosa White Fleurette, a park or shrub rose

Rosa Austriana®, a ground cover rose

few years, also in private gardens. The shrubs are usually tall and wide and are particularly suitable for shrub borders. They should be lightly pruned. Because they tend to bloom throughout summer and fall, they are also known as continuous-flowering shrub roses. Cultivars that do not grow very tall, but are very bushy and require little pruning, are known as low shrub roses.

Symbol ↔: ground cover roses: The ground cover roses actually belong to the group park or shrub roses. They spread out so vigorously that the combination of branches and leaves covers the entire ground surface. This is certainly the case for roses

with branches on the ground; however, views differ considerably regarding the taller growing varieties. Some people still consider certain shrub roses of about forty inches height as ground cover roses.

Symbol ⟋: climbing roses. There are two basic types of climbing roses – climbers and ramblers. Climbers have sturdy thick stems, whereas ramblers have long thinner stems.

They often need help holding on to the climbing support. Tying helps. Once they have reached the top, the stems hang down and the flowers bloom

Rosa Salita, a continuous-flowering climbing rose

usually in very rich trusses, often once per season. These days true climbers often have many continuous-flowering varieties, which are therefore also called continuous-flowering climbers.

Symbool _h: height. The figure indicates the average height in inches. The final height of a rose is affected by many factors, including the soil type, the nutritional condition of the soil, protection against the wind and the pruning method.

Symbool ♀: once-flowering. A once-flowering rose concentrates the annual blooms in one particular period of the season. Afterwards there are no further blooms.

Symbool ♀♀: remontant. A remontant rose, also called a repeat-flowering rose, produces blooms several times a year, but not constantly. There are therefore periods when there are no blooms at all.

Symbool ♀♀♀: continuous-flowering. A continuous-flowering rose produces uninterrupted blooms throughout the season, often in flushes and not always equally profuse, but the bush is never without flowers.

Symbool ⌒: the rose has no fragrance or it is so slight that it can be regarded as practically fragrantless.

Symbool ⌒⌒: the rose has a light fragrance.

Symbool ⌒⌒⌒: the rose has a strong fragrance. The fragrance can be detected, especially if you smell the flower.

Symbool ⌒⌒⌒⌒: the rose has a very strong fragrance. This includes remarkably fragrant roses that can be smelled from a distance. Roses with the symbols ⌒⌒⌒ or ⌒⌒⌒⌒ in this encyclopedia are a good choice if you like fragrant roses.

Symbool ✪: this symbol, for roses with a good resistance to rose diseases, is awarded to roses that have been shown through tests to be very disease-resistant and recognized as such by specialists in breeding strong roses. However, the absence of this symbol does not necessarily mean that the rose is prone to disease, as the resistance of many roses has not yet been sufficiently tested.

2 Explanation of terms

This book avoids using technical terms as much as possible. The terms you will come across are explained here.

Bed (rose bed)
Part of the garden where various rose bushes (usually the same variety) are planted alongside one another.

Bourbon rose
A group of old roses that originated on the island Réunion, which at the time was called Île de Bourbon. This was a spontaneous crossing between the

Rosa Royal Bonica® in a plant border of landscape architect Heikie Hoeksma

Chinese rose 'Old Blush' and a Damask rose. From the latter the Bourbon roses inherited the pleasant fragrance, and from the Chinese rose the ability to repeat flower. They bloom twice per year.

Breeding
Breeding involves the creation of new varieties. This usually occurs by crossing different varieties with each other. The often hundreds of seedlings are planted in test fields and closely monitored. The rose breeder checks to see whether any plants with new, good characteristics arise among these seedlings. If a good plant is found it is cultivated even further, by grafting, budding (also a form of grafting) or taking cuttings.

Budding
A method of grafting whereby a leaf bud on the side

The English rose Rosa Mary Rose combined with *Clematis* 'Dorothy Walton'

of a stem that has not yet developed is cut off and only the 'eye' is grafted onto the root stock. For this reason it is known as bud grafting.

Calyx
Undermost wreath of flower leaves, usually green with roses.

Cleaning
The degree to which petals fall after flowering. The petals of a good cleaning rose fall completely off after the flower is spent. With a badly cleaning rose they remain, rotting or affected by fungus on the flower.

Cluster-flowered rose
Another name for floribunda rose.

Combining
Roses come in all colors (apart from pure blue). Each rose can therefore be combined with other particular plants. This can be a combination of a rose with one other plant, a Clematis, for example, or a rose in a border combined with several other types of flowers.

Corolla
Uppermost crown of petals.

Corymb
Cluster-flowered manner of flowering whereby the flowers are at around the same height due to the flower stalks of unequal lengths. In many roses this manner of flowering is referred to as corymbiform with paniculiform branching. See also 'truss'.

Cut rose

A rose that you can cut off and place in a vase. This encyclopedia describes primarily garden roses, a number of which are suitable as cut roses. Florists sell cut roses that have been cultivated specifically for the cut rose market. They have been specially developed by professional breeders to produce an optimum yield. Important characteristics include the number of cut roses that can be harvested per square foot, the perishability, the length and sturdiness of the stem as well as the color, shape and fragrance – all things that consumers consider when buying a bouquet of flowers. Not so much attention is spent on how these cut roses perform in the garden. After all, cut roses are usually grown in greenhouses. These days there is a growing interest in breeding cut roses outdoors. Rosa Mambo® (TANobmam) of Tantau is such an outdoor cut rose. The beautifully formed flowers in various shades of yellow, copper and orange are borne on stems approximately twenty-five inches long. They can keep for twelve days in a vase.

Cuttings

A method for propagating roses. Shoots (often from the top) are cut from a bush and then replanted to then take root. In the past this method was practically only used for propagating root stocks. These days this is done increasingly with bushes that have to flower from cuttings, particularly with roses for public green areas.

Damask rose

One of the oldest groups of old roses, also known as Rosa x damascena. The origins of the Damask rose are uncertain, but some people believe that it is a crossing between the French rose and the musk rose. Damask roses are characterized by a loose, elegant flower shape and a very strong fragrance. See also Rosa x damascena in Roses from A to Z.

Grafting

A method for propagating roses. A part of the variety with the beautiful flowers is cut off (scion) and attached to the root stock. The root stock is cut to allow the scion to be inserted so that both parts grow together.

Graft union

The place where the root stock and scion have been attached and subsequently grown together.

Floribunda rose

An important group of roses, also known as cluster-flowered. Originated from a crossing between large-flowered roses and Polyantha roses. This latter rose came from the multiflorous rose. This explains why the flowers are not single, but appear in many-flowered clusters. Floribunda roses inherited the ability to flower the whole summer from the large-flowered roses.

Full

The flower has twenty to forty petals.

Roses in public green areas, here below Rosa Bonica® in the heart of a roundabout

Hybrid Tea

Old name for large-flowered bushes.

Modern roses

Originated from the continuous-flowering roses that were introduced to Europe from China (which at the time were called tea roses due to their fragrance) which were then hybridized. The first modern rose dates back to 1867.

Moschata hybrids

See 'musk hybrids'.

Rosa Katharina Zeimet, a polyantha rose

Musk hybrids

These are distant relatives of Rosa moschata. This

The Rosarium at Winschoten, the Netherlands

musk rose does not occur naturally in the wild. Perhaps they originated from a crossing between other wild roses. The result is a rather diverse variety of hybrids known as musk roses. The roses that are now called musk hybrids or moschata hybrids are merely distantly related to the musk rose. The moschata hybrids generally produce rich and long-lasting blooms that appear early. They develop shoots from the base, which then bend. The first flower cluster forms at the top. During the flowering period new flower clusters form lower down the stem. The moschata hybrids, in fact, flower from top to bottom with slightly fragrant flowers. An unpruned shrub will flower from as early as May.

Petals
Leaves of the flower that together form the corolla.

Polyanthas
A group of roses that originated in 1875 through crossing the multiflorous rose *(Rosa multiflora)* with a continuous-flowering Chinese tea rose. From its parents the polyantha rose inherited the characteristics of multiflorous trusses and continuous flowering, respectively.

Prickles
A sharp outgrowth on the surface (See 'thorn').

Public green areas
All plants that have been planted and maintained by the government. Roses that require little care are frequently used.

Quartered
A form of very full flowers whereby the petals are folded into four distinct sections.

Reverted sports
Rosa Pink La Sevillana® is an example of a sport:

Rosa Mambo®, a cut rose

a spontaneous genetic change (see also 'sport'). Sometimes the old genes get the upper hand, however. We then refer to 'reverted sports' or reversion. In a rose bed of Pink La Sevillana® one may find, for example, a vermilion-flowering plant that looks exactly like the original parent plant – *Rosa* La Sevillana®.

Root stock
Rose on top of which another rose has been grafted (see also 'grafting').

Rosarium
A park or garden that is planted primarily with roses.

Rugosa hybrid
Descendant of the ramanas rose *(Rosa rugosa)*, a botanical rose that grows wild in many parts of Europe. This rose grows upright with very thorny stems and has highly fragrant, single flowers that develop into large hips. After the first bloom of flowers in early summer there is usually reduced flower production throughout the rest of summer. It is also known as the Japanese rose. See also *Rosa rugosa*.

Scion
Cut-off part of a rose that is to be grafted on a root stock.

Semi-double
The flower has more than ten petals but less than

Rosa Excelsa as tree rose, together with Rosa Baby Carnaval

Reverted sport of the Pink La Sevillana

twenty. On opening, the eye of the flower (which is the center where the color is distinctly different from the rest of the flower) is usually visible.

Sepals
The flower leaves covering the bud that together form the calyx.

Single-flowered
The flower has the natural number of petals, usually five (sometimes up to ten) arranged in a circle around the open heart.

Solitary
Stands on its own.

Sport
A spontaneous genetic change producing a new rose variety. An example is Rosa La Sevillana®, a floribunda rose with vermilion red flowers. Amid these red flowers a pink version was found. This was cultivated further and given the name Pink La Sevillana®. Only the color of this sport is different; all other hereditary characteristics are the same as La Sevillana®. See also 'reverted sports'.

Tea rose
Name given to a group of Chinese roses that are able to flower the whole summer. This characteristic led to a sensation for European rose lovers who, up until then, had to suffice with roses that flowered once or twice per year. As the Chinese tea roses do not grow vigorously and are not very frost hardy, they were crossed with more robust roses in order to combine all the good characteristics. Modern roses originated in this way.

Thorns
A stipule, leaf or branch that has been transformed into a stiff, sharp, pointed projection. Strictly speaking, roses do not have thorns, but prickles. But as 'thorn' is the word in common usage, we will refer to thorns in this encyclopedia.

Tree rose
A rose that has been grafted on a stem, which only begins to branch afterwards. The branches may spread outwards or grow vertically, but when a variety with weak branches is grafted as high as possible, a weeping tree rose is formed. The British name is standard rose.

Truss
Form of flowering where a number of flowers are connected by their footstalks to a single stem. Although there are quite a few blooms that botanically can be regarded as paniculiform corymbs, this encyclopedia will use everyday speech and refer to any branched form of flowering as a truss.

Upright
The branches grow primarily vertically, producing a bush that is usually higher than it is wide.

Very full
The flower has more than forty petals.

Weeping tree rose
See also 'tree rose'.

3   Rose Care

The emphasis in this Illustrated Encyclopedia of Roses is the selection of the right roses. As we wish to show as many different roses as possible, we will limit the description of the care and the specific characteristics of roses to the essentials. The information in this chapter is sufficient to help you grow beautiful roses in your garden.

Location

The location of the roses is by far the most important factor for successful growth. Although roses originate from various parts of the world, where they grow in nature is generally much the same for all varieties.

The typical location of a wild rose can be divided into four categories:

A Sunny
B Ventilated
C Fertile
D Well-drained

A Sunny

Roses like the sun. They grow and flower the best where there is plenty of light. Most varieties can withstand partial shade, and there are even others that thrive in these conditions. However, a completely shaded area is not suitable. The plants would become vulnerable to all sorts of diseases and will flower badly.

B Ventilated

In nature, roses tend to be pioneer plants. They germinate in open ground and grow quickly to form a sturdy bush, which will remain established for some time. It is only when all sorts of other plants start to germinate among the roses and suffocate them with their growth that they start to deteriorate and eventually die from fungus and other diseases.

In open spaces there is always sufficient wind to quickly blow the rose dry. In their evolution, roses have therefore equipped themselves inadequately against damage from fungi, and are consequently susceptible to them. You should therefore plant the rose bushes where the wind can help to quickly remove dew from the bush. This is also one of the most important reasons for pruning modern rose varieties each year. By leaving less wood (especially in the heart), the air can move more freely.

However, do not place the roses in a drafty site or directly in the wind. Roses tend to grow badly where there is cold wind and become more susceptible to aphids.

C Fertile

The open sites where roses often grow in nature tend to be areas of mineral-rich and fertile soil. Loose, chalky clay soil is the favorite type of soil, but other soils can be sufficient for effective growth. This is especially the case on slopes. When the soil is eroded (through shifting, drifting, and washing away) nutrients are released. This is low in nitrogen. Roses grow the best in chalky, clay, loess and sulfate soils, but can also grow satisfactorily in fertile and water-retaining sandy soils.

The worst soils are dry and sodden soils; these are totally unsuitable for roses. If growing on sandy soil, compost must be added. See also 'Fertilizing roses'.

D Good drainage

The roots of rose bushes are adapted to soils in which they have to root in the wild. The surface dries out in the sun in their open sites. The roots search deeper into the soil in search of water and nutrients. On slopes the water drains or runs off very quickly. Here the roots are never in contact with stagnating moisture.

In the garden the absence of stagnant moisture is an important condition for healthy roses. In groundwater – especially in the winter – where the groundwater levels are high, the deep-rooted rose roots will rot or be more prone to freezing with frost. Therefore, only start growing roses if the groundwater level does not exceed twenty inches below ground level.

Planting roses

The best time for planting

The best time to plant a dug-up rose bush (with bare roots) is the fall, from the moment that the leaves have fallen from the bush. At that time the soil is still warm enough for root activity. The bare bush only loses water from the green branches and the ground no longer dries out in the fall. Newly planted roses will quickly produce hair roots in that warm and moist soil, which will compensate for the moisture loss from the branches in the winter. Only in areas where frost is severe may it be better to plant the bushes in the spring.

During the spring, roses can be planted the moment that there is no longer any frost on the soil and up to the point that the leaves begin to grow. Spring has two disadvantages compared to planting in the fall. The soil in spring is still cold, which slows down root growth. And when the leaves begin to grow they start to lose moisture. Sometimes the badly developed root system is not able to compensate for the moisture loss and the bush consequently dies.

Rose traders were rather unhappy about the fact that it was only possible to plant roses in a period when there were no flowers. They missed the impulse buying from customers who would respond to seeing splendid flowers displayed in the show garden. But breeders have found an answer to this. They sell the plants throughout the year in pots. The customer can now place a flowering rose bush in the garden just like that. And through the use of dissolvable walls, the roses can be planted with pot and all in the ground. This helps to avoid damaging the roots.

How to plant the rose

Because roses have long roots, you will have to dig a deep hole. You may prune the roots a little, but the remaining roots have to hang freely straight down into the hole. The planting hole therefore has to be deeper than the length of the remaining roots. If the roots lay around the hole the rose will grow badly for some time.

The old custom of putting barnyard manure in the planting hole in order to enrich the soil is not done so much these days. Too many roots have been infected by fungus through the compost. It is, however, possible to place some soil improvement products or special rose compost in granular form. Personally, I prefer to allow the rose to develop roots on its own and then add compost after the first growth season.

The depth at which the bush goes into the ground is very important for good growth. Most roses have been grafted. A stem or eye of a selected rose variety is inserted and attached to a well-growing root stock. The place where the two roses meet is called the graft union.

This is often a thickened area and can therefore be easily recognized. But as this is not always the case, it is best to assume that the site of grafting is where the bush begins to branch out.

When planting, there is a trick to ensure that the graft union is at the right height: let the roots of the rose hang into the planting hole and fill the hole with your free hand while your other hand keeps the rose in position. Press the soil around the roots. As this will cause the rose to sink a little you should pull upwards while doing so. Ensure that the graft union ends up precisely at the height of the surrounding ground level. Once this has been done, stamp the ground around the bush firmly and carefully. In doing so the graft union sinks a little below the surface, which is ideal for growth.

If the ground is dry, pour a bucket of water at the foot of the bush and add soil where the soil sinks down.

One last thing now has to be done, especially if you have planted the rose in the spring. The young bush has to be pruned, regardless of how small it is. By shortening the stems there will initially be fewer leaves. This reduces the chance of drying out. Bushes planted in fall require less rigorous pruning. However, you should prune in the following spring once the likelihood of frost has disappeared.

Fertilizing roses

In the past only barnyard manure was used for fertilizing roses. This was placed around the base of the rose bush in fall, which also helped to protect against the effects of frost. In this way the graft union was covered. This is still a good method, particularly on sandy soil. The decomposing manure – with added straw – increases the humus content of the soil and ensures that the sandy soil is better able to retain any moisture. The winter rains would then wash the nutrients into the soil to the deeper roots. There are, however, a few disadvantages to this method. In the first place, it is increasingly difficult to get hold of barnyard manure, especially in urban areas. Secondly, the nitrogen level of barnyard manure is quite high and it is precisely this particular nutrient that roses require less. And finally, the nitrogen not only reaches the roots of the rose, it spreads out gradually, especially in loose soil, significantly affecting the environment and causing explosive algal growth in ponds and ditches. These days, specific fertilizers for roses are available in shops. They have relatively low nitrogen (N) levels, with particularly high levels of phosphates (P) and potassium (K). The nitrogen promotes the growth of the leaves, while the phosphates and potassium encourage rich blooms and strong tissue. The special fertilizer is usually applied twice per year: in March-April and in June-July.

2 Rake the granules through the top layer of the soil. Roses are deep-rooted, so the raking will not damage any roots.

3 Water the area where the fertilizer granules have been raked into the soil. It is only once the granules become wet that they begin to release their nutrients, which have to sink towards the roots. For quicker results, you can dissolve the recommended amount in water and pour at the foot of the rose.

Applying special rose fertilizer

1 Pour the recommended dosage of fertilizer in a cup. Scatter the fertilizer evenly around the foot of the rose bush.

Protection against frost

Severe temperatures can damage roses, and although certain roses are more vulnerable than others, the winter hardiness of roses has not been dealt with in this encyclopedia. First of all, this is because the roses featured in this book are sufficiently winter hardy in our region to remain healthy and beautiful. Only in cases where a rose is particularly vulnerable to frost have we mentioned this. Secondly, winter damage is not only related to the lowest temperature, but also the humidity, the period at which it begins to freeze and the care of the rose.

Frost in inland areas results in less damage than the same temperatures below zero would in an oceanic climate. In continental areas the air is drier, the low temperatures come less as a surprise and the wood has had a better chance of maturing in the summer. In areas with wet, mild winters, a sudden freeze is felt more severely. The ground would have been warm and wet for some time, resulting in the wood of the rose bush containing much water. Wood with a high water content is particularly vulnerable to freezing temperatures, especially the graft union where the rose had been grafted onto the root stock (often a bud graft). If this joint is swollen through too much water, the graft may split and the grafted rose will be lost.

Covering the graft union with soil can reduce the chance of this happening. This should be done in fall (a job that used to be, and still is, combined with the application of barnyard manure). Cover the foot of the rose bush, including the graft, with soil and then top up with barnyard manure as required. Do not let the compost touch the rose directly. Always ensure that some soil separates the two.

Tree roses are the most vulnerable to frost, as the graft union is high above the ground, and can therefore not be covered by soil. It is possible, however, to wrap straw or conifer leaves around the graft. You can also place a makeshift roof over this area to keep the insulation material dry. Never wrap with plastic, as this would increase the risk of rotting and freezing.

The graft is now protected, but the ends of the stems may still freeze. This may seem disastrous, but in most cases not much harm results. Except for the more sensitive roses, partial freezing causes no problems. When pruning in spring you simply cut away the frozen parts. First of all, the green ends of the stems will freeze. These are the youngest part of the plant. They have not matured and so contain relatively much moisture and few fibers.

That's why it is best not to apply any nitrogen-rich fertilizer after the first growth period in the spring, until the leaves have fallen and growth stops. Nitrogen (symbolized by the letter N, often seen in packaging in the combination: N+P+K) promotes rapid growth with succulent, large cells, and it is these sorts of cells that freeze first. The rose fertilizer that is applied in June-July therefore contains a relatively small amount of nitrogen and more phosphate (P) and potassium (K). This last element in particular encourages the formation of sturdy tissue. As compost is only effective as a combination of these elements, even the most specialized rose compost will contain some nitrogen. That is why you should not apply any more fertilizer as of August. The wood has to mature and should no longer grow as of September, or if so, then slowly.

Pruning roses

There seems to be no subject more controversial than the pruning of roses. It is therefore important to put the pruning rules into clear perspective. Below we will explain how the various types of roses can be pruned. 'Can' is the appropriate word, as many people have their own methods they swear by. However, in practice not too much importance should be attached to the various methods, as tests have shown that even the roughest of methods can produce very good results. In one such test, a rose garden containing the same types of roses was pruned according to two methods:

1 skilled gardeners pruned according to the rules;
2 all roses were simply trimmed to a particular height.

The roses that were pruned according to the second method actually seemed to grow and bloom better. These were roses that should in theory have been pruned according to method A described in this chapter (see pruning methods). And the differences between the methods do seem to be important. For this reason it is important to know the type to which a rose belongs.

The tens of thousands of different roses can be classified in various ways. They are often subdivided in great detail, which can be important to professionals working with roses. However, the average rose enthusiast would simply drown in this sort of detailed classification (which is not always that consistent). Particularly the various hybrids from the various types confuse matters further. The approach to the classification of roses in this encyclopedia has been based on the following question: "How should a particular rose be pruned?" Generally speaking, roses can be placed into two categories:
- roses that grow and bloom better through hard pruning;
- roses that are best pruned moderately.

In this encyclopedia the following groups belong to the first category:

- large-flowered roses, also known as Hybrid Teas (indicated by the symbol ✼);

- floribunda roses, also known as cluster-flowered roses (indicated by the symbol ✼✼);

- patio, miniature or dwarf roses (indicated by the symbol ▣).

In this encyclopedia the following groups belong to the second category:

- botanical or wild roses (indicated by the symbol ⊛);

- old or historical roses (indicated by the symbol ◉);

- English roses (indicated by the symbol ❦GB)

- park or shrub roses, including polyantha roses (indicated by the symbol ◍);

- ground cover roses (indicated by the symbol ↔);

- climbing roses, including ramblers (indicated by the symbol ♪).

Below you can read how best to prune each of the two categories of roses. The pruning methods A, B and C are explained in the following section.

✼ Large-flowered roses, or Hybrid Teas

The buds of these roses are formed on the new wood. This rose may therefore receive hard pruning, which encourages the growth of sturdy fresh shoots, without making it too large. Method A is often applied to large-flowered roses in a rose garden. If you prefer to have this rose in the background of a border, you can leave the thickest stems a little longer.

✼✼ Floribunda roses, or cluster-flowered roses

Pruning is carried out in the same way as with large-flowered roses (see above). Floribunda roses are used in rose beds even more than large-flowered roses. Method A therefore gives us an excellent view of the desired pruning effect.

▣ Patio, miniature and dwarf roses

All roses that grow to less than twenty inches tall belong to this group of roses, with the exception of ground cover roses, which are pruned in a completely different way. Patio roses and the genuine miniatures or dwarf roses are in effect smaller versions of large-flowered roses or floribunda roses and so are also pruned according to method A.

⊛ Botanical or wild roses

In nature, roses are pruned solely by animals. These roses have developed an aversion to this and so protect themselves against grazing animals with thorns. They eventually form a compact bush that is usually quite high and wide. It is only in natural gardens, parks and other public green areas that we really accept this kind of vigorous growth and enjoy such a wonderfully developed bush, which blooms just once a year and then leaves behind hips that nearly always look attractive. Sometimes pruning will be necessary when the bush becomes too large or when parts of the stems die off or begin to rub against one another, causing damage. In that case, use method B. It is best to prune directly after flowering, so that the bush has the entire summer to recover and so can bloom again the following year. With moderate pruning some hips may still develop. Only cut off dead wood or living stems that have to be removed for one of the above reasons.

◉ Old roses or historical roses

True rose enthusiasts can be quite lyrical when describing the romantic, full blooms and sumptuous fragrance of the old roses.

They will readily admit that these roses, however, only bloom once or twice in one season, often grow to quite a large size and are rather vulnerable to disease. Old roses do not have to be pruned much, and in this respect are similar to botanical roses. The best time for pruning is after flowering. The continuous-flowering Bourbon roses and repeat roses and climbers do not require any pruning, or pruning method B at the most, preferably after flowering.

⚘GB English roses

English roses are derived from crossing modern roses with old roses. They form a transitional group and it is therefore possible to prune them according to method A. This would result in bedding roses with few, though large flowers that remain relatively low. However, English roses are pruned more frequently in the same way as park or shrub roses (Method B). See below.

⚘ Park or shrub roses

The charm of these continuous-flowering shrub roses is their rough exterior. The stems grow high and wide and bear flowers from early summer till deep into fall. A rich bloom in the following year can only be guaranteed by pruning. Method B describes how best to prune this type of rose.
In the case of polyantha roses, the pruning is slightly different: in the growing season (if required) only cut off the flower clusters once the flowering is over to guarantee a good further flush of blooms. If you wish to see hips, do not cut stems that have flowered in late summer. After the winter only cut off the trusses with hips. The shrub will then flower early. Pruning in the summer will then again be limited to cutting away trusses that have flowered. However, you will also have to cut back to the ground any stems that have bloomed for two successive years. They will then make room for new shoots.

↔ Ground cover roses

The ground cover roses belong to the park or shrub rose group, but have a different form. The shoots grow sideways or first vertically and then droop. Often new long shoots form above the older shoots. In this way the soil beneath disappears from view. Ground cover roses are used frequently in public green areas, as they are easy to maintain and keep weeds at bay. They are sometimes cut on a large scale using a mowing bar which cuts off the top most level. For the home garden it is best not to prune at all.

✂ Climbing roses, including ramblers

Old, repeat flowering climbing roses do not require much pruning after the first bloom. For the rest, climbing roses and ramblers can be treated according to pruning method C.

So when buying roses be sure that you note not only the name but also the group to which they belong. Only then would you know the height and method of pruning.

Pruning methods

Pruning method A; for the majority of modern roses

Modern large-flowered roses, floribunda roses, patio roses and miniature roses are pruned according to method A.

1 First all the dead wood is cut away from the bush. Cut the brown stems as close as possible to the ground.

3 Remove all stems that grow towards the center of the bush. This gives the plant more light and air in the summer.

2 It is best to remove all diseased and frozen stems as well, or cut them to where there are no more brown areas. Sometimes a branch may be green on the outside but brown inside.

2a If when cutting a stem you see a brown spot in the cut end, cut as many times as necessary until the pith is totally white, then cut another inch off.

4 Thin shoots will never grow strongly or bloom well. Cut as close as possible to the ground.

25

5 Remove the least strong shoots that cross one another from the stems, so that the strongest have space to grow.

7 Use long-handled pruners for any old thick stems and dead knots.

6 Remove also the old, wooden stems by cutting them away at the base.

8 Shorten the remaining stems to about a hand's width above the ground.

9 Cut each stem about one sixth of an inch above a bud. The cut should be diagonal with the highest part on the side of the bud.

10 The end result looks drastic, but in the course of spring the rose will develop beautifully and produce richer blooms the coming summer.

Normal and dormant buds

The buds at the end of healthy stems already begin to develop by spring. They are easy to recognize. When pruning you also need to be aware of the dormant buds further down the stems. They will develop after pruning.

Tree roses

For pruning tree roses the category to which they belong is of importance. A rambler budded onto a tree rose will form a weeping tree rose which will have to be pruned moderately to maintain its weeping character (see method B). A floribunda rose on a tree rose is pruned in the spring just above the graft union, leaving behind only small stumps (see method A).

Pruning method B

This is the most suitable pruning method for park or shrub roses and for English roses, as well as for old and botanical roses, for as far as pruning is necessary.

1 First examine the bush to see where the strongest stems are. Leave these for the moment: they are dealt with later.

2 Cut away the thin, entangled shoots at the base of the bush to give you space for further pruning.

3 Also for this group of roses, remove any wooden stems and those affected by frost and disease.

4 Thin, spindly shoots should all be removed. Cut them from the base, so that they can no longer develop.

5 Three to seven stems now remain. Cut about half of these stems to half their height.

6 Remove all sideshoots from the remaining stems and cut off the top from where they begin to branch out.

7 When cutting off the sideshoots, leave short stumps, each with preferably at least two dormant buds that can develop later.

8 This eventually leaves you with stems of varying lengths. The bush will grow full and flower from June into fall.

Pruning method C: for climbing roses.

Climbing roses are classified into two groups according to their growth habit: the true climbers and the ramblers. They can be identified through the sturdiness of the branches: roses with stiff vertical stems that remain upright when leaning against a support we usually call climbing roses. Varieties that have less rigid stems and cannot remain upright without help are called ramblers. These have to be tied. However, the charm of weaker stems is that th flower trusses droop under their own weight, creating a cascade of flowers. They usually produce profuse, but short-lived, blooms. Climbing roses have varieties that produce rich and short-lived blooms as well as varieties that are continuously flowering.

You have to be restrained in your pruning for both types. This is to ensure that the plant can develop optimally, and rich blooms are encouraged. The once-flowering climbing roses and ramblers have to be pruned immediately after the flowers are spent, and continuous-flowering climbing roses after the first bloom.

1 Leave the vertical shoots (the main shoots), intact as much as possible, regardless of whether or not attached. Only shorten the ends as required. Cut off much of the length of the side shoots of the main shoots. Only three eyes should remain on the side shoots.

2 Every summer a few fast-growing shoots will spring up from the base. These are not wild shoots that have to be cut off, as is often thought. On the contrary, these fast-growing shoots should be nurtured, as they form the future main shoots. Eventually older main shoots will harden and produce fewer blooms. These old main shoots should be completely removed in spring. A saw is often necessary for this, as the stem can be thick and hard; pruning shears would simply not do the job.

3 In spring new eyes are already visible on the old stump. New shoots will develop from these. If you wait too long with cutting off the old branches, they will completely turn to wood and no more new shoots will develop on the base. Guide the new shoot from the previous summer to where the old one was, and the replacement is complete. How many main shoots you retain depends on the space available. Always ensure that the main shoots do not grow too closely to one another. They all produce side branches that can become entangled with one another, making the plant

more susceptible to disease and adversely affecting the flowering.

Rose diseases

Disease is part of the natural life of plants, animals and man. We need to realize this in order to overcome the disproportionate fear for every blemish or irregularity. This should not get in the way of enjoying roses. Of course, this is different if the damage is so extreme that the plant hardly grows, scarcely blooms or even dies. In this case something has gone wrong. What do you have to do to keep roses healthy?

1 The correct location. First of all you have to see whether the rose is in the correct location (see Location). If sited correctly, the rose will grow optimally and so be less susceptible to disease and plagues, regardless of what and how often you spray.

2 Compost. Bearing in mind that optimal growth is the most important condition for a healthy rose, you can promote growth by applying compost at the right time. See further Fertilizing roses.

3 Pruning. If you simply let the bush grow freely year after year it will develop into a mass of branches and leaves. Less light and air will get to the leaves in the center and the bush will become sick. Fungal disease in particular would then spread throughout the plant. Pruning therefore helps to combat disease. When pruning ensure that the heart of the bush gets enough light and air (see further Pruning roses)

4 Choose disease-resistant roses. If you meet all the above conditions and your rose still becomes sick, you probably have a rose variety that is susceptible to disease. In past decades breeders (those who crossed roses to create new varieties) paid little attention to disease. "All you have to do is spray them anyway," was a common view. Breeders concentrated on producing roses with beautifully formed flowers, striking colors and – recently again – a pleasant fragrance. And such varieties would also have to bloom the whole summer. This led to many varieties coming onto the market that were susceptible to fungal disease.

But those who had bought their roses there for their own gardens would soon be disappointed. Once planted at home the bushes became sick, as the average gardener does not spray the entire garden with pesticides.

There has recently been a significant turnaround, mainly as a result of government measures. Regulations regarding the use of pesticides have become more and more stringent. As a result, rose varieties that are sensitive to disease will slowly disappear. A few rose breeders have already been looking at resistance to disease for some time. The others will have to follow suit, as only reasonably healthy roses will have a future. Unfortunately, not many tests have been carried out into resistance to disease. The few tests have been inconclusive, for example, because a reasonably healthy variety can also weaken after a few decades. So consumers should pay as much attention as possible to the information provided on the resistance of the roses that they buy. The first results of comparative tests have already been published (though sporadically) in gardening magazines. In the A to Z section of this encyclopedia the symbol [●] has been given to those roses that have succeeded in these tests for disease resistance.

5 Use natural pesticides. Further to point 4 we can note that there are more and more sub-

stances being tested that do not so much combat the disease inflicting the rose but rather increase the resistance of the rose to that disease. Some substances help to combat all fungal diseases. They often work on the basis of organic fatty acids and silica (sand). They strengthen and harden the outer skin of the plant, making it more difficult for fungi to enter.

A very simple substance can help against mildew: milk. Use a plant sprayer and spray pure milk over the young leaves. They will become glossy as a result and be less susceptible to mildew.

Fungal diseases of roses

The most important diseases to affect roses are those caused by fungi. The conditions under which they multiply best differ per type. In general we can say that fungi are more active in damp air.

FALSE MILDEW

In roses this disease is caused by the fungus Peronospera sparsa. Purple spots become visible on the upper side of the rose leaves. If you look at the underside of the leaf you will see furry fungal threads. The fungus penetrates the leaf and stems, thereby damaging the plant. Although the disease is seen in garden roses it occurs more frequently in greenhouse roses, as the air is much more damp in the greenhouse.

MILDEW

This is the most widespread rose disease, which is normally seen as of the middle of summer. This is because the responsible fungus (Shaerotheca

Mildew

RUST

Rust can severely affect a rose, and can even be fatal. The disease is caused by a fungus, usually Phragmidium tuberculatum. Initially this can be recognized as small orange swellings on the underside of the leaf. These later become brown or black. Orange pits develop later on the upper side of the leaves. The fungus can also spread to the branches. With severe attacks the leaves will eventually drop off and the branches die (or even the entire rose), due to the disrupted flow of sap. Removing the affected leaf early on (and destroying through burning, for example) can keep the spread of the disease at bay.

BLACK SPOT

Black spot is the most feared rose disease in North-West Europe. The fungal spores of Diplocarpon rosae are spread through water (water splashing up from the ground or water running along the branches). The fungus develops the quickest at temperatures of around 65°F and can therefore occur early in the season, particularly with high humidity.

pannosa var. rosae) thrives at temperatures of around 72°F with high humidity.

The plant, particularly the young shoots with leaf and buds, is covered by a white film. This makes the plant less attractive, hampers photosynthesis, but does not do the rose any significant harm. The fungus does not penetrate the rose. The spores are spread by the wind. A healthy rose will continue growth once the climate is less favorable for the fungus.

Black spot

Rust

Balling

The disease has less of a chance in less dense bushes that have been pruned well. Preventative spraying with substances that assist in strengthening the leaves can help to keep the disease under control. However, your most important weapon is the selection of rose varieties that are less vulnerable to this serious disease.

BALLING

The very full flowers of certain rose varieties can be particularly sensitive to changing weather conditions. What we have here is not so much a disease but a phenomenon. The outer petals of such a flower, in the picture Rosa Octavia Hill, become damaged by rain and then become a little slimy. If this is followed by a period of bright sunshine, this outer layer of the bud dries out and turns hard and brown. The flowers are often not strong enough to push open this outer layer. Consequently the whole flower rots and eventually drops off. You can help the flower by removing this outer layer at an early stage. The bud will then still open up and bloom.

Rose pests

Roses are visited by all sorts of feeding animals. The damage they cause is usually less threatening than damage from fungal diseases. Try to accept that your roses will always be nibbled at. Don't try to reduce the number of animals visiting your garden. Do the opposite. The greater the variety of animals in your garden, the smaller the chance that the number of certain feeding animals will develop into plague proportions. Birds, such as tits, the willow warbler, the chiffchaff and the wren eat many insects from roses. Provide nest boxes for the tits, low bushes and shrubs as nesting areas for the willow warbler and the chiffchaff, and a thick hedge or ivy as a nesting area for the wren, and you will notice the difference. Never use insecticides in the garden. These will also kill the lacewing flies, ladybugs and other useful insects. And as aphids, for example, recover more quickly from the chemical onslaught than their enemies, the use of insecticides will actually eventually lead to a plague. A plague is said to exist once harmful animals suddenly appear in large numbers. In a garden where there is a good biological balance roses will be eaten a little, but there will never be a plague.

Pests on roses

FROGHOPPER

Around the base of a bud or leaf, a mass of foam may appear. This is sometimes called 'cuckoo-spit', which has nothing to do with the bird. The foam is produced by the froghopper. This yellow-green animal (Philaenus) hides inside this foam.
It sucks the sap of the plant but causes no appreciable damage. If you do not like the look of the foam just spray off with a garden hose, preferably

Froghopper

while the leaf is still wet from dew or rain, so that this does not encourage any fungal growth.

ROSE SAWFLY

In the spring you may suddenly see curled up leaves hanging from their stalks. They look as if they have been rolled inwards. This is the work of the rose sawfly (Blennocampa phyllocolpa). The insect is active in the summer and spring, particularly on warm days, making it look as if the leaves have curled up as a result of the heat. In reality the sawfly injects a liquid into the tissue around the leaf vein causing the leaf to curl. After piercing the leaf the sawfly lays a number of eggs on the underside of the leaf. The larvae that emerge are protected from predators in the rolled up leaves. They eat the leaf and once they fully mature in the summer they fall to the ground where they pupate, to emerge the following spring as a flying insect. If you roll out the leaf you should be able to see these larvae.

You may be tempted to remove and destroy the rolled up leaf. However, this would cause the plant yet more damage (less photosynthesis) than if you just let the larvae get on with their business. This phenomenon returns every year but causes the rose little harm.

ROSE SLUG

The larvae of the rose slug, a type of sawfly (Endelmyia aethiops), seem to scrape away the outer layer (mesophyll) from the underside or top of the rose leaf, causing transparent areas. Light attacks do not cause any significant damage. Some of the larvae will be eaten by birds.

ROSE LEAFHOPPERS

White areas may appear on the upper leaf surface. This is due to the cells of the leaf being sucked empty by leaf hoppers (Edwardsiana rosae). If you

Rose slug

Rose sawfly

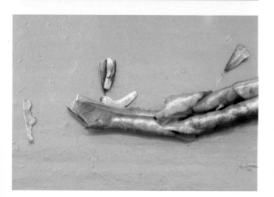

turn the leaf over you will see a yellow-white long insect, about the same length as an adult aphid but narrower. The larger ones can fly. Leafhoppers search out roses located in warm and sheltered places (so in the sun and sheltered). This is only a temporary problem and usually hardly affects the growth and flowering of the rose.

In the event of serious attacks you can spray the underside of the plant with a garden hose full on from the bottom at a time that the leaves are already wet from rain or dew. This does not directly kill the

Rose leafhoppers

insects but hampers their development, especially that of the younger insects that cannot fly. They are seldom able to climb back up the rose.

ROSE CHAFER

If you find the flower buds perched tilted on the stalk this is usually due to damage caused by feeding insects at the base. These are usually beetles that eat away at the young bud. If they get no further than the plant skin, the bud will simply unfold. If the damage is deeper the stamens will bulge outwards and the bud will no longer open. The

Caterpillars

problem usually occurs in only a few buds, so action is not really required. Unattractive buds can simply be cut off.

CATERPILLARS

Caterpillars prefer the most succulent parts of the plant. Particularly the caterpillars of moths can be found on roses, and they are especially active at night. The often eat the bud until it is hollow. During the day these caterpillars are difficult to see. They usually rest parallel to a stalk unnoticed by birds. You can give the birds a helping hand by moving the caterpillars to another plant, preferably a member of the rose family (such as apple, pear, strawberry, blackberry, rowanberry or Juneberry).

APHIDS

Everyone is familiar with the sight of aphids on the top of stems and particularly on rose buds making a meal of these succulent young parts. However, the plant will only be subjected to a continuous plague of these pests if there is something not quite

Rose chafer

right somewhere. If that's the case, check the following: is the rose located in a drafty area?
Or on a muggy site? Have you sprayed the rose with a chemical that may have killed off the aphids' natural predators? If the rose is in a suitable location in the garden and there are enough aphid predators in your garden (birds such as the wren,

the willow warbler, the chiffchaff, the garden warbler, the blackcap and the bluetit), spring will often bring some aphids for a while, but they will either completely disappear or so few will remain that they will not pose any problems. However, if you wish to rid yourself of all aphids, use a garden hose full on to spray them off the young shoots and buds. Always spray in the direction of growth (so from under upwards): in this way you will not cause any damage. It is best to spray when the plant is already wet from rain or dew, so that fungal growth is not encouraged.

Aphids

Aphids

4 Roses from A to Z

Rosa 21 Again

(MEInimo)
see *Rosa* Regatta®

Rosa A Shropshire Lad

(AUSled) Austin (1996)
A Shropshire Lad is a shrub-like English rose around
five feet tall with spreading branches, making the
shrub reach three-and-a-half feet wide. The very full
flowers have a peach-colored heart, with the outer
petals turning to the lightest pink imaginable. They
have a delicious, fruity fragrance. There is also
a climbing version of this rose: Rosa A Shropshire
Lad Climbing, which resembles this in everything
apart from the fact that it can reach around seven feet
tall when trained. Do not confuse this rose with Rosa
Shropshire Lass, another rose from David Austin Sr.
This is an alba hybrid with single, almost white
flowers with a pink tinge.
🌿GB 60h ♣♣♣ ෴෴

A Shropshire Lad

Rosa Aachener Dom

(MEIcapinal)
see *Rosa* Pink Panther®

Rosa Abbaye de Cluny®

(MEIbrinpay) Meilland (1996)
The very full apricot flowers of this large-flowered
rose fit in wonderfully with the romantic yearning for

Abbaye de Cluny®

old-fashioned respectable beauty. The color goes very
well with those of many perennials and annuals in the
border. This is where the over thirty-inch-tall plant
looks its best. For a large-flowered rose the medium
to dark green leaves remain relatively healthy. This
variety is one of the new roses of Meilland (registered
in 1996) from the Fleur Romantica® series that aims
to produce romantic looking roses – such as the English roses – combined with resistance to rose diseases.
The flowers have a light fragrance. Despite this
Abbaye de Cluny® has received numerous awards,
including the Golden Medal of Lyon in 1994.
✳ 35h ♣♣ ෴෴

Rosa Abendglut

(POUlcs001)
see *Rosa* Valiant Heart™ Floribunda Poulsen®

Rosa Abigaile®

(TANelaigib) Tantau (1988)
With a maximum size of one-and-a-half feet this is
a low floribunda rose, which can be used as a patio
rose, is highly suitable for small gardens, flower
boxes and even for pot cultivation.
The beautifully formed, full flowers open out from
carmine-pink buds. They have a cream-colored

Abigaile®

heart, which on opening dominates the overall look. It has a mild fragrance though from close by it gives a full perfume. The red wine-tinged leaves are on a well-branched, healthy bush.
✹✹ 20h ❦❦❦ ☁☁ ✚

Rosa Abraham Darby™

(AUScot) Austin (1985)
Not all roses that David Austin bred originated from crossing old roses with modern roses. Abraham Darby is the 'son' of the modern climbing rose Rosa Aloha and the floribunda rose Rosa Yellow Cushion. The result is a practically spherical bush of about

Abraham Darby™

five feet height and width, making it very suitable for combining with shrubs as well as for borders with high perennials. The very full flowers bloom in a few adjacent clusters. They have subtle colors, with hints of pink, apricot and yellow, and have an intense fruity fragrance. They appear throughout the summer on the high shrub, which has large frosty green leaves. The leaves are vulnerable to rose diseases.
❦GB 60h ❦❦❦ ☁☁☁☁

Rosa Abrikoos Queen Elizabeth

see Rosa Aprikot Queen Elizabeth

Rosa Acapella®

(TANallepa) Tantau (1994)
It is only when the cherry-red buds fold open into large, full flowers that you see the two colors. The outside is a silvery-white. The wonderful fragrance and long stems make this a perfect cut rose. The glossy, dark green leaves are quite resistant to fungal diseases. The upright bush grows strongly.
✿ 30h ❦❦❦ ☁☁☁ ✚

Rosa Adele Duttweiler

(POUltroi)
see Rosa Troika™ Hybrid Tea Poulsen®

Acapella®

Rosa x alba

(-) botanical rose (-)

No one knows exactly how this white rose came about. Its cradle is somewhere in the garden. It is possible that *Rosa gallica* and *Rosa arvensis* crossed spontaneously with each other, but perhaps *Rosa corymbfera*, *Rosa canina* or *Rosa damascena* also played a role. In any case a tall shrub with dull gray-green leaves was produced. The fragrant flowers appear in early summer. They are moderately full and pure white, though sometimes a light pink color. In spring round, red hips are formed. A typical rose for natural gardens.

❀ 80h ♀ ◌◌ ✚

Rosa alba Maxima

Rosa alba Maxima

(-) old rose (certainly before 1500)

The origins of the Jacobite rose are unknown. It orig-

Rosa x alba

inated many centuries ago, possibly as a crossing between the dog rose and the French rose or the Damask rose. The result is a robust shrub with long, thin stems. In addition to rose-red hooked thorns they also bear many large, blue-green leaves. However, we are more interested in the flowers. These are large and very full and have a delicious fragrance. They bloom only in early summer, with ivory-white flowers.

❀ 60–100h ♀ ◌◌◌ ✚

Rosa alba Meidiland®

(MEIflopan) Meilland (1987)

Some shrub roses that until recently were only planted in public green areas can be increasingly seen in private gardens. *Rosa alba* Meidiland® is a good choice, also for smaller gardens. The shrubs grow up to thirty inches in height and grow strongly outwards due to their branched growth. The foliage is glossy and medium green. The snowy-white, odorless, full flowers are not large but there are many. After an initial rich flush of blooms, further modest blooms continue for some time. They are often planted in large groups in order to cover a large area.

In small gardens they are very suitable for combining with perennials. This variety is also suitable as

Rosa alba Meidiland®

a weeping rose. This rose is a little vulnerable to black spot but not at all to mildew.

↔ 25h ♀♀ ⌒ ✚

Rosa alba Meillandécor

see *Rosa* alba Meidiland

Rosa Albéric Barbier

(-) Barbier (1900)

One of the most popular old rambling roses, with very full, cream-colored flowers with a hint of yellow. The open flowers are rather flat, with the petals forming a compact mass. This has a disadvantage after blooming as the petals turn brown and remain on the flower, especially in rainy weather. The flowers have a light, fresh fragrance. The stems are thin and flexible. It is therefore best to tie them at the desired height, whereby they droop down with rich blooms. The flower blooms in June-July. The plant has beautiful thin leaves that change from light green to dark green with age. The leaves are vulnerable to black spot.

↗ 80–200h ♀ ⌒⌒

Alcantara®

under the weight of the rich, full flower trusses. The dark red, single flowers of approximately one-and-a-half inches width bear a striking amount of pollen in the heart. They flower profusely throughout summer. The leaves stay on the plant for a long while, and are very resistant to fungal disease.

↔ 25h ♀♀♀ ⌒⌒ ✚

Rosa Alchemist

see *Rosa* Alchymist

Rosa Alchymist

(-) Kordes (1956)

The very full flowers of this climbing rose are initially yellow, but then change to soft pink, with hints of salmon, orange and apricot.

Alchymist

Albéric Barbier

Rosa Alcantara®

(NOAre) Noack (1999)

A ground cover rose from the famous Flower Carpet® series of the German breeder Noack. The stems branch out profusely and bend towards the ground

The plant blooms profusely but not for long. The large flowers produce an intense fragrance. The shrub itself grows vigorously with glossy, bronze-green young leaves, which later turn dark green. It is a little vulnerable to mildew. Alchemyst is also suitable for fairly shady walls.
↝ 80–160h ⚘ ◌◌◌

Rosa Alchymiste

see *Rosa* Alchymist

Rosa Alden Biesen®

(-) Lens (1996)

Although this moschata hybrid (see also Rosa moschata) has marzipan-pink blooms, they have a characteristic that enables double use. After flowering they do not dry, but turn green as with the flowers of some hydrangeas. The very full clusters are therefore very sought after as a cut rose, and keep well as a dried flower. The flower trusses are large and long. They bloom throughout summer on curved stems that can grow to five feet.

⊛ 50h ⚘⚘⚘ ◌◌

Alden Biesen®

Rosa Alec's Red

(COred) Cocker (1970)

This large-flowered rose is still popular today, primarily thanks to its wonderful fragrance. The roses have a delicious old-fashioned rose perfume. The five-inch-

Alec's Red

wide, bright rose-red petals are very full. They are borne singly or in trusses on an upright shrub that grows slowly and so therefore does not have constantly repeating blooms. The foliage is large and dark green.

✻ 30h ⚘⚘ ◌◌◌

Rosa Alexander

(HARlex) Harkness (1972)

This somewhat older large-flowered rose has already won many prizes. Way back in 1974 it received the ADR award, just before this reputable German inspectorate became very strict regarding the health of roses. However, in subsequent inspections in the period 1995-1998 the Alexander rose was shown to be one of the most robust large-flowered roses. The glossy, clear-green foliage is still remarkably resistant to fungal diseases.

Alexander

The bush has sturdy vertical stems of about four feet, but grow to less than one-and-a-half feet wide. It is therefore best to plant these roses close to one another (fifteen inches) to effectively fill a flower bed. Alexander is also suitable as a solitary rose and cut rose. The full flower has the characteristic bud form of a Hybrid Tea, but opens to form a rather flat flower. The flower is vermilion red and has a light fragrance.
✳ 35h 🌷🌷🌷 ⌒⌒ ✛ ADR

Rosa Alexandra

(POUldra)
see *Rosa* Prinsess Alexandra™ Renaissance®

Rosa Alexandra Rose

(AUSday)
see *Rosa* The Alexandra Rose

Rosa Alléluia®

(DELatur) Delbard (1980)
Alléluia® is a rose that steals the show and did so during exhibitions in Paris (Bagatelle) and Madrid, where it won several prizes. The full flower develops slowly from a long bud, allowing enthusiasts the pleasure of enjoying the silver underside of the petals for some time. The inside of each petal is exquisite: velvet-like and deep red. The flowers have hardly any fragrance. This bushy rose has glossy, dark-green foliage.
✳ 30h 🌷🌷🌷 ⌒

Rosa Alliance®

(MEIbleri) Meilland (1985)
The pointed buds of the Alliance® unfold to reveal

Alléluia®

beautifully formed moderately full flowers. They are ivory-white with a hint of pink. They have slight fragrance, but remain beautiful for some time. Because the flowers are perched on long reddish green stems, they are very suitable as cut rose. The mat leaves are dark green. The shrub can grow up to thirty-five inches tall. As many other older large-flowered roses the Alliance® is susceptible to black spot.
✳ 35h 🌷🌷🌷 ⌒

Alliance®

Rosa Alpine Sunset

(-) Cants of Colchester (1973)
Only if you live in a mild climate can you make the most of this large-flowered rose, as the plant is rather sensitive to severe frost.

Alpine Sunset

It has upright stems that in early summer bear many large, full flowers that smell wonderful. The flowers show subtle variations of salmon-pink, apricot and cream. The large flowers require a great deal of energy, as the blooms appear in distinct flushes, except when the rose is given sufficient feed.

⚘ 30h ♣♣ ☁☁☁

Rosa Altissimo®

(DELmur) Delbard (1966)

Simplicity characterizes this continuous-flowering climber. The clear, red, single flowers have a tuft of yellow stamens in their eye. They appear deep into autumn on this robust bush with dark green foliage. This is particularly suitable for covering a wall. Attach the stems horizontally as much as possible in order to correct the strong vertical growth as well as to stimulate blooms further down the plant.

↗ 120h ♣♣♣ ☁

Altissimo®

Rosa Ambassador®

(MEInuzeten) Meilland (1979)

The buds and flowers of Ambassador® are yellow on the outside. As the flower opens the inner orange becomes more visible, the flower eventually blooming with a salmon-pink color. The flowers can be up to four inches wide and are perched on top of long stems bearing glossy, dark green leaves (deep red with new growth). A good large-flowered rose for the vase. In oceanic climates Ambassador® is susceptible to mildew.

⚘ 45h ♣♣♣ ☁☁

Ambassador®

Rosa Amber Queen®

(HARroony) Harkness (1984)

What strikes you immediately about this rose is the healthy appearance of this well-branching bush and the wonderful glossy foliage. It starts with a reddish hue then goes from olive-green to dark green. The full, amber-colored flowers retain their young form and only later open out fully. They are approximately three inches wide, cup-shaped and compact. Despite this they do not suffer much from bad weather and clean quite well. You can smell their wonderful sweet, spicy fragrance from a distance. Recommended.

✿✿ 30h ♣♣♣ ☁☁☁ ✛

Amber Queen®

Rosa Ambiance®

(-) Lens (1994)

A moschata hybrid (see also Rosa moschata) that grows remarkably low. The spreading branches form a bush that grows to an average of one-and-a-half feet high. It bears wide trusses of pink, single flowers throughout the season. The flowers have a lighter, almost white, eye with yellow stamens.

🌐 20h 🌷🌷🌷 ☁☁

Rosa Ambridge Rose

(AUSwonder) Austin (1990)

This is one of the lower growing English roses. It grows rather bushy and bears many large, mat, medium green leaves. In the summer single buds form on the long, thin stems. The very full flowers open up to reveal light pink petals and an apricot-yellow eye. They are initially cup-shaped, often quartered. Later they bloom more open. By then they hang to the side

due to their own weight. They smell strongly of myrrh.

🌷GB 35h 🌷🌷🌷 ☁☁☁☁

Rosa American Pillar

(-) Van Fleet (1902)

The vigorous shoots of this rambler can reach up to twenty feet height. It does not require much tying to keep it stable. Clusters of full flowers bloom profusely in July. They are approximately three inches wide, and open up to reveal bright red petals which discolor throughout the season. They have an ivory-white eye boasting golden pollen, making the young rose even more attractive.

This is an excellent rose for providing a powerful effect against a high wall, rose pillar or pergola. The

Ambridge Rose

American Pillar

American Pillar

flowers have a light, spicy fragrance. The gray-green, glossy foliage is susceptible to mildew.

120–240h

Rosa Amoretto

(KORpastato)

see *Rosa* Sebastian KNEIPP®

Rosa Amstelveen®

(MEIpopul) Meilland (1994)

Amstelveen® is one of those modern, vigorous shrub roses that can remain beautiful without chemicals. The bushes grow to about thirty-five inches tall and can become equally wide, covering the ground with a blanket of flowers. These flowers remain in bloom

Amstelveen®

Amstelveen®

later on in the season. The single, open pink flowers have a lighter eye, and insects have good access to the yellow stamens. A perfect shrub for planting in groups (approximately three plants per ten square feet), but also as a solitary between perennials or other shrubs.

35h TOP

Rosa Amsterdam®

(HAVam) Verschuren (1972)

Amsterdam® is a winner of the Golden Rose at the rose show in The Hague. And quite rightly, it is a striking rose. The leaves are initially reddish brown and stay this mahogany color for some time, with half of the leaf having this color. Later they turn mat, deep green with a brown hue. Well above the foliage bloom clusters of wonderfully contrasting orange-red flowers of about two-and-a-half inches width. They are moderately full and cup-shaped and have a fresh fragrance. After blooming they clean well, also with rainy weather. The bush grows vigorously, prettily and regularly, and branches out profusely. New flower clusters de-

Amsterdam®

Amsterdam®

Angela®

velop throughout the summer. An outstanding rose for beds, borders and public green areas. The only negative aspect of this rose is that it is susceptible to mildew. ☀☀ 30h 🌷🌷🌷 ☁☁☁

Rosa Amulett®

(TANtaluma) Tantau (1991)

The rose-red flowers have the color and form of 'old roses': full and cup-shaped. However, they have no fragrance and bloom on a shrub of only ten to twenty inches height. It branches out profusely, grows primarily outwards and bears glossy, medium green leaves. As it flowers continuously this variety is ideal for small gardens as well as flower boxes and large pots. ▦/☀☀ 15h 🌷🌷🌷 ☁

Rosa Angela®

(KORday) Kordes (1984)

The cup-shaped, pink flowers appear in such profusion that this low shrub is completely covered by

Amulett®

blooms in the high season. The long stems, which have the tendency to grow outwards, bend under the weight. The heart of the moderately full flower is of a considerably lighter pink. The flowers have hardly any fragrance. Thanks to the good disease-resistance of the leaves in particular, Angela® was granted the ADR rose award.

� 40h 🌷🌷🌷 ☁ ✚ ADR

Rosa Angelica

(KORday)

see *Rosa* Angela®

Rosa Anna Ford®

(HARpiccolo) Harkness (1980)

It is as if yellow stars twinkle in the eye of the red-orange flowers of this somewhat older patio rose. In its day it caused much amazement and won numerous prizes during international rose shows. The moderately full flowers appear throughout the summer and fall in clusters above the shiny, medium green foliage. The bush grows to about one-and-a-half feet tall

Anna Ford®

and wide, and is highly suitable for cheerful beds and as foreground in an orange-yellow border.
▣ 20h ⚘⚘⚘ ☁☁

Rosa Anna Livia

(KORmetter)
see *Rosa* Trier 2000®

Rosa Anne Boleyn

(AUSecret) Austin (1999)
This is one of the more recent English roses. The bush grows with bending stems to about three-and-a-half feet tall and wide. Throughout the summer the rose produces very full flowers in luscious clusters. They are light pink in color and have a mild fragrance.
⚘GB 35h ⚘⚘⚘ ☁☁

Rosa Anne Harkness®

(HARkaramel) Harkness (1980)
This rose produces rich blooms as of mid-summer. The moderately full, amber to apricot-colored flowers bloom simultaneously in large trusses on sturdy stems. The flushes are particularly lush in August and September. Sometimes there may be up to thirty flowers in one truss, so by cutting a single stem you have a complete bouquet. The cluster has a mild but pleasant fragrance and keeps well in a vase. The cup-shaped flowers remain for a long time in the garden as well. They are borne on strong vertical stems. The entire bush grows usually up to more than three-and-a-half feet tall, and is therefore suitable for a border with large perennials. It can also be used as hedging.
✲✲ 45h ⚘⚘⚘ ☁☁

Anne Boleyn

Anne Harkness®

Rosa Anneke Doorenbos

(-) Doorenbos (1956)
The remarkably rich flushes of this floribunda rose immediately catch the eye. The flowers are borne by a very strong, vertical bush which branches very well. New full trusses with moderately full, light pink flowers appear throughout summer and fall. They are approximately two-and-a-half inches wide and eventually fade to a creamy pink color. The rose can withstand bad weather, as it can clean well. It has a light fruity fragrance.
The bush has reddish foliage which slowly turns olive-green and then a glossy, medium green.
✲✲ 45h ⚘⚘⚘ ☁☁

Anneke Doorenbos

Rosa Annelies®

(LENplero) Lens (2000)

This was one of the last moschata hybrids of Louis Lens, who died in 2001. Numerous full and fragrant flowers bloom on this plant. On opening they are a light pink color. As they unfold further they become increasingly white, leaving a very light pink tint. The bush initially grows vertically, then later tilts bearing glossy, light green leaves and long subdivided trusses. The long stems are ideal for tying, to produce a low rambler.

⊛ / ⅋ 50h–60h 💐💐💐 ⌒⌒

Rosa Anthony Meilland®

(MEIbaltaz) Meilland (1990)

The canary-yellow flowers of Anthony Meilland® grow to over three inches wide, which is large for a floribunda rose. That is why only a few flowers bloom on

Annelies®

a truss at one time. Rich flushes alternate with poorer ones. As the rose remains quite low and relatively large, with somewhat glossy, medium green leaves, they retain their beauty even with fewer blooms.

✻✻ 25h 💐💐 ⌒

Anthony Meilland®

Rosa Antique Silk

(KORampa)

see Rosa Champagner

Rosa Aotearoa-New Zealand

(MACgenev)

see Rosa New Zealand

Rosa Apricot Bells®

(LENtrichin) Lens (1999)

In this moschata hybrid of Lens (see also Rosa moschata) you can also see the genes of the Rosa chinensis 'Mutabilis' come through. The color of this form of Chinese rose changes during its bloom from yellow with orange to copper, then salmon and finally pink. A similar change of color is seen in the moderately full flowers of Apricot Bells®. The apricot-colored buds unfold to reveal cream flowers with a hint of apricot. They slowly change to a light pink color. The leaves with thin leaflets have tinges of red-brown. The flowers are borne on vertical stems that reach five feet in height and then start to bend.

⊛ 60h 💐💐💐 ⌒⌒

Rosa Apricot Queen®

(INTertrico) Interplant (1998)

Apricot is quite a striking color for a shrub rose. The single to semi-double flowers of the Apricot Queen® that open up from pointed buds have this very color. As they get older this color fades to salmon-pink. From early summer to fall more and

Apricot Bells®

Apricot Queen®

Apricot Queen Elizabeth

more new trusses appear on this vigorous rose, which in 2000 won gold in the category park or shrub rose during the Dutch International Rose Show in The Hague.
☉ 40h 🌱🌱🌱 ⌣ ✛

Rosa **Apricot Queen Elizabeth**

(-) Verschuren (1980)
A highly valued rose, which is nevertheless not widely sold. In tests on resistance this floribunda rose scored as one of the best. It is hardly affected by any rose diseases. The young foliage has a red tint. Later this changes from olive-green to dark gray-brown.

Apricot Queen®

The bush branches out profusely at the base and bears leaves deep into fall. From this strong base the bush extends shoots to about three-and-a-half feet in height. These bear trusses with subtly colored flowers: apricot with a yellow heart and a pale salmon edge. They have a wonderful fragrance and once the

bloom is finished they clean well. The good growth enables trusses to be formed throughout the season on very thorny stems.
✿✿ 40h 🌱🌱🌱 ⌣⌣⌣ ✛ TOP

Rosa **Aprikola**®

(KORorbe) Kordes (2000)
The golden basic color of this new rose changes with age into an apricot or soft pink. The full flowers appear in trusses from pointed buds.
They have a mild fruity fragrance. The medium green leaves become very dark green throughout the season. The leaves are very shiny and have good resistance to fungal diseases.
✿✿ 30h 🌱🌱🌱 ⌣⌣ ✛

Rosa **Aquitaine**

(POUlnoz)
see *Rosa* Pink Cover™ Towne & Country®

Aprikola®

Rosa **Arielle Dombasie**

see *Rosa* Arielle Dombasle

Rosa **Arielle Dombasle®**

(MEIhourag) Meilland (1991)

Due to its striking orange-red color, which becomes tinted with pink during flowering, this climbing rose doesn't suit all walls. So ensure that the color of the wall goes with the flowers. A green or brown background is ideal for this beautiful large-flowered climber that blooms continuously. It grows up to six to ten feet tall.

✂ 100h 🌹🌹🌹 ☁

Rosa **Arioso®**

(MEImucas) Meilland (1995)

The flowers of the Arioso® could actually be considered a model for the ideal tea rose. This is a modern Hybrid Tea, or large-flowered rose. The flowers have a wonderful soft pink color and a strong, fresh, spicy fragrance.

✳ 30h 🌹🌹 ☁☁☁

Arielle Dombasle®

Rosa **Armada®**

(HARuseful) Harkness (1988)

The form of the flowers are reminiscent of the popular rose 'New Dawn' which happens to be the mother of Armada®. Armada®, however, is a much deeper red. The semi-double flowers are borne in

Arioso®

large trusses, which eventually change into green hips. By cutting off the spent flowers you will stimulate new blooms. Even though the bush has a branching and wide-spreading growth habit, it can reach up to five feet tall. The shiny, bright green foliage remains attractive and disease-free.

☻ 50h 🌹🌹🌹 ☁☁ ✚ ADR

Rosa **Arnoud Delbard®**

(DELtep) Delbard (1972)

One of the older floribunda roses, which once won the biggest American prize but never gained popularity in Europe. Nonetheless, Arnoud Delbard® blooms continuously throughout summer with beautifully formed full flowers in bright colors between pink and orange. They have a light honey fragrance. The light green foliage goes well with the

Armada®

Arnoud Delbard®

Ashram®

wonderful bright flower colors. The plant has good branching growth and remains compact. Ideal bedding rose.
✿✿ 25h ❦❦❦ ⌒⌒

Rosa Art Deco®

(-) Lens (1993)

A moschata hybrid that can be planted as a tall shrub as well as a low rambler. The trusses of bright red, single flowers are borne on vertical stems of around five feet length. If you support Art Deco® and cut away the weaker shoots, the plant can grow even taller.
◔ / ✗ 60h ❦❦❦ ⌒⌒

Rosa Ashram®

(TANmarsa) Tantau (1998)

From a distance the full flowers appear a warm brown-orange color. On close inspection they appear blotched and stripy, with copper-yellow and warm brown. They fold out from long buds and can withstand rain well. Due to the long stems and light,

Art Deco®

fruity fragrance these flowers are also suitable as cut roses. The large, healthy, dark olive-green leaves are borne on vigorous vertical stems.
✗ 30h ❦❦❦ ⌒⌒ ✿

Rosa Aspen

(POUlmulti)
see *Rosa* Snow Cover™ Towne & Country®

Rosa Aspen

(POUlurt)
see *Rosa* Sun Cover™ Towne & Country®

Rosa Aspirin

(TANiripsa)
see *Rosa* Aspirin®-Rose

Rosa Aspirin®-Rose

(TANiripsa) Tantau (1997)

The flower color of this shrub-like floribunda rose varies with the weather. When warm and sunny the relatively large flowers are white, in cooler periods, soft pink. They appear throughout the summer (profusely first, then later in smaller numbers) above the shiny, clear olive-green foliage.

They are slightly fragrant. The shrub has branching growth, up to thirty inches tall and twenty inches wide, and is sometimes used for ground cover, particularly in public green areas. The rose is also very suitable for private gardens as it is very resistant to fungal disease.
✿✿ / ↔ 30h ❦❦❦ ⌒ ✿ ADR

Aspirin®-Rose

Aspirin®-Rose

Rosa Astrid Lindgren™ Floribunda Poulsen®

(POUluf) Poulsen (1990)

This highly rewarding floribunda rose covers a whole bed with mat, gray-green foliage and trusses of wonderfully formed flowers. The flowers are semi-double, almost four inches wide and give a light, fresh fragrance. During blooming they open out to form cup-shaped to flat flowers, which are visited by bees. With lengthy periods of bad weather they clean moderately well, though they can put up well with damp. Astrid Lindgren™ has good resistance to fungal disease and so can be recommended for borders of private gardens.

✹✹ 40h 🌷🌷🌷 ∽∽ ✚ TOP

Astrid Lindgren™ Floribunda Poulsen®

Rosa Atlantic Star

(FRYworld) Fryer (1993)

The well-formed, full flowers open out from orange buds. They are an apricot to light salmon-pink color, and have a mild but pleasant fragrance. The upright shrub bears glossy, dark green leaves, with the flowers contrasting beautifully. Atlantic Star is wonderful for bedding, and is also suitable for borders.

✹✹ 30h 🌷🌷🌷 ∽∽

Rosa Atlantis™ Palace®

(POUlsiana) Poulsen (1998)

Although this is not a true miniature rose, this low floribunda rose can be used in small beds and large tubs. They are planted as a solitary and grow to about twenty inches.

With good feeding and sufficient water they bloom the whole summer and fall with semi-double yellow flowers approximately two inches wide.

▣/✹✹ 20h 🌷🌷🌷 ∽

Atlantic Star

Rosa Auckland Metro

(MACbucpal)
see *Rosa* Metro

Atlantis™ Palace®

Rosa Audrey Hepburn

(TWOadore) Twomey (1991)
The beautifully formed, full flowers develop from pointed buds in trusses of approximately seven flowers per stalk. They are pale pink with a somewhat deeper pink color towards the edges. They can sometimes also reveal a yellow to apricot heart. They have a light, fruity fragrance, with an unpleasant hint of camphor. The upright growing rose branches out regularly. It bears mahogany-colored leaves, which turn olive-green and later a mat gray-green.
⚘ 30h ♥♥♥ ◌◌

Rosa Augusta Luise®

(TANgust) Tantau (1999)
Augusta Luise® is one of the new 'nostalgic roses' of

Audrey Hepburn

the German breeder Tantau, which aims to be the answer to the great popularity of the English roses. The full flowers vary in color from apricot to soft pink with a lot of cream. They have a delicious sweet, fruity fragrance and a lovely classic form. They are borne on long stems, making them ideal for cutting. The glossy, olive-green leaves have a good resistance to fungal diseases.
⚘ 30h ♥♥♥ ◌◌◌ ✚

Rosa Auguste Renoir®

(MEItoifar) Meilland (1994)
The impressionist painter Renoir was a great rose lover, and in his lifetime a rose was even named after him: Rosa Painter Renoir. The story goes that Renoir used the fleshy tones of the rose as example when he could not get hold of a model of flesh and blood. The shrub rose Rosa Painter Renoir is said to still grow in his former garden in the southern French

Augusta Luise®

town of Les Colettes. The modern Meilland rose Auguste Renoir® from the Fleur Romantica® series recreates the atmosphere of the time in which Renoir painted his masterpieces, with its powerful pink hues, romantic forms and lovely perfumes.
The large flowers are so lusciously full that they bend under their own weight. The stems are very thorny.
⚘ 30h ♥♥♥ ◌◌◌

Rosa Austriana®

(TANanaistrua) Tantau (1996)
The rich blooms of this modern shrub rose last throughout summer and fall. The laterally growing

Auguste Renoir®

plant is covered with blood red flowers. They are semi-double and quickly reveal their heart stuffed with pollen, but they have no fragrance. Bad weather has hardly any effect on the plant, and after blooming the petals simply fall off. Even under bright sunshine the flowers retain their color. The shrub branches vigorously, becomes over one-and-a-half feet tall and equally wide. The shiny, medium green leaves remain healthy and attractive in the fall. This highly recommended rose has won many prizes including the highest distinction for park and shrub roses during the International Rose Show in The Hague.

/↔ 25h

Rosa Azulabria

(RUIblun)

see *Rosa* Bluenette

Austriana®

Austriana®

Rosa Baby Carnaval

(TANba)

see *Rosa* Baby Maskerade®

Rosa Baby Carnival

(TANba)

see *Rosa* Baby Maskerade®

Rosa Baby Mascarade

(TANba)

see *Rosa* Baby Maskerade®

Rosa Baby Maskarade

(TANba)

see *Rosa* Baby Maskerade®

Rosa Baby Maskerade®

(TANba) Tantau (1955)

Since the appearance of this rose in 1955 numerous synonyms have come about with diverse ways of spelling. The names, however, are all similar to either Baby Maskerade or Baby Carnaval.

These are all miniature roses with separate, full, multi-colored flowers with hardly any fragrance. They appear to be yellow with pink-red, but display further nuances of apricot and cream. Its rich and long flowering makes this miniature rose very popular and available at many outlets. The bushes grow vertically. They bear glossy, dark green leaves that for a fairly old variety shows good resistance to disease.

15h

Baby Maskerade®

Rosa Baby Masquerade

(TANba)
see *Rosa* Baby Maskerade®

Rosa Bad Birnbach®

(KORpancom) Kordes (1999)

The salmon-pink flowers are relatively large in comparison with the small size of the bush. They are full, yet display a heart which reveals light stripes and yellow stamens. The scentless flowers appear in trusses above the glossy, dark green foliage. Due to its limited height Bad Birnbach can also be regarded as a patio rose.

✲✲ 20h ✿✿✿ ☁ ✚

Rosa Ballade®

(TANedallab) Tantau (1991)

The clear pink, full flowers of Ballade® open to reveal a cup-shape. There are a few flowers to a cluster but unfortunately they have only a very slight fragrance. However, they have good resistance to fungal diseases. This is one reason why they are often planted in public places. The glossy, grass-colored foliage stays green for a long time and contrasts wonderful-

Bad Birnbach®

ly with the bright flowers. The plant is compact and branches well.

✲✲ 30h ✿✿✿ ☁ ✚

Rosa Bantry Bay®

(-) McGredy (1967)

This is one of the most rewarding climbing roses of the moment. The sturdy stems grow up to ten feet tall, but by keeping them short the bush grows lower with many vertical and sideward trusses that cover the entire plant during July.

Afterwards it blooms less but constantly. The cup-shaped, full, baby pink flowers grow to almost four

Ballade®

inches wide. At the end of the bloom the flowers begin to fade: in bright sun they even turn ivory-white, exposing the heart with yellow pollen. They give a light but delicious fragrance of apples. The light leaves become glossy, dark green with age. It is vulnerable to black spot.

60-120h ✿✿✿ ☁☁

Bantry Bay®

Rosa Barbara Austin

(AUStop) Austin (1997)

The bushy plant initially grows upright but the stems then bend. In summer lilac-pink flowers appear. They are full but with the loose form of many old roses, giving a romantic look. This is enhanced by the powerful fragrance of old roses.

🌹GB 40h 🌹🌹🌹 ☁☁

Rosa Barkarole®

(TANelorak) Tantau (1988)

The velvety, rich red flowers unfold from long, almost black buds. Barkarole® is one of the deepest red roses and so is much in demand as a cut rose, also because they have a strong but not pronounced fragrance. The flowers appear regularly throughout

Barbara Austin

the summer. They can withstand rain well. The large, dark green leaves have good resistance to fungal diseases. The flowers are borne on vigorously growing stems that can sometimes reach five feet tall, although they are usually no more than three-and-a-half feet. The bush itself looks somewhat untidy.

✻ 35h 🌹🌹🌹 ☁☁☁ ✚

Rosa Barock®

(TANbak) TANtau (1999)

Under the label 'Nostalgic Roses' Tantau introduces varieties that are reminiscent of country gardens: rich flowers with a delicious fragrance.

This is the German breeder's answer to the popular English roses. Barock® has a pleasant though fairly weak fragrance. But it certainly does not disappoint. The very full flowers have tints of yellow, apricot and a hint of salmon. They do well in bad weather and continue to produce good blooms. The shrub can reach up to five feet in height. Barock® has medium green leaves that are fairly disease-resistant.

🌀 50–60h 🌹🌹🌹 ☁☁ ✚

Barkarole®

Rosa Barry Fearn

(KORschwama)
see *Rosa* Schwarze Madonna®

Barock®

Bassino®

Rosa Bassino®

(KORmixel) Kordes (1988)

The long stems of this shrub rose bend under the weight of the foliage and flowers, and consequently mainly grow sidewards: bushy yet providing good ground cover. The full trusses with bright red, single flowers have their richest flushes at the start of summer, after which this is repeated a few more times but not so intensely. The yellow pollen in the cup-shaped flowers contrast beautifully and entice insects to visit. Bassino® has light green, glossy leaves, which unfortunately are prone to black spot.

↔ 10h 🌺🌺 ☁

Rosa Bavaria

(KORmun)

see *Rosa* Gruss an Bayern®

Rosa Bavaria München

(POUlkalm)

see *Rosa* Kalmar™ Castle®

Rosa Bayerngold®

(TANyab) Tantau (1990)

Many yellow roses are vulnerable to rose diseases. Bayerngold® is a remarkable exception.

The medium green foliage has good resistance to fungal disease and stays attractive late into the season. The flowers are borne on compact bushes of approximately one-and-a-half feet in height. The canary-yellow flowers extend from these bushes the whole summer through to fall. They are well formed but have no fragrance.

🌺🌺 20h 🌺🌺🌺 ☁ ✪

Bayerngold®

Rosa Bayernland Cover™ Towne & Country®

(POUlrijk) Poulsen (1996)

The glossy, dark green leaves hide practically all the ground from view. The shrub has good branching growth and grows up to one-and-a-half feet tall, but some flowering stems can grow up to three-and-a-half feet tall. They bear trusses with semi-double, pink flowers, which are approximately two-and-a-half inches wide and have a mild, fruity fragrance.

🌑 25h 🌹🌹🌹 ☁☁

Rosa Beaulieu

(TANzahde)

see *Rosa* Red Haze®

Bayernland Cover™ Towne & Country®

Rosa Bella Rosa®

(KORwonder) Kordes (1981)

Bella Rosa® is characterized by its extremely rich flushes of full, pink flowers. The yellow pollen can eventually also be seen. The flowers have a mild fragrance of wild roses. The compact growth of the bush and the long flowering duration make the rose ideal for bedding. The young olive-green and older dark green foliage are quite striking.

�֎�֎ 25h 🌹🌹🌹 ☁☁

Bella Rosa®

Rosa Bella™ Castle®

(POUljill) Poulsen (1997)

The bush has regular branching growth. They grow to about thirty inches tall, but according to Poulsen they can reach as much as five feet. Above the glossy, dark green foliage are trusses of semi-double, light yellow flowers, which grow to about three inches wide.

The flowers are cupped when open, and once flowered they don't clean easily. This is a rather dull rose with hardly any fragrance.

�֎✖ 30h 🌹🌹🌹 ☁

Bella™ Castle®

Rosa Belle de Londres

see *Rosa* Compassion

Rosa Benjamin Britten

(AUSencart) Austin (2001)
The full flowers of this recent English rose resemble those of the peony rose. They open slowly to a wide cup-shape and have a distinctive brick-red color with touches of orange. It has a strong, fruity fragrance. The flowers of Benjamin Britten – named after the English composer – develop within small trusses on a medium-sized yet compact shrub, which bears many medium green leaves.

🌹GB 50h 🌹🌹🌹 ☁☁☁

Rosa Berendina

(DELdog)
see *Rosa* Pimprenelle®

Benjamin Britten

Rosa Bering™ Renaissance®

(POUlberin) Poulsen (1998)
Attempts at breeding blue roses have so far failed, as the pale mauve color of this flower bears testimony. The perfume is both strong and sweet. The half-inch-wide flowers initially have a round form. The ball later opens allowing insects to visit the yellow pollen and red stigma. Unfortunately, the flowers are sensitive to rain and so do not clean well.

☁ 40h 🌹🌹🌹 ☁☁☁☁

Bering™ Renaissance®

Rosa Berkshire

(KORpinka)
see *Rosa* Sommermärchen®

Rosa Berleburg™ Castle®

(POUlbella) Poulsen (1996)
The trusses with full red flowers bloom cup-shaped above the shiny, dark green leaves. These leaves have tinges of mahogany. The bush is a little too large to be regarded as a patio rose, but is suitable for smaller gardens, and possibly flower boxes or large pots.

✸✸ 25h 🌹🌹🌹 ☁

Rosa Bernhard Dänike

(TANweieke)
see *Rosa* Ingrid Weibull®

Berleburg™ Castle®

Rosa Bernina®

(-) De Ruiter (1979)

A wonderfully formed cut rose, which can also be used in beds and borders. The bushes do not branch much and because they primarily grow vertically they give a rather small impression. The almost four-inch-wide flowers have a splendid form: they are full with cream and a touch of apricot in the heart of the young flower. They blemish somewhat with rain but clean well. They have a light, fresh, fruity fragrance. The leaves are of medium size and are a light gray-green when they first unfold, then become a mat dark gray-green color with age.

✺✺ 30h 🌸🌸🌸 ☁☁

Rosa Bernstein-Rose®

(TANeitber) Tantau (1987)

The yellowish orange of this floribunda rose reminded the German rose breeder Tantau of amber, in German Bernstein. The large, cup-shaped flowers are very full, have a pleasant spicy fragrance and bloom constantly throughout the summer. They have

Bernina®

the form of old roses or English roses. Tantau prefers to talk of 'nostalgic roses', and Bernstein-Rose® belongs to this category. The bush grows low and bears dark green foliage that is very resistant to mildew and black spot.

✺✺ 25h 🌸🌸🌸 ☁☁ ✚

Bernstein-Rose®

Rosa Berolina®

(KORpriwa) Kordes (1986)

Large-flowered yellow roses are not really in fashion, certainly when the bush grows very upright. However, this ADR rose does have the great advantage of problem-free growth, without any noticeable susceptibility to fungal disease.

Plant it in the background of a border or fill a bed, to give excellent cut roses. The flowers have a light, sweet fragrance.

✳ 40–80h 🌸🌸🌸 ☁☁ ✚ ADR

Berolina®

Rosa Berries 'n Cream

(POUlclimb)
see *Rosa* Calypso™ Courtyard®

Rosa Best of Friends

(POUldunk)
see *Rosa* Kaj Munk™ Paramount®

Rosa Betty Harkness

(HARette) Harkness (1998)
An exuberant flowering floribunda rose with orange-pink to salmon-pink flowers. Yellow can be seen at the base of the numerous petals. The buds appear in luscious trusses, which branch out like a screen. The three-inch-wide full flowers have a delicious sweet, fruity fragrance. Due to the many flowers it can be smelt from a distance. In 2000 Betty Harkness won the Fragrance Prize at the International Rose Show in The Hague. The bush grows up to thirty inches tall, has good branching growth and bears many large, glossy, dark green leaves that look very healthy.
✾✾ 30h ❦❦❦ ◌◌◌◌

Rosa Betty Prior

(-) Prior (1935)
When in full bloom this old-fashioned floribunda rose looks impressive. The single flowers are flat. Initially they are cherry-red in color, but then change to a reddish pink exterior and a light pink interior, giving a bi-colored effect. The flowers have a slight

Betty Harkness

Betty Harkness

musty fruity fragrance. New full trusses are formed regularly on strikingly thin stems which, however, successfully hold the flowers away from the abundant foliage. The foliage is initially light green with a purple edge and leaf stalk, but turns a grayish green with age.
✾✾ 30h ❦❦❦ ◌

Rosa Bewitched

(POUlbella)
see *Rosa* Berleburg™ Castle®

Betty Prior

Rosa Bijou d'Or

(TANledolg)
see *Rosa* Goldjuwel®

Rosa Bingo Meidiland®

(MEIpotal) Meilland (1994)

The combination of the bright color of the buds and the soft pink of the flowers is quite striking. On opening, the single flowers reveal a white eye with yellow stamens. The bush branches profusely to about chest height. The dark green, glossy foliage stays attractive throughout summer, as Bingo Meidiland® is very resistant to black spot and mildew.

🌾 30h 🌹🌹🌹 ⌁ ✚ ADR TOP

Rosa Bingo Meillandecor

see *Rosa* Bingo Meidiland

Bingo Meidiland®

Rosa Bischofsstadt Paderborn®

(-) Kordes (1964)

The bright red, semi-double flowers of this shrub rose are an impressive sight even from a distance. As you come closer you will see that this dazzling effect is in part due to the light eye of the fully developed flowers. They bloom the whole summer and fall on the profusely growing bush, which can reach five feet tall. The mat, olive-green foliage is fairly resistant to disease, and due to its vigorous growth the bush is well covered in foliage late in the season. It is sometimes used as a low climbing rose, but more often as a hedge.

🌾 40–60h 🌹🌹🌹 ⌁ ✚ ADR

Bischofsstadt Paderborn®

Rosa Black Madonna

(KORschwama)

see *Rosa* Schwarze Madonna®

Rosa Blenheim

(TANmurse)

see *Rosa* Schneesturm®

Rosa Blessings

(-) Gregory (1967)

The reddish brown young leaves go well with the soft and yet prominent coral-red to salmon-pink color of the full flowers. They have a pleasant fragrance and make excellent cut roses.

The bush grows vigorously upright and looks healthy.

✻ 30h 🌹🌹🌹 ⌁⌁⌁

Left to the front *Rosa* Blessings; adjacent *Rosa* Dame de Coeur and *Rosa* Maria Mathilde

Blessings

Rosa Blue Bajou®

(KORkultop) Kordes (1993)

Blue is the only color not seen in roses and that is probably why so much effort goes into trying to achieve this. With Blue Bajou® the rose breeder Kordes hasn't quite succeeded in this, but has managed to produce a dazzling, low-growing floribunda rose with fragrant, grayish lilac-colored flowers. They develop from cone-shaped buds, from which the petals slowly unfurl to later reveal the heart and stamens. By that time the full flowers are wide and saucer-shaped. They contrast well with the glossy, dark green leaves. For healthy growth, plant in a good location and provide sufficient nutrients.

✿✿ 25h ❦❦❦ ☁☁

Rosa Blue Monday

(TANnacht)
see *Rosa* Mainzer Fastnacht

Blue Bajou®

Rosa Blue Moon

(TANnacht)
see *Rosa* Mainzer Fastnacht

Rosa Blue Nile

(DELnible)
see *Rosa* Nil Bleu®

Rosa Blue Parfum®

(TANfifum) Tantau (1978)

Give this rose the best possible care and you will be rewarded with beautiful violet-blue flowers. They have an intense fragrance and are very suitable for cutting, although some will find the fragrance too strong. The well-formed, full flowers usually appear in early summer. They are sensitive to bad weather. Therefore place in the best possible location for roses: sunshine, good ventilation – but not drafty – and fertile, loose soil. The bushy shrub grows to around two feet tall.

✿✿ 25h ❦❦❦ ☁☁☁☁

Rosa Blue Perfume

(TANfifum)
see *Rosa* Blue Parfum®

Blue Parfum®

Rosa Blue Peter

(RUIblun)
see *Rosa* Bluenette

Rosa Blue Rambler

(Schmidt)
see *Rosa* Veilchenblau

Rosa Blue River®

(KORsicht) Kordes (1984)
The large, full flowers bloom singly or with a few next
to one another on the upright yet well-branching bush.
The flowers combine color well: the lilac petals are
often colored magenta on the edges, whilst towards
the middle the petals turn a gray-white color. They
have a wonderful fragrance. The leaves of Blue River®
are dark green. It is an excellent rose for warm summers in areas with a continental climate.
⚹ 30h 🌹🌹🌹 ☁☁☁☁

Rosa Blue Rosalie

(Schmidt)
see *Rosa* Veilchenblau

Blue River®

Rosa Bluenette

(RUIblun) De Ruiter (1983)
Numerous lilac flowers bloom on a low shrub,
which is equally suitable as a patio rose in containers as grafted on a stem. The compact growth
ensures that the rose stays in shape. The semi-
double, mildly fragrant flowers are saucer-shaped
when open, revealing their yellow pollen. They are
very vulnerable to bad weather and can look messy
after rain. The compact bush bears attractive, light
green leaves.
▣ 15h 🌹🌹🌹 ☁☁

Bluenette

Bluenette

Rosa Bluesette®

(LENmau) Lens (1984)
Once the full flowers have completely opened they
reveal a very special form. The lilac-mauve petals bend
backwards, closely overlapping one another. They
overlap in spirals, like roof tiles and reveal their yellow-
gold pollen in the heart. The flowers are almost two
inches wide. Bluesette® has a light fragrance. The flowers are in trusses on the low, well-branching shrub.
▣ 10h 🌹🌹🌹 ☁☁

Rosa Blühwunder®

(KORedan) Kordes (1995)
Sometimes up to fifty roses appear on a single stem of
this extremely richly blooming floribunda rose. At the
height of its blooms this bush is covered with semi-
double, light salmon-pink flowers, which have a mild

Bluesette®

Blythe Spirit

apple fragrance. After the initial profuse blooms, there is a subsequent flush lasting months. Blühwunder® has upright growth with much branching. The glossy, dark green leaves are not very susceptible to rose diseases. In France Blühwunder® is sold under the name Ponderosa, but do not confuse this with the orange-red Kordes rose Ponderosa (KORpon), which is no longer available but can still be found in some rosariums and gardens. Take care if you come across the name Flower Power, as this is used not only for this rose but also for a low-growing shrub rose from Fryer.

✿✿ 30–35h ❦❦❦ ✿✿ ✪ ADR

Rosa Blythe Spirit

(AUSchool) Austin (1999)

Full trusses of pale yellow flowers appear on this profusely branching shrub, which grows equally wide as tall. The full flowers appear the entire summer above the gray-green foliage. They have a mild musk fragrance. Until recently, David Austin classified Blythe Spirit as a continuous-flowering shrub rose. This makes no difference to the care required. Light pruning, as with park or shrub roses, is advised.

❦GB/◍ 50h ❦❦❦ ✿✿

Blühwunder®

Rosa Bobbie James

(-) Sunningdale Nursery (1961)

The spectacular blooms in early summer make Bobbie James one of the top ramblers.

The thin, light green stems require support or need to be tied, but then still manage to reach some seventeen feet. It bears attractive foliage of the same light green color of Granny Smith apples. This light appearance is reinforced by the two-inch-wide semi-double flowers. They are mildly fragrant and reveal their golden pollen. Together with the golden stamens they resemble a bride's bouquet, and the fresh

Bobbie James

Bobbie James (middle)

fruity fragrance enhances this party mood. A stunning rose to grow against a tree or high arch.

⚘ 120–200h ♀ ☁☁☁

Rosa Bolchoi®

(MElzuzes) Meilland (1996)

Under the name Parfums de Provence® the French rose breeding family Meilland produces highly fragrant roses. Meilland describes the fragrance of Bolchoi® as a 'a blend of lemon, fruit and rose perfume'. The blooms are distinctly bi-colored, full, and large flowered. The exterior of the petals are a yellowish cream, the inside rose-red. The flowers remain the entire summer and look wonderful in a vase.

✳ 30h ♀♀♀ ☁☁☁☁

Rosa Bolero™ Courtyard®

(POUlbota) Poulsen (2000)

The over three-inch-wide, single flowers combine beautifully with the reddish, later glossy, gray-green leaves: the flowers are creamy white, but with a small hint of soft pink. They have a light fragrance. The shrub branches profusely, but particularly upwards, and is therefore primarily used as a rambler.

⚘ 100h ♀♀♀ ☁☁

Rosa Bonanza®

(KORmarie) Kordes (1983)

On opening, the flowers of Bonanza® reveal golden petals with rose-red edges, giving a clear bi-colored effect. The colors fade somewhat with age. The heart of the semi-double flower is clearly visible. The flowers appear in trusses on the tall bush that can grow up to seven feet tall under favorable conditions. The

Bolero™ Courtyard®

glossy, dark green leaves stay fairly healthy, which earned the rose the ADR award.

🌑 60–80h ♀♀♀ ☁ ✪ ARD

Bolchoi®

Bonanza®

Rosa Bonbon™ Hit®

(POUlbon) Poulsen (1996)

The golden color of the flowers of this patio rose is contrasted wonderfully by the orange to red markings, particularly on the edges. The semi-double flowers are approximately two inches wide, and bloom in trusses above the glossy, dark green foliage.

15h

Rosa Bonica®82

(MEIdomonac) Meilland (1985)

This shrub rose has been heaped with distinctions, including the German ADR award and the title of Top Rose in the Netherlands. No wonder, because this variety has much to offer: lengthy blooms until deep into fall, light pink flowers and a loose bush form that hides the ground from view. Although this variety is reputed to be very healthy it is somewhat susceptible to black spot. Insects are able to penetrate the heart of the full flowers, so that this waist-high bush produces hips after a beautiful summer.

25h ADR TOP

Bonbon™ Hit®

Bonica®82

Bonica®82

Rosa Bony Meilove®

(MEIboniov) Meilland (1999)

Patio roses are ideal for small gardens as they remain small and yet produce rich flushes. Bony Meilove® has full, saucer-shaped, pink flowers.

In the ground the bush can grow up to one-and-a-half feet tall, but will also thrive in a large pot.

20h

Bony Meilove®

Rosa Bordure Camaïeu®

(DELcapo) Delbard (2001)

This is the latest variety in the popular Bordure series of the French breeding family Delbard. The semi-double, cup-shaped flowers are multi-colored. They open from orange-red buds, bloom yellow to apricot and turn pink with age. As flowers of different ages bloom at the same time, a multi-colored visual feast is produced. The bush has profuse branching growth and is wide-spreading with glossy, olive-green leaves.

🌸 20h 🌷🌷🌷 ☁

Rosa Bordure d'Or®

(DELbojaun) Delbard (1985)

The golden flowers bloom on an upright bush, fifteen to thirty inches tall, which sometimes reaches forty

Bordure Camaïeu®

inches. The bush grows well and bears rich blooms. The full, cup-shaped flowers are three inches wide, and have a mild, fresh fragrance. The young foliage is light green, changing to a mat, dark gray-green.

🌸 25h 🌷🌷🌷 ☁

Bordure d'Or®

Rosa Bordure de Nacrée

(DELcrouf)

see *Rosa* Bordure Nacrée®

Rosa Bordure Nacrée®

(DELcrouf) Delbard (1973)

The full, fragrantless flowers have a striking blend of colors, from yellow to pale pink. They bloom in trusses on a low, well-branching bush of approximately twenty inches tall.

🌸 20h 🌷🌷🌷 ☁

Rosa Bordure Rose®

(DELcoussi) Delbard (1993)

This is the successor to the earlier edition of Bordure Rose, which bore the cultivar name of DELbara. Whilst that rose had cream-colored flowers with pink edges, the flowers of the new Bordure Rose® are completely pale pink with a more intense color in the full heart.

Bordure Nacrée®

They have no fragrance, but bloom the whole summer on a well-branching bush with glossy, dark green leaves.

✿✿ 30h 🌷🌷🌷 ☁

Rosa Bordure Vermillon®

(DELbover) Delbard (1990)

The charm of this miniature rose lies in the bi-color of the full flowers. The inside of the flower is bright

Bordure Rose®

Bordure Vive®

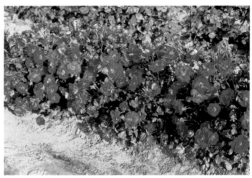

red; the outside has touches of cream. They have no fragrance and bloom in luxuriant trusses on a low and limp bush.
🏵 15h ❦❦❦ ☁

Rosa **Bordure Vive**®

(DELboviv) Delbard (1985)
This wide-spreading bush, with relatively large, medium green foliage, remains very low. It bears carmine-red flowers that have no fragrance.
🏵 15h ❦❦❦ ☁

Bordure Vermillon®

Rosa **Bossa Nova**

(POUloma)
see *Rosa* Meine Oma™

Rosa **Bouquet Parfait**®

(-) Lens (1989)
Each truss on this upright rose forms a bouquet in itself, so close are the full flowers next to one another. They open up from round swollen buds to look like full peony roses, but in reality they are much smaller: around two inches. The color varies per flower. They are primarily milky white with hints of pink, particularly on the edges. Light pink flowers also develop, particularly in cooler weather. Its light musk fragrance adds to its popularity as a cut rose. The color of the flowers combines well with many other flowers in a vase. The shrub grows upright with fresh green leaves.
🌼 50h ❦❦❦ ☁☁

Rosa **Bouquet Vanille**®

(DELblatine) Delbard (1993)
The attractive, pointed buds are salmon-pink, but when they open out to saucer-shaped flowers they quickly fade to vanilla. What's more, the flowers have a mild vanilla fragrance. This is a beautiful floribunda rose, which forms a well-branching upright bush with

Bouquet Parfait®

Bouquet Vanille®

long-lasting rich blooms. Bouquet Vanille® bears many large, dark green leaves. Highly recommended.
�֎�֎ 35h 🌹🌹🌹 ☁☁

Rosa Bournonville™ Courtyard®

(Poulyc001) Poulsen (2000)

This is the new addition to the Courtyard series of the Danish breeder Poulsen. This includes a number of ramblers that have a distinctive, vigorously branching growth, covering the base of the plant well with leaves. Bournonville™ doesn't grow especially tall and bears semi-double, pale pink flowers with an open heart. They have no fragrance.
⚶ 🌹🌹🌹 80h ☁

Rosa Braithwaite

(AUScrim)

see *Rosa* L.D. Braithwaite

Bournonville™ Courtyard®

Rosa Breath of Life

(HARquanne) Harkness (1982)

The apricot-colored flowers of Breath of Life are large for a climber, but unfortunately they do not appear in large numbers. A cluster comprises of no more than three of the full flowers. They have a mild but pleasant fragrance. To encourage rich blooms, plant in a warm, sufficiently fertile location. The branches can reach up to ten feet tall and bear glossy, dark green leaves.
⚶ 100h 🌹🌹🌹 ☁☁

Rosa Bremer Stadtmusikanten®

(KORterschi) Kordes (2000)

The cream to pale pink flowers unfold from yellow,

Breath of Life

cream buds. The flowers are full and hemispherical, and have a mild sweet perfume. A few flowers appear on each stem of the upright bush that bears dark green, glossy leaves. This promising new rose from Kordes grows up to three-and-a-half feet tall.
⚘ 50h 🌹🌹🌹 ☁☁

Bremer Stadtmusikanten®

Rosa Brian Rix

(HARflipper) Harkness (1999)

Being five feet tall and three-and-a-half feet wide this shrub is highly suitable for hedging when placed in a row. The lilac-pink flowers appear in trusses throughout the whole summer. They are semi-double and open from attractive, pointed buds, and then bloom wide open, spreading their delightful fragrance. Brian Rix also functions well as a solitary.

🌐 60h 🌹🌹🌹 ☁☁☁

Rosa Briant Hill®

(-) Poulsen (1994)

The flowers of this miniature rose are only two-and-a-half inches wide, but well formed. They are semi-double and have a bright red-orange color, but hard-

Brian Rix

ly any fragrance. The bush grows upright and somewhat irregularly, so they are not suitable for bedding. The decorative leaves are glossy, dark green. The bush is highly suited to be grown as a tree rose.

🔲 20h 🌹🌹🌹 ☁

Briant Hill®

Rosa Bride's Dream

(KORoyness)

see *Rosa* Märchenkönigin®

Rosa Bridge of Sighs

(HARglow) Harkness (2000)

In early fall this climbing rose is a feast for the eyes. Numerous trusses are borne of orange flowers, which from close by show more subtle hues. Inside they are pure orange, changing to pale orange and amber on the edges. When open the cup-shaped semi-double flowers reveal golden pollen in an apricot heart. They have a pleasant fragrance. If fed well and planted in a favorable location the rose will grow well and produce some good blooms. Each flower only blooms for a short while but cleans well. This climber grows up to ten feet tall.

🌿 120h 🌹🌹 ☁☁☁

Rosa Brilliant™ Hit®

(POUlbril) Poulsen (-)

A miniature that is sold as an indoor pot rose, but actually grows better outside in a container or pot. The full, orange-red flowers have the perfect shape of a large-flowered rose, but then in miniature. The bush grows up to about ten to fifteen inches tall.

🔲 15h 🌹🌹🌹 ☁☁

Bridge of Sighs

Rosa Brite Lites®

(HARtanna)

see *Rosa* Princess Alice

Brilliant™ Hit®

Rosa Broadlands

(TANmirsch)
see *Rosa* Sonnenschirm®

Rosa Brother Cadfael™

(AUSglobe) Austin (1990)
This English rose with its colossal flowers is named after the fictional novel character Brother Cadfael, a medieval monk and detective. The flowers resemble those of the full peony rose. The pale pink petals of the moderately full flowers overlap one another, eventually revealing – unintentionally – the heart of the flower, which has an old rose perfume.
♀GB 50h ♀♀♀ ☁☁☁

Brother Cadfael™

Rosa Bruocsella

(LENbru) Lens (1980)
A large-flowered rose with a wonderful perfume. The full, yellow flowers develop from pointed buds and are wide, open and globular. This regularly growing bush with grayish green leaves grows constantly and is seldom without flowers in the summer. The flowers are suitable for the vase.
✳ 25h ♀♀♀ ☁☁☁

Rosa Bryce Canyon

(POUldrik)
see *Rosa* Frederiksborg™ Castle®

Rosa Buck's Fizz

(POUlgav)
see *Rosa* Gavnø™ Hybrid Tea Poulsen®

Bruocsella

Rosa Buff Beauty

(-) Bentall (1939)
With this musk hybrid the rose enthusiast has the choice of growing the rose high and wide to form a hedge or to let it grow as a rambler. In the height of summer the rose blooms only once but with rich flushes of very full flowers. They develop from ochre-yellow buds and initially retain that color.
With age the flowers turn a yellowish cream color. They have the typical musk fragrance after which this rose group has been named. Buff Beauty is still highly recommended.
◍ / ⚘ 50–80h ♀ ☁☁☁

Buff Beauty

Rosa Buffalo Gal

(UHLwa)
see *Rosa rugosa* Foxi®

Rosa Bukavu®

(-) Lens (1998)
This rose was named after the area around the Congo region and city Bukavu. The revenues from the first two years of sales of Bukavu® went to the health authorities in that area. This floribunda rose is closely related to the popular Rosa Rush from the same breeder. Bukavu® has trusses of carmine-red, single flowers that have an almost totally white heart. They have good resistance to bad weather. Although formally a floribunda rose, Bukavu® forms a shrub that is also highly suitable as a hedge.
✲✲ 50h ✿✿✿ ☁☁

Rosa Burghausen®

(KORonto) Kordes (1991)
This shrub grows so profusely that after a few years it is already the height of an average man and sometimes reaches up to eight feet. The stems are thick and sturdy. The shrub grows primarily upright, but

Bukavu®

Burghausen®

can eventually reach five feet wide. It therefore makes an ideal hedge, for which you only need one plant per ten square feet. In early summer Burghausen® is overladen with semi-double, bright red flowers. The flowers are saucer-shaped and reveal a heart with yellow stamens and a lighter spot. The medium green, glossy foliage has good resistance to fungal disease.
⊛ 80h ✿✿✿ ☁ ✚ ADR

Rosa Buttercup™

(AUSband) Austin (1998)
Cup-shaped, butter-yellow flowers characterize the Buttercup™. The buds form in full trusses on the long vertical branches. On unfolding the flowers are deeper in color, apricot even, but fade with age.
Under their weight the branches begin to droop, forming a loose shrub that blends in well in a romantic border with other shrubs and perennials. The flowers are semi-double and have a light and fresh fragrance.
✿GB/⊛ 55h ✿✿✿ ☁☁

Buttercup™

Rosa Butterflies Cover™ Towne & Country®

(POUlbut) Poulsen (1998)

Bees are frequent visitors to these single flowers, which entice the insects with their mass of pollen. The one-and-a-half-inch-wide flowers are pale pink. They have hardly any fragrance. Each truss bears dozens of buds that protrude just above the mat, green foliage. After a rich initial flush in early summer, further blooms follow, which though less intense last for some time. There is profuse branching, helping to cover the ground well.

⊚ /↔ 20h 🌷🌷🌷 ✿

Rosa Calypso™ Courtyard®

(POUlclimb) Poulsen (1998)

The three-inch-wide semi-double flowers of this rambler are eye-catching due to their color combination. They are cream-colored with dashes of pink. New

Butterflies Cover™ Towne & Country®

trusses are produced throughout the summer, which smell slightly of apples. The leaves have a mahogany tinge on the edges and turn shiny dark green with age.

🪡 120h 🌷🌷🌷 ✿✿

Calypso™ Courtyard®

Rosa Cambridge

(POUlrust)

see *Rosa* Lavender Cover™ Towne & Country®

Rosa Camille Pisarro®

(DELstricol) Delbard (1996)

A spectacular rose that bears the name of the impressionist painter, Camille Pisarro® belongs to a series of multi-colored roses with the names of painters. This rose displays every conceivable shade of red, pink and yellow with some white, in spots, blotches and stripes on the petals of the mildly fragrant flowers. New trusses are formed throughout the summer on a fairly strong growing bush.

❋❋ 30h 🌷🌷🌷 ✿✿

Rosa Canary®

(TANcary) Tantau (1976)

The large, full flowers are only canary yellow in the heart. The outer petals are tinged orange-red. Due to the spectacular shape, pleasant perfume and

Camille Pisarro®

long stems they are highly suitable as cut rose. Canary® is quite weather resistant and so makes a good rose for the garden as well. The bush grows upright to about thirty inches and bears large olive-green leaves that have good resistance to fungal disease.

Although the rose is known as a continuous bloomer, there are sometimes pauses in the blooms.

❋ 30h 🌷🌷🌷 ✿✿✿ ✚

Canary®

Rosa Candide

(POUlgav)
see *Rosa* Gavnø™ Hybrid Tea Poulsen®

Rosa Candy Cover™ Towne & Country®

(POUlbico) Poulsen (1993)
The basic color of the semi-double, two-inch-wide flowers is bright red, with blotches and stripes of pink and white. The saucer-shaped flowers display golden pollen, which attracts insects. Candy Cover™ has a slight fragrance. The shrub blooms throughout summer and fall.

⊛ 25h ❦❦❦ ☁

Candy Cover™ Towne & Country®

Rosa Candy Sunblaze™

(MEIdanclar)
see Romantic Meillandina®

Rosa Canicule

(TANmirsch)
see *Rosa* Sonnenschirm®

Rosa canina

(-) botanical rose (-)
The dog rose grows throughout Europe and the neighboring areas of Asia and Africa. It is the most common wild rose in Europe. In early summer single flowers appear on the drooping branches. This drooping form of growth distinguishes the dog rose from other wild roses. The flower color differs considerably from one plant to the next. Flowers may be totally white or pink, but they are more frequently white with pink blotches on the edges. They are slightly fragrant. After flowering in early summer long orange-red hips are formed, which in winter are eaten by birds. A good rose for natural gardens.

⊛ 80h ❦ ☁☁ ✛

Rosa Cantabrigiensis

(-) botanical hybrid (1931)
This special shrub came about simply by chance in a botanical garden in Cambridge, probably as a hybrid of Rosa xanthina f. hugonis and Rosa sericea. The single, yellow flowers appear already in May. They have a pleasant perfume. After flowering,

Rosa canina

round orange-red hips form in the fall, which are hidden amongst the dense green foliage. The very healthy leaves are divided into smaller, light green leaflets. The stems initially grow upwards, then later bend outwards.

⊛ 80h ⚥ ⌒⌒⌒ ✚

Rosa Canyonlands

(POUlmax)
see *Rosa* Fredensborg™ Castle®

Cantabrigiensis

Rosa Cappa Magna®

(DELsap) Delbard (1965)
If looking for a healthy, upright rose with large, clear scarlet flowers, Cappa Magna® is the ideal choice. The glossy, dark green leaves are seldom affected by any rose diseases. The leaves are borne on branches of up to five feet long, which droop under the weight of the full trusses. The flowers, which hardly have any fragrance, are clustered in groups of up to twen-

Cappa Magna®

ty or thirty on the well-branching shrub. They are single flowers with ruffled petals, and open out cup-shaped up to four inches wide. The hearts have a prominent tuft of yellow pollen. The healthy leaves are initially mahogany, which later turn to a glossy dark green.

⊛ 50h ⚥⚥⚥ ⌒ ✚ TOP

Rosa Caprice de Meilland®

(MEIsionver) Meilland (1998)
The candy-pink flowers give off an intense fruity fragrance: it is for this reason that the breeder family Meilland has included this large-flowered rose in the Parfums de Provence® brand. Despite this southern European name these flowers are hardy when it comes to rain and wind, and last long in a vase.

✳ 35h ⚥⚥⚥ ⌒⌒⌒

Rosa Cardinal Hume®

(HARregale) Harkness (1984)
As soon as the buds begin to color, it looks like the flowers will be black. Once open the flowers display

Caprice de Meilland®

a deep purple-red similar to this cardinal's head gear. The heart reveals golden pollen and often has white lines.

The shape and growth of the Cardinal Hume® resembles that of an old rose. It was introduced by Harkness in 1984 and is a continuous-flowering shrub rose. The three-inches wide flowers have a fresh, light musk fragrance. They bloom the whole

Cardinal Hume®

Caribia®

summer on a profusely branching shrub, which droops due to the weight of the flower trusses, producing wide growth. You could say the plant is semi-ground covering. Cardinal Hume® is best as a solitary, preferably with other perennials, as the dark green foliage is susceptible to black spot.

🌑 45h 🌹🌹🌹 ☁☁

Rosa Carefree Delight™

see *Rosa* Bingo Meidiland

Rosa Carefree Wonder™

(MEIpitac)
see *Rosa* Dynastie®

Rosa Carefully Wonder

(MEIpitac)
see *Rosa* Dynastie®

Rosa Caribia®

(Harry Wheatcroft) Wheatcroft (1973)
This is a bit of a freak of nature. The rose from which Caribia® originated (Rosa Piccadilly) has petals that are golden at the back and orange-red inside. The stripy pattern of the Caribia® sport arose spontaneously from this. The full flowers appear singly on a strongly upright growing bush, which remains fairly low and bears medium green foliage. The leaves are somewhat susceptible to black spot, but still look quite healthy in the fall. The bush blooms the entire summer and fall.

✳ 30h 🌹🌹🌹 ☁☁

Rosa Carl Philip Kristian IV

(KORpeahn)
see *Rosa* Mariandel®

Rosa Carrot Top

(POUltop)
see *Rosa* Top™ Hit®

Rosa Cascade

(POUlskab)
see *Rosa* Nordina™ Courtyard®

Rosa Casque d'Or®

(DELcascor) Delbard (1979)
Casque d'Or® is sometimes classed among the large-flowered roses, and indeed under favorable conditions can produce four-inch-wide flowers. Breeder Delbard rightly classifies it as a floribunda rose: the full yellow flowers appear in trusses on the vertical bush looking very much like a floribunda.
The flowers have no fragrance but do appear the whole summer above the medium green foliage of the vigorously growing bush.

✳✳ 35h 🌹🌹🌹 ☁

Rosa Castella®

(TANallet) Tantau (1984)
This continuous-flowering shrub rose can grow up to five feet tall and is therefore suitable for low hedging.

Casque d'Or®

The upright shrubs are full with large, glossy, dark green leaves. They are fairly resistant to rose diseases and stay attractive into the autumn. The full, red flowers initially appear in very large numbers. Later there are fewer but the blooms continue throughout summer and fall.
⦿ 60h ♀♀♀ ☁

Rosa Castle Howard

(TANtasch)
see *Rosa* Goldschatz®

Rosa Cathedral City

(KORtanken)
see *Rosa* Domstadt Fulda®

Castella®

Rosa Catherine Deneuve®

(MEIpraserpi) Meilland (1981)
The flowers of this large-flowered rose vary somewhat in color: apricot to coral-pink. They have an attractive shape and are mildly fragrant. Catherine Deneuve® blooms practically constantly throughout the summer. The bushes are robust and are usually planted alongside one another in beds.
✻ 35h ♀♀♀/♀♀ ☁☁

Rosa Cécile Brünner

(-) Pernet-Ducher (1881)
The loose structure of the trusses are quite striking in this polyantha rose. The one-and-a-half-inch-wide flowers seem to float alone in the air. They are semi-double and have the shape of a beautiful large-flowered rose but in miniature. The flowers are pale pink, becoming white later. They have a light, fruity, sweet fragrance. The bush has few thorns and relatively few

Catherine Deneuve®

medium green leaves, whereby the smooth stems are quite noticeable.
▣ 15h ♀♀♀ ☁☁

Rosa Celeste

see *Rosa* Celestial

Rosa Celestial

(-) unknown (end of 18th century)
The origins of this old rose are unknown, but it is assumed that they were in Holland. Celestial belongs to

Cécile Brünner

the alba hybrids, which can be clearly seen by its large, bluish gray-green foliage. The bush can grow up to six-and-a-half feet tall and almost as wide. The rose blooms only well once it has sufficient space. Hard pruning leads to an explosion of new shoots, which then hardly bloom. The flowers are semi-double, silvery-pink with yellow pollen in the heart and have a pleasant fragrance. ❀ 70h ⚘ ☁☁☁

Rosa Celina®

(NOAson) Noack (1997)

The single to semi-double, yellow flowers appear from as early as May. They bloom in trusses on an upright shrub, where the older branches bend so much that they effectively cover the ground. The foliage is retained well on the bush and is very resistant to rose diseases.

↔ 30h ⚘⚘⚘ ☁☁ ✚ ADR

Celestial

Rosa Céline Delbard®

(DELcéli) Delbard (1983)

On opening, the full flowers of Céline Delbard® have a wonderful form. They eventually become saucer-shaped and display a heart with a small tuft of stamens. They have no fragrance.

They continue to form trusses throughout the summer and fall with five to ten flowers on each. The

Celina®

bush with its glossy, dark green foliage looks very healthy.

✿✿ 35h ⚘⚘⚘ ☁

Céline Delbard®

Rosa Centenaire de Lourdes

(DELge)
see *Rosa* Centenaire de Lourdes® Rose

Rosa Centenaire de Lourdes® Rouge

(DELflor) Delbard (1992)
The three-inch-wide flowers of this floribunda rose are crimson, often with white stripes. They are semi-double and cup-shaped when open. They have rich flushes, which can last some time. They give off only a mild perfume. The very rich trusses are borne on thick stems. The young leaves are light green (with some red), and later turn a glossy, dark gray-green. It stays very healthy, and because the bush has such vigorous growth it is very suitable for bedding and borders.
✿✿ 40h ❦❦❦ ⌣ ✚

Rosa Centenaire de Lourdes® Rose

(DELge) Delbard (1958)
This rose was originally called just Centenaire de Lourdes®. The 'Rose' was added when breeder Delbard also introduced a red flowering variety. The bright pink floribunda rose stands out through its extremely rich blooms. The trusses with full, practical-

Centenaire de Lourdes® Rouge

ly scentless flowers appear until deep into fall. This 'old rose' remains strikingly healthy; that's why they are often used in public green areas.
✿✿ 40h ❦❦❦ ⌣ ✚

Rosa Centenary

(KOReledas)
see *Rosa* NDR1 Radio Niedersachsen®

Centenaire de Lourdes® Rose

Rosa x *centifolia* Muscosa

(Moss rose) unknown breeder (around 1796)
The name moss rose comes from the moss-like growths on the sepals. The very full flowers are soft pink and have a pleasant fragrance. After a few weeks the summer blooms finish. It is then best to shorten the stems by a third to encourage further blooms the next summer. Rosa x centiflora Muscosa grows up to five feet tall.
The stems bear olive-green leaves and many vicious thorns.
❀ 40–60h ❦ ⌣⌣⌣⌣ ✚

Rosa CentrO® Rose

(TANoronez) Tantau (2000)
This is one of the so-called Stecktii® roses, as they are propagated using cuttings. Roses grown from cuttings initially develop slowly, but in their second year

Rosa x *centifolia* Muscosa

their growth catches up and they flower as well as a grafted rose. CentrO® Rose grows luxuriously, as wide as it is tall, and bears thick foliage. However, it does not cover the ground so well. They are often used in public green areas, in part due to their good resistance to fungal diseases. The foliage is bronze-green and changes to glossy dark green. The bush looks good up into fall. The trusses are practically scentless, with semi-double, crimson flowers that appear in rich flushes in early summer. They continue to bloom throughout summer and fall.
ⓦ 20h �👑🌷 ☁ ✚

Rosa **Century Sunset**

(TANsaras)
see *Rosa* Herz Ass®

Rosa **Cerise Bouquet**

(-) Kordes (1958)
The drooping branches of the seven-feet-tall rose produce an elegant bush that is ideal for any natural

CentrO® Rose

or romantic garden. Early summer the bush is covered by cherry-red flowers. The flowers are moderately full and loose with a flat shape and have a pleasant scent. Cerise Bouquet is once flowering and has light green leaves.
ⓦ 80h 🌷 ☁☁

Cerise Bouquet

Rosa **Cesar**®

(MEIsardan) Meilland (1993)
A rose that looks like an ornamental cabbage would be quite special. And this Cesar® with its ruffled buds is just that. The forty to sixty petals are curled and primarily creamy pink, with salmon-pink in the heart. They are so heavy that the stems tilt under the weight, making them look like the fullest of English roses. The Fleur Romantica® series should therefore be seen as the breeder Meilland's answer to the extremely popular English roses of David Austin.
They can be used in the same way: in combination with perennials that would give the rose a little support.
ⓦ 30h 🌷🌷🌷 ☁

Rosa **Cevennes**

(KORlirus)
see *Rosa* Heidesommer®

Cesar®

Rosa Champagner

(KORampa) Kordes (1983)

Although the flowers have the typical shape of a large-flowered rose, this is actually a floribunda rose that is grown primarily in greenhouses as a cut rose. Outside it should be grown only in areas with warm summers. The pointed buds develop into fragrant, star-shaped flowers, which also stay attractive in a vase for a long time. They are ivory-colored with a hint of pale pink. They appear in smallish groups throughout the summer. The stems have few thorns and bear many mat, dark green leaves. The bush is upright and has good branching growth.

✹✹ 25h ♚♚♚ ◌◌

Rosa Champagnerperle

(KORampa)

see *Rosa* Champagner

Rosa Champs Elysees

(MEIcarl) Meilland (1957)

This well-known rose is slowly getting out of favor. The rose blooms throughout the season with large, intense red flowers on fairly soft stems, which bend

Champagner

easily under the weight of the full flowers. They are practically scentless. The healthy leaves are dark green.

✲ 25h ♚♚♚ ◌

Rosa Chantoli

(FRYxotic)

see *Rosa* Warm Wishes

Rosa Charentes™

see *Rosa* Astrid Lindgren™ Floribunda Poulsen®

Champs Elysees

Rosa Charity™

(AUSchar) Austin (1997)

The name refers to the typically English practice of opening gardens to the public for charity purposes through the National Garden Scheme. This rose has the character of an old rose: full and a shallow cup shape. Charity™ does, however, have a very contemporary color, namely apricot-yellow, but the rich scent of old roses remains.

♚GB 50h ♚♚♚ ◌◌◌

Rosa Charles Austin®

(AUSfather) Austin (1973)

This somewhat older English rose is still popular. Stems extend upwards from the branching bush, bearing trusses of apricot which fade to a light salmon-pink with age. The flowers are very full and have a wonderful sweet scent of old roses. The foliage is large, mat and medium to dark green.

♚GB 40h ♚♚♚ ◌◌◌◌

Charity™

Rosa Charles de Gaulle®

(MEllanein) Meilland (1974)

Pure blue roses do not exist, but with Charles de Gaulle® the rose family Meilland have come pretty close. The fragrant flowers have a striking lilac color, a little more pink than in the photo. The flower has the form of a classic Hybrid Tea, which we now tend to call a large-flowered rose. The robust bush thrives particularly in warm settings, and therefore less so in a cold and wet climate.

✻ 30h ❀❀❀ ☁☁☁

Charles Austin®

Rosa Charles Rennie Mackintosh

(AUSren) Austin (1988)

The full flowers are initially spherical, later opening out into a deep cup-shape. They have a lilac pink

color, which depending on the weather tends towards either pink or lilac. The heart contains smaller curled petals. The flowers have light, pleasant fragrance and appear singly on the end of slender stems. The stems bend slightly under the weight, but the rose is still suitable as a cut rose. The stems bear extremely sharp thorns and relatively dark green leaves.

❀GB/◍ 55h ❀❀❀ ☁☁

Charles de Gaulle®

Rosa Charlotte

(AUSpoly) Austin (1993)

Charlotte begins flowering mid-summer and continues lightly into the fall. The bush bears full flowers, with soft yellow towards the center and cream on the outside. They have a light and pleasant fragrance of tea roses. The upright shrub remains compact and grows almost as wide as it is tall. The bronze green leaves eventually turn dark green.

❀GB 35h ❀❀ ☁☁

Charles Rennie Mackintosh

Rosa Charmant®

(KORpeligo) Kordes (1999)

The tapered round buds on this miniature rose betray the very rich contents: cup-shaped, full flowers with pink petals, which turn a yellowish white towards the heart. The rear of the flowers is noticeably lighter. They have hardly any scent.

In early summer the compact bushes are covered in flowers. A moderate second flush follows later in the season.

The foliage is small, dark green and very glossy.

🔲 15h 🌹🌹 ◠

Charlotte

Charmant®

Rosa Charming Cover™ Towne & Country®

(POUlharmu) Poulsen (2000)

Semi-double, cup-shaped, bright red flowers bloom on this low bush. There is no discernable fragrance. The rose has glossy, medium green leaves.

◉ 25h 🌹🌹🌹 ◠

Rosa Charming Decumba®

(HANchade) Hanekamp (1999)

This is first and foremost a ground cover rose, which has slender stems creeping off in all directions. They bear hooked thorns, which help the plant climb up as soon as they find support. The leaves (usually with seven leaflets) are a fresh light green color, and later grass-green. This is one of the healthy cutting roses from the Stecktii series, which are bred primarily for

Charming Cover™ Towne & Country®

use in public areas. The scentless, single, ivory-white flowers grow to one-and-a-half inches wide.

They bloom in early summer, with occasional further flushes.

↔ 15h 🌹 ◠ ✚

Rosa Chartreuse de Parme®

(DELviola) Delbard (1996)

In its year of introduction this large-flowered rose was awarded the fragrance prize in Paris. The very full carmine-pink flowers open from round buds.

Charming Decumba®

Château de Versailles®

They are very suitable as cut rose, but sensitive to bad weather. The bush grows to thirty inches tall.
✱ 30h 🌹🌹🌹 ☁☁☁

Rosa Château de Versailles®

(DELricos) Delbard (1986)

Do not confuse this rose with Rosa Versailles (DELset): this pale pink large-flowered rose from the same breeder was introduced back in 1967. Château de Versailles® produces very full flowers, which are borne singly on the stems and are cup-shaped. Their charm is primarily due to their dual color. The inside of the petals are bright red and the outside are white.

Chartreuse de Parme®

Although they have no fragrance this rose is very suitable for the vase.
✱ 30h 🌹🌹🌹 ☁

Rosa Château Pavie

(POUlduce)
see Rosa Tivoli 150™ Hybrid Tea Poulsen®

Rosa Chatsworth

(TANotax)
see Rosa Mirato®

Rosa Chaucer®

(AUScon) Austin (1970)

Chaucer® is the parent plant of numerous other English roses. However, particularly due to its sensitivity to mildew it is no longer a favorite of even David Austin. These days there are better cultivars than this 'oldie' from 1970.

Nonetheless, this bush has a clear look with its mat, light to medium green leaves and lightly colored flowers. The light pink, very full and deep cup-shaped flowers appear in trusses. They have a mild myrrh perfume. The bush grows upright and bears very sharp, red thorns.
🌹GB 40h 🌹🌹🌹 ☁☁☁

Chaucer®

Rosa Cherry Brandy® '85

(TANryrandy) Tantau (1985)
The wonderfully formed large flowers are copper-or-ange. They are borne singly or with a few other flowers on long stalks. This, together with the wonderful fragrance typical of tea roses, make them very suitable as cut roses. Due to the vigorous growth of the vertical bush, new flowers are produced throughout summer and fall. The leaves are initially burgundy, later turning olive-green then dark green. The plant is very resistant to fungal diseases.

✿ 35h ♀♀♀ ☁☁☁ ✚

Rosa Cherry Cover™ Towne & Country®

(POUlerry) Poulsen (2000)
This sister of Rosa Charming Cover™ blooms pink instead of red, and the flowers are somewhat larger. There are no other significant differences: semi-double flowers with hardly any scent, above glossy, dark green leaves.

@ 25h ♀♀♀ ☁

Cherry Brandy® '85

Rosa Cherry Meidiland®

(MEIrumour) Meilland (1995)
The flowers of this shrub rose have no scent, but are still visited by insects. The open, white heart clearly displays the stamens. The edges of the flowers are

Cherry Cover™ Towne & Country®

cherry-red. The flowers are grouped in dense plumes at the end of the branches. The shrub itself grows wider than it is tall and can be used for ground cover. The glossy, dark green leaves are fairly resistant to mildew but can on occasion be affected by black spot.

@ 30h ♀♀♀ ☁

Rosa Cherry Meilandecor

see *Rosa* Cherry Meidiland

Rosa Chianti

(AUSwine) Austin (1967)
When old roses were crossed with the more modern groups much of the character of the old roses remained with Chianti: the carmine-red color that

Cherry Meidiland®

later turns a purple hue, the wonderful fragrance, but unfortunately also the once flowering. Flowers are formed only in the height of summer, but then in large numbers. They are usually in trusses, sometimes singly, on a vigorously growing shrub, which grows to be as wide as it is tall. Particularly suited to large gardens. The mat leaves are dark green. A forerunner of English roses.

⊛ 60h ♥ ✿✿✿✿

Rosa Chicago Peace®

(JOHnago) Johnston (1962)
The immense popularity of the rose 'Peace' ensured that breeders studied every deviation of roses. After all, so-called sports can spontaneously arise: mutations with other characteristics. A total of nineteen sports of 'Peace' have been recorded, Chicago Peace®

Chianti

being one. The flowers of Chicago Peace® have somewhat intenser colors: salmon-pink, a little apricot tending towards orange-yellow, and with the Chicago variety a little more yellow. At a favorable site the bush remains healthy.

✳ 30h ♥♥/♥♥♥ ✿✿ ✚

Chicago Peace®

Rosa Child of Achievement™

see *Rosa* Bella™ Castle®

Rosa Chimo®

(INTercher) Interplant (1988)
The bright red, single flowers carry a thick tuft of stamens, which bear clearly visible golden pollen. The flowers appear throughout the summer in trusses between the long branches of the ground cover shrub, which can also be bred as a weeping tree rose. The foliage is a fresh, glossy light green. It is susceptible to black spot, which is hardly ever a problem to this vigorous plant.

↔ 25h ♥♥♥ ✿

Rosa Chitina

(Poulmulti)
see *Rosa* Snow Cover™ Towne & Country®

Rosa Chitina

(POUlurt)
see *Rosa* Sun Cover™ Towne & Country®

Chimo®

Rosa Christopher Columbus

(POUlbico)
see *Rosa* Candy Cover™ Towne & Country®

Rosa Cinderella

(-) De Vink (1953)

Cinderella has all the characteristics necessary to grow in a pot: compact growth with many leaves, thorn-free stems and well-spread blooms of slightly fragrant small flowers. The full flowers are ivory-white with pink to cherry-red blotches on the outside and near the ends. New trusses appear throughout the summer. This excellent and popular miniature rose has many attractive, light green leaves, and combines well with other plants in a pot.

🔲 10h 🌹🌹🌹 ☁☁

Rosa City Livery®

(HARhero) Harkness (2000)

This is one of the latest floribunda roses of the British breeder Harkness. He gave this rose the official cultivar name that he had previously used himself

Cinderella

for the shrub rose Rosa Marjorie Fair. That rose with its pink flowers and white eye is also called Rosa Red Ballerina or Rosa Red Yesterday. Do not confuse these roses with one another. City Livery® bears full, lemon yellow flowers, which have a fresh

City Livery®

fragrance. They bloom in trusses on a thirty-inch tall bush.

❀❀ 30h 🌹🌹🌹 ☁☁

Rosa City of Birmingham

(KORholst)

see Rosa Holstein 87®

Rosa City of London®

(HARukfore) Harkness (1988)

The light pink flowers have a delicious sweet and pleasant fragrance. They appear in full trusses throughout summer and fall, are semi-double and open to reveal pink stamens and ochre-colored pollen within their heart. The flowers eventually fade to a cream color. Unfortunately the petals remain on the spent flowers: the bush cleans moderately. City of London® grows upright and has good and regular branching. The vigorous growth continually sends new flower trusses upwards. The olive-green leaves have an attractive shine.

❀❀ 35 🌹🌹🌹 ☁☁☁

Rosa Clair Matin®

(MEImont) Meilland(1960)

A delightful, richly blooming climbing rose with semi-double soft pink flowers. They open out in full

City of London®

corymbs from bright pink, pointed buds.
The blooms last all summer and fall. The flowers are moderately fragrant, with a sweet and fruity scent. Young stems and leaves are brownish red, the mature leaves dark green. Mildew is not a problem if locat-

Clair Matin®

ed in a suitable location. Ensure that there are sufficient nutrients, as its rapid growth requires much energy: this climber can reach seven to fourteen feet tall, depending on the support. Although insects have easy access to the yellow stamens and stigma, no hips are formed.

🌱 80h–120h ♥♥♥ ⌒⌒

Rosa Clair™ Renaissance®

(POUlsyng) Poulsen (1997)

After an initial rich flush more modest blooms follow. But the flowers are worth the wait. They are cup-shaped with an open heart full with red stamens and golden pollen. The flower is a creamy light pink with some apricot when first open. Enchanting with a fresh sweet scent. The shrub grows upright with flower trusses proudly above the glossy, gray-green foliage.

🌼 30h ♥♥♥ ⌒⌒⌒

Clair™ Renaissance®

Rosa Claude Monet®

(JACdesa) Jackson & Perkins/Delbard (1992)

With blotches and stripes of yellow, pink and cream, the flowers of this large-flowered rose are quite striking. They are slightly fragrant and despite their loose cup-shape are popular as cut roses. A disadvantage is that the bush is not very vigorous, resulting in blooms of short duration. Claud Monet® is sold as a tree rose.

✲ 30h ♥♥♥ ⌒⌒

Rosa Clementine®

(TANogrew) Tantau (1997)

Do not confuse this rose with the pink rose of the rubiginosa type, which bears the same name and is also known as Rosa Janet's Pride.

Claude Monet®

Tantau's Clementine® is a miniature rose with very full, scentless flowers in the popular color apricot. Towards the edges they fade to sulfur yellow. The bush has rich blooms, which continue if you keep the bush growing. The foliage is medium green.

🎴 40h ♥♥♥ ⌒

Clementine®

Rosa Climbing Gites de France

see *Rosa* Gites de France®

Rosa Climbing Gold Badge

(MEIgronurisar)
see *Rosa* Climbing Gold Bunny

Rosa Climbing Gold Bunny®

(MEIgronurisar) Meilland (1991)
The over three-inch-wide lemon yellow flowers can cover an entire wall. Choose, therefore, a warm wall, so that the plant is better kept free of diseases such as black spot. The rose originates from the non-climbing Gold Bynny®, which displays the same permanently colored flowers, but which only grows up to thirty inches. This climbing sister reaches heights of seven feet.

꙰ 80h 🌷🌷🌷 ♡

Rosa Climbing Iceberg

(-) Cant (1968)
Apart from the fact that this rose usually grows taller than the Schneewittchen® there are few differences between the flowers of the popular Kordes rose. The dark green leaves are susceptible to black spot. Some bought specimens of Climbing Iceberg have been

Climbing Iceberg

Rosa Clos Fleuri® Bicolore

(DELrula) Delbard (1992)
The bi-colored, well-shaped flowers of this rose are in themselves worth a mention here. Inside the petals are pinkish red, outside creamy, sometimes with a hint of yellow.

✿✿ 40h 🌷🌷🌷 ♡

Rosa Clos Fleuri® Blanc

(DELblan) Delbard (1989)
Clos Fleuri® Blanc grows so vigorously that it is used not only as a bush but also a low climber.
Supported against a rose pillar or arch the rose can reach five feet. In summer Clos Fleuri® Blanc blooms with very full, white flowers with a butter-yellow

Climbing Gold Bunny®

Clos Fleuri® Bicolore

known to climb poorly due to incorrect cutting or grafting. Pauses between blooms can be reduced by feeding the rose until august and removing the old flowers.

꙰ 80–200h 🌷🌷 ♡♡

heart. They are slightly fragrant. Removing old flowers encourages new blooms. The rose has bright green leaves.

✿✿/꙰ 40h/60h 🌷🌷 ♡

Rosa Clos Fleuri® Jaune

(DELjaune) Delbard (1989)

This floribunda rose from the Clos Fleuri series is similar in its growth habit to Rosa Clos Fleuri® Blanc. The flowers of Clos Fleuri® Jaune are, however, less full (semi-double) and the color is different. They open ochre-yellow but turn amber with age, often

Clos Fleuri® Blanc

with a carmine-red edge. The bush sometimes has sparse foliage.
✻✻/✤ 40h/60h ♥♥♥ ☁

Clos Fleuri® Jaune

Rosa Clos Fleuri® Rose

(DELodive) Delbard (1994)

This rose is also known as Rosa Clos Fleuri® Rose No. 2, because in 1989 Delbard had already introduced a rose with the same trade name and the cultivar name: DELpomp. You can still find this older version at nurseries. The latest of the two has rich blooms which last the whole summer and fall with very full, cup-shaped flowers. The flowers grow to three inches wide, are bright pink but fade with age. They have a light, sweet, spicy perfume. This is one of the best floribunda roses of Delbard. The bush branches well and bears many glossy, dark green leaves. The old Clos Fleuri® Rose (DELpomp) from 1989 was particularly suitable for areas with good summers. The flowers clean badly.
✻✻ 35h ♥♥♥ ☁☁

Rosa Clyde Meilove®

(MEIclydov) Meilland (1999)

The very full white flowers of the patio rose Clyde Meilove® protrude well above the bronze-tinged foliage. The bushes remain small enough to be kept in a pot on a terrace.

Clos Fleuri® Rose

Also attractive in a small garden.
▣ 20h ♥♥♥ ☁

Clyde Meilove®

Colette®

Rosa **Colbert®**

(DELcolb) Delbard (1989)

The unusual color combination of the large, full flowers of Colbert® are very eye-catching. They initially seem to have the bright pink color of candy, but on closer inspection this is only on the edges. The base color is a silvery white, making the plants stand out in any border or bed. The foliage of this upright plant is glossy dark green.

✿ 35h ♚♚♚ ☁

Rosa **Colette®**

(MEIroupis) Meilland (1996)

The extremely full, fragrant flowers sometimes have

Colbert®

up to 135 petals. No wonder that the stems bend. This effect is reinforced by the broad, loose growing style of the shrub. The flowers are solitary, so Colette® can be regarded as a large-flowered rose. However, prune this rose as a park or shrub rose. The loose growth

and pale salmon-pink flowers make wonderful combinations with perennials possible. The breeder therefore included Colette® in the Fleur Romantica® series. The long stems can also be tied together giving the effect of a low climbing rose.

◐ /✿ 40h ♚♚♚ ☁☁☁

Rosa **Color Wonder**

(KORbico)

see *Rosa* Königin der Rosen®

Rosa **Commonwealth Glory**

(HARclue) Harkness (1999)

The buds unfold as you would expect from a perfectly formed large-flowered rose.

On opening the large, full flowers are apricot in the center, sometimes with salmon-pink. The outside of the petals fade quickly to ivory-white with a hint of pink. A very charming combination. The flowers

Commonwealth Glory

have a sweet perfume. The upright plant bears glossy, dark green foliage.

☀ 35h ✿✿✿ ☁☁

Rosa Compactila®

(HANcomp) Hanekamp (1990)

Even when this ground cover rose is not in bloom it is a pretty site. This is due to the fine, pinnate blue green foliage on the very thorny red stems. In April-May the rose has rich flushes of small cream flowers, in the form of wild roses. A splendid and highly robust rose for public green areas and for large areas in natural gardens. Compactila® is propagated using cuttings.

↔ 25h ✿ ☁ ✚

Rosa Compassion®

(-) Harkness (1973)

Compassion® is one of the most popular continuous-flowering ramblers and has won numerous

Compactila®

prizes. The flowers appear the whole summer on the thin stems. The full flowers have a mix of colors: an apricot pink base with salmon-pink towards the edges. A particular color will dominate depending on the conditions, usually salmon-pink. The flowers have a pleasant sweet fragrance. By bending the red, thorny stems, Compassion can also be grown over low hedges. The normal height is six-and-a-half to eleven-and-a-half feet. The large, healthy dark green foliage provides a good background for the flowers.

✎ 120h ✿✿✿ ☁☁☁ ✚ ADR TOP

Compassion®

Rosa Comtesse de Segur®

(DELtendre) Delbard (1994)

The very full, pink flowers have the scent of fruit and roses. They flower the whole summer in trusses on a vigorous bush.

☀ 35h ✿✿✿ ☁☁☁

Rosa Concerto®94

(MEIhaitoil) Meilland (1994)

The very full flowers of Concerto®94 (Take note: there is also a rose called 'Concerto', but with red

Comtesse de Segur®

flowers) display a variety of colors: pale yellow, salmon and apricot to orange-red.

The individual flowers vary in color depending on their age. They grow in trusses on the wide upright bush, which can reach up to three-and-a-half feet. The foliage is mat, dark green. Concerto®94 com-

Concerto®94

bines splendidly with perennials. The rose is very resistant to mildew but susceptible to black spot.
@ /✿✿ 40h ♀♀♀ ⌒

Rosa Conquest

(HARbrill) Harkness (1994)
Soon after the warm yellow flowers open from the pointed buds they reveal their golden pollen. They have a light and delicious fruity perfume. The flowers fade a great deal with age, but remain attractive. However, when they wilt they do not look so good as they clean quite badly. Therefore place the rose in a warm, sunny site.
The medium-sized bush bears large, shiny, dark green leaves.
✿✿ 30h ♀♀♀ ⌒⌒

Conquest

Rosa Constance Finn

(HAReden) Harkness (1997)
Each truss of the soft pink flowers of Constance Finn forms a complete bouquet. The flowers open simultaneously, releasing a pleasant fragrance. They are very full and soft pink, fading to ivory-white with a hint a pink at the edges. For a floribunda rose the bush grows very vigorously, with healthy looking dark green leaves.
✿✿ 40h ♀♀♀ ⌒⌒⌒

Rosa Constance Spry®

(AUSfirst) Austin (1969)
AUSfirst, the patent name of Constance Spry®, was the first rose to be referred to as an English rose, although it did not have all the characteristics that

Constance Finn

were attributed to that category of rose. This vigorous rose, for example, only flowers in summer without any subsequent blooms. Despite this it is still very popular due to its enormous, soft pink flowers, which under their weight droop gracefully sidewards. They are very full and release a strong scent of myrrh. The rose has limp stems that should be fastened, otherwise it soon becomes too difficult to lift the mass of stems and flowers.
⚘ 120h ♀ ⌒⌒⌒⌒

Rosa Constanze Spry

(AUSfirst)
see *Rosa* Constance Spry®

Constance Spry®

Rosa Coral Border™ Towne & Country®

(POUlalo) Poulsen (1998)

The full, bright red flowers appear in trusses. They are three inches wide and have a light and fresh fruity fragrance. The flower color contrasts wonderfully with the light green of the young leaves of the flowering shoots. The leaves turn a glossy, medium green with age. Coral Border™ is a well-branching low shrub with long stems bearing flowers which bend under the weight, producing a more or less ground cover form.

🌼 30h 🌷🌷🌷 ☁☁

Rosa Coral Gables

(POUlalo)

see *Rosa* Coral Border™ Towne & Country®

Coral Border™ Towne & Country®

Rosa Coral Palace

(POUldron)

see *Rosa* Schackenborg™ Castle®

Rosa Cornelia

(-) Pemberton (1925)

The English clergyman Pemberton developed numerous musk hybrids (see also Rosa moschata), the flowers of which appear in trusses throughout summer, and smell of musk. Cornelia, too, has continuous blooms. Full, loose flowers are borne on a high and wide shrub. The flower color varies considerably: from soft apricot to pink, with all possible hues in between, depending on the soil and season. Cornelia smells delicious and can be used as a cut rose, but is at its best when combined with perennials.

🌼 45–60h 🌷🌷🌷 ☁☁☁

Rosa Cottage Rose

(AUSglisten) Austin (1991)

The full flowers of Cottage Rose are cup-shaped when open, with a messy but charming appearance.

Cornelia

The heart, full with soft pink petals is sometimes quartered. The lightly fragrant flowers appear in trusses on the shrub. For an English rose the plant stays quite low and has rather bushy growth with very thorny stems.

The rose flowers the whole summer.

🌷GB 35h 🌷🌷🌷 ☁☁

Cottage Rose

Rosa Countess Celeste

(POUldron)
see *Rosa* Schackenborg™ Castle®

Rosa Country Touch

(KORpinka)
see *Rosa* Sommermärchen®

Rosa Countryman

(AUSman)
see *Rosa* The Countryman®

Rosa Courage™ Paramount®

(POUlduf) Poulsen (1998)
This full, dark red rose is from the Paramount series, which includes low-growing, large-flowered roses. The flowers have a pleasant fragrance. They bloom the whole summer on a bushy shrub of twenty-five to forty inches tall.
☼ 30h 🌹🌹🌹 ☁☁☁

Courage™ Paramount®

Rosa Courtoisie®

(DELcourt) Delbard (1984)
The wide full flowers appear from elegantly formed buds. The flowers have a light but pleasant fragrance and are mild orange in color, with a tint of yellow on the outside. They will flower the whole summer in a warm climate and if fed well. The bushes branch well and have vigorous upright growth. Foliage is medium green.
☼☼ 40h 🌹🌹🌹/🌹🌹 ☁☁

Rosa Cream Abundance

(HARflax) Harkness (1999)
We could call the very full flowers of Cream Abundance 'cream-colored-extra', because through the cream we

Courtoisie®

can see a haze of soft yellow and sometimes soft pink. The lightly fragrant flowers bloom the whole summer and fall on a profusely branching bush with dark green foliage.
☼☼ 35h 🌹🌹🌹 ☁☁

Cream Abundance

Rosa Crêpe de Chine®

(DELtop) Delbard (1970)

The large, bright pink flowers of Crêpe de Chine® are borne high on the vigorously growing stems. Sometimes the semi-double, cup-shaped flowers bloom five feet above the ground. They are usually solitary, and can reach up to five-and-a-half inches wide. They have a light and fruity fragrance with a light scent of roses. The upright bushes reach three-and-a-half to five feet high and bear very large dark green leaves. Sometimes you have to be content with this foliage as there may be pauses between the blooms. Most suitable as cut rose or for bedding, as the bright pink is difficult to combine with other colors.

⚘ 45h ❦❦ ◌◌

Rosa Crimson Glory

(-) Kordes (1935)

This is one of the famous 'golden oldies' that is still very much loved. First and foremost for its Damask perfume. And secondly for the blooms spread

Crêpe de Chine®

throughout the whole summer and early fall, not always the case for an old large-flowered rose. What's more, the solitary flower is perfect: full, velvety, scarlet and drooping gracefully on the stem. The dark green foliage contrasts well. However, the leaves are fairly sparse and susceptible to mildew, which will gradually affect its popularity among rose enthusiasts. The plant is bushy and compact.

⚘ 30h ❦❦❦ ◌◌◌

Crimson Glory

Rosa Crimson Meidiland®

(MEIouscki) Meilland (1996)

This is one of the new, vigorous shrub roses. They bloom luxuriantly and long, even in less favorable locations. The rose-red flowers (with small white accents) of Crimson Meidiland® are semi-double and appear in masses on the profusely branching shrub, which is almost as wide as it is tall.

The medium green leaves are hardly affected by mildew and black spot.

☽ 30h ❦❦❦ ◌ ✚ ADR

Rosa Crimson Meillandecor

see *Rosa* Crimson Meidiland

Crimson Meidiland®

Rosa Crown Princess Margareta

(AUSwinter) Austin (1999)

Due to its considerable size you can determine yourself how to use this English rose: in a border, together with other shrubs or perennials, or as a climbing rose. The very full, cup-shaped flowers appear in trusses. They are apricot in color, but with generous amounts of orange and a little yellow. They have a wonderful fruity fragrance.

🌻GB/🌱 60h/100h 🌷🌷🌷 ☁☁☁

Crown Princess Margareta

Rosa Crystal™ Palace®

(POUlrek) Poulsen (1996)

A low floribunda rose, which when planted in beds can grow to 20 inches wide and tall. When in a pot or container to ensure permanent blooms give sufficient water and feed. The flowers reach 3-inches wide. They have a very light, creamy pink color.

▣/✿✿ 20h 🌷🌷🌷 ☁

Rosa Cyclamen Meillandecor

(MEIpelta)

see *Rosa* Fuchsia Meidiland

Rosa Cymbaline

(AUSlean)

see *Rosa* Cymbeline

Rosa Cymbeline

(AUSlean) Austin (1982)

This English rose grows wider than it is tall. The stems are so thin that they bend under the weight of the flower trusses and the dark green foliage, and very often end up lying close to the ground. The rose is therefore not able to support itself and so has to be grown alongside other plants. But herein lies its strength. The full flowers are a silvery soft pink and can therefore be combined with almost any other flower. They have a strong myrrh fragrance. The flowers are sensitive to rain and the leaves to black spot. This is perhaps why David Austin continues to sell this rose, but no longer promotes it.

🌻GB 50h 🌷🌷🌷 ☁☁☁

Cymbeline

Crystal™ Palace®

100

Rosa Dagmar Hastrup

(-) Hastrup (1914)

Dagmar Hastrup is a rugosa hybrid (related to the ramanas rose) and so has heavily thorned stems and rough gray-green leaves. The plant grows relatively low (30 inches) with profuse sidewards branching and is thick with foliage. The flowers are thee inches wide, single, light pink and have a pleasant sweet fragrance. Though the first bloom produces large hips, the flowering continues.

🌑 30h 🌷🌷🌷 ✿✿✿✿ ✚

Rosa Dama di Cuori

(Lens)

see *Rosa* Dame de Coeur

Dagmar Hastrup

Rosa x *damascena*

(-) botanical rose (-)

The Greeks probably prepared rose oil from the petals of the Damask rose for several centuries BC. Later the Romans had this rose cultivated in vast quantities in Egypt to add luster to their banquets. During one such event so many petals were cascaded on top of the guests that some actually suffocated. The Damask rose is probably a hybrid of the French rose and the musk rose. The flower varies greatly in intensity, from intense pink to pale, almost white. They flower once or twice a season on a shrub of almost six-and-a-half feet tall and wide. They have a wonderful fragrance.

🌑 80h 🌷 ✿✿✿✿ ✚

Rosa x *damascena*

Rosa Dame de Coeur

(-) Lens (1958)

Large-flowered roses have been grown for many centuries on the basis of their flower shape and color. For some decades now attention has been paid again to their fragrance. Hardly any attention was given to their resistance to disease. However, exceptions have arisen, such as Dame de Coeur. The full, cherry-red flowers appear in trusses next to one another. New, light though pleasantly fragrant roses appear throughout summer and fall on a vigorous upright bush of approximately 30 inches high.

In the ADR tests for disease resistance of large-flowered roses (between 1995 and 1998) Dame de Coeur was one of the few roses shown to be resistant.

✳ 30h 🌷🌷🌷 ✿✿ ✚ TOP

Dame de Coeur

Rosa Dapple Dawn

(AUSdapple) Austin (1983)

This continuous-flowering shrub rose of David Austin bears rich blooms throughout the summer and fall. The flowers are saucer-shaped in wonderful, mild colors: soft pink with tints of apricot and salmon, with a lighter colored heart. The heart is soft yellow to cream and houses a striking tuft of stamens. The flowers have a mild musk fragrance.

Apart from its color this variety is similar to the red Rosa Red Coat. Dapple Dawn is also characterized by its upright growth and dark green foliage.

60h

Rosa Dark Lady

(AUSbloom)

see *Rosa* The Dark Lady

Dapple Dawn

Rosa Day Light

(INTerlight)

see *Rosa* Daylight®

Rosa Daylight®

(INTerlight) Interplant (1990)

The dark leaves of the profusely branching bush contrast wonderfully with the three-inch-wide flowers. They are semi-double and primarily creamy yellow, with pink tints. They open immediately from the amber-colored buds into cup-shaped flowers revealing their heart of yellow pollen. Fortunately the fragrance is not strong, as it is unpleasant. It is a splendid rose for bedding and borders, in part due to their attractive brown-red foliage.

30h

Rosa Delbir®

(DELbir) Delbard-Chabert (1965)

The bright pink flowers contrast wonderfully with the glossy, light green leaves. They are full, three inches wide and appear in trusses on the fairly slack, bending stems. This makes the rose ideal for intertwining with perennials in a romantic border. The rose has won many prizes, though has the disadvantage of not cleaning well. Dead-heading therefore needs to be done after rainy periods.

30h

Daylight®

Rosa Della Balfour

(HARblend) Harkness (1994)

The flowers of this climber have very subtle shades of pink and orange. They are full, with a pleasant

Delbir®

fresh lemon perfume, but do not flower long or in great numbers. The plant grows vigorously upright to around ten feet.

🔧 120h 🌺🌺 ☁☁☁

Della Balfour

Rosa Denise Grey

(MEIxetal)
see *Rosa* Make Up®

Rosa Dentelle de Bruges®

(-) Lens (1991)
In early summer the flowers hang like a white veil on the branches of the Dentelle de Bruges®. They are single to semi-double and open from pink buds to saucer-shaped flowers. Insects visit the heart of yellow pollen of the slightly fragrant flowers. The

Dentelle de Bruges®

shrub can be used as a low climber. It bears fairly rough medium green leaves, consisting of long leaflets.

🌣/🔧 60h 🌺 ☁☁ ✚

Rosa Dentelle de Bruxelles®

(-) Lens (1988)
This is the deeper pink counterpart of Rosa Dentelle de Malines®, which resembles this shrub rose in many respects. Both can also be used as a low climber. The thinner stems are cut off to give more strength to the rest. In early summer the shrub produces luxuriant blooms of semi-double, pink flowers with a white heart. The branches and the young leaves are burgundy, giving a rose-red impression.

🌣/🔧 70h 🌺 ☁☁ ✚

Dentelle de Bruxelles®

Rosa Dentelle de Malines®

(-) Lens (1986)
The parent plant of this shrub was Rosa filipes, which explains its impressive growth. The rose can reach the height of a man without any support; with support it grows as a low climbing rose.

Dentelle de Malines®

By pruning away the thinner stems, the remaining stems can grow more vigorously. In early summer Dentelle de Malines® produces luxuriant blooms of cup-shaped, semi-double flowers, which from a distance look like the blossom of an ornamental cherry tree. Once fully developed, they are white with a hint of pink. Young leaves are a single shade of light pink. The foliage consists of relatively large olive-green leaflets.

🌸 / 🌿 70h 🌷 ⌒⌒ ✛

Rosa Devon

(POUlrijk)
see *Rosa* Bayernland Cover™ Towne & Country®

Rosa Diadeem

(TANmeda)
see *Rosa* Diadem®

Rosa Diadem®

(TANmeda) Tantau (1986)
The flower trusses are borne on long stems, making these roses very suitable as cut roses. Even the still-closed buds open well in the vase. For the best results the supplier Tantau advises breaking off the central bud at the top. The full, pink flowers have a very slight fruity perfume. The color fades with age. New trusses appear throughout the summer and fall on the upright bush. The bush is rich in dark green foliage, which is fairly resistant to disease and so remains attractive in the fall.

✳✳ 30h 🌷🌷🌷 ⌒

Diadem®

Rosa Diamond Border™ Towne & Country®

(POUldiram) Poulsen (1997)
Insects love the semi-double, cream flowers, with their golden pollen. The almost saucer-shaped flowers have a light fresh fragrance. The tapered trusses bear large numbers of flowers. The flower shoots first grow upwards, sometimes higher than five feet, but they quickly bend under the weight. This shrub therefore needs either space or support. Diamond Border™ has many glossy, healthy looking leaves.

🌸 50h 🌷🌷🌷 ⌒⌒

Diamond Border™ Towne & Country®

Rosa Diamond Head

(POUldiram)
see *Rosa* Diamond Border™ Towne & Country®

Rosa Die Welt®

(DieKOR) Kordes (1976)
Die Welt® thrives particularly in areas with a continental climate. Otherwise in order to enjoy its splendid flowers it has to be planted in a sunny location where there are warm summers, because it is not a pretty sight after rain. The flowers unfold from promising large, tapered buds. The buds seem to indicate a red flower, but the orange-yellow gradually becomes clear. During flowering the red edges change to pink/salmon-pink.

Die Welt®

Dirigent®

The large, dark green foliage shines intensely. The flowers are borne on thick, long, straight stems, making it ideal as cut rose.

✻ 30h 🌻🌻🌻 ∽∽

Rosa Directeur H.J. Bos®

(INTerby) Interplant (1985)

The relatively thin stems have a red tint and form an attractive whole with the dense, shiny, medium green leaves. Above the foliage bloom the semi-double, cup-shaped, soft pink flowers which give a pleasant soft rose fragrance. The shrub grows vigorously and healthy.

⊚ 40h 🌻🌻🌻 ∽ ✛

Directeur H.J. Bos®

Rosa Dirigent®

(-) Tantau (1956)

The scarlet, semi-double flowers bloom in richly full trusses on a vigorous shrub with light green foliage. The red of the flowers does not even fade in bright sunlight. The flowers remain attractive for a long time and clean well. In the wild Dirigent® grows to a shrub of over three-and-half feet, but with support it can

sometimes reach heights of five feet. Dirigent® is a healthy rose.

⊚ 40–60h 🌻🌻🌻 ∽ ✛ ADR

Rosa Dolly Dot

(-) Jackson&Perkins (1998)

Yellow, semi-double flowers are borne above the shiny, dark green foliage. For the rest, this low floribunda rose has little to offer.

▣ 15h 🌻🌻🌻 ∽

Dolly Dot

Rosa Domstadt Fulda®

(KORtanken) Kordes (1994)

The pointed buds open to reveal relatively wide cup-shaped flowers. They are semi-double and bright florescent crimson. The color is heightened by the dark green, shiny leaves with hints of deep red. After profuse blooms in early summer regular blooms follow throughout the summer and fall. In part because it has dense foliage the plant remains attractive the whole season. The thick stems display a striking upright growth.

✻✻ 30h 🌻🌻🌻 ∽∽ ✛

Domstadt Fulda®

Rosa Dorothy Perkins

(-) Jackson&Perkins (1901)

The flower color of this rambler is a lighter pink but for the rest it is very similar to the popular Rosa Excelsa. The two-and-a-half inch flowers are as full, and bloom in early summer in splendid richly full trusses, which droop gracefully. As with Excelsa, Dorothy Perkins is also suitable as a tree rose or weeping tree rose. The foliage remains attractive and shiny for some time, but the buds and flowers are frequently affected by mildew. Despite this they are highly recommended for large gardens where there is room for both the once flowering ramblers such as Dorothy Perkins as well as the continuous-flowering variety. An improvement to this variety is Rosa Super Dorothy (HELdoro), introduced by Hetzel in 1986. This rambler remains in flower quite well and is less susceptible to mildew.

✿ 120–240h ♀ ⌔

Dorothy Perkins

Rosa Dortmund®

(-) Kordes (1955)

When given the opportunity Dortmund® will climb up to six to thirteen feet high against a fence, arch or pillar. From this high position the climber develops a cascade of single, red flowers with a white heart. They appear throughout the summer in multi-florous trusses on the ends of bending stems. The small leaves have a striking shape. Their edges are wavy, sometimes even serrated like a holly leaf and almost as dark green. Vigorous growth combined with sturdy foliage make it quite resistant to fungal diseases.

✿ 80–160h ♀♀♀ ⌔⌔ ✚ ADR

Dortmund®

Rosa Doux Parfum

(HARzola)

see *Rosa* L'Aimant

Rosa Dreaming

(KORrei)

see *Rosa* Träumerei®

Rosa Dreams Come True

(MEIvestal)

see *Rosa* Senator Burda®

Rosa Dronning Margrethe™ Palace®

(POUlskov) Poulsen (1996)

The full, three-inch-wide flowers of this low shrub rose look as fresh as they smell.

Dronning Margrethe™ Palace®

The flowers fade from soft pink to cream with a hint of pink. They are not affected by rain and have a light, pleasant, fruity scent. The foliage is light to medium green. The shrub grows compact and branches extremely well, covering a bed with leaves. This rose can also be used in large pots and tubs. The best rose from the Palace series of Poulsen.

�",☻ 25h 🌷🌷🌷 ☁☁

Rosa Drottningholm

(POUlasor)
see *Rosa* Rosenborg™ Castle®

Rosa Dublin Bay®

(MACdub) McGredy (1976)
Throughout the summer new trusses of crimson flowers appear on this low climber. The full flowers open wide and are eventually a round cup-shape. They have hardly any fragrance. This red rose is particularly popular in warm countries. They combine good growth and rich blooms with a small stature, and so

Dublin Bay®

are usually planted against rose arches and pillars. The flowers appear across the entire length of the seven-feet climber. Dublin Bay can also be planted without support. It then displays a bushy growth.

🌿 80h 🌷🌷🌷 ☁

Rosa Duftgold®

(TANdugoft) Tantau (1981)
Full, bright yellow flowers above the grass-green, glossy foliage of an upright bush: Duftgold® in summer and early fall. With good growth the plant will flower for some time. It has a spicy scent. The flowers have good resistance to rain and the foliage stays attractive for a long time.

✳ 30h 🌷🌷🌷 ☁☁☁

Duftgold®

Duftrausch®

107

Rosa Duftrausch®

(TANschaubud) (1986)

The large, mauve-colored, full flowers have a very strong spicy scent as expected from a Damask rose. The bush branches profusely and blooms fairly constantly throughout the summer. For a large-flowered rose the dark green leaves have good resistance to black spot and mildew. An excellent bedding rose, but also suitable for combining with perennials. Highly recommended.

✳ 35h ♀♀♀ ⌀⌀⌀⌀ ✚

Rosa Duftwolke®

(Tanellis) Tantau (1963)

The beautifully formed, full flowers have a striking bright coral-red color. They appear already in early summer on the low bush. They do honor to the name of the rose with their very strong fragrance: fruity and yet spicy, with a lot of citrus. Because of this wonderful fragrance, Duftwolke® was for a long time one of the most popular roses and has received numerous prizes. An excellent cut rose. Although the glossy, medium green leaves can be affected by black spot and mildew the plant quickly recovers and remains attractive into the fall. The flowers are sensitive to rain.

✳ 30h ♀♀♀ ⌀⌀⌀⌀ADR

Duftwolke®

Rosa Duftzauber 84®

(KORzaun) Kordes (1984)

Not to be confused with the rose-red flowering Duftzauber (KORdu) that was bred by Kordes in 1969. Duftzauber 84® was introduced in 1984. The parent plant was Feuerzauber, impregnated by the pollen of an unknown seedling. The result has since won many

Duftzauber 84®

international prizes. The bushes are vigorous and upright, making the rose even suitable for hedging. The plant can grow up to four feet tall and so is excellent for bedding. The leaves are mat, dark green and resistant to fungal disease. The full, velvety red flowers have a pleasant fragrance. They are either solitary or several may be grouped together on the long stems. Makes a good long-lasting cut flower. The bush cleans well: the old flowers fall off in their entirety.

✳ 40h ♀♀♀ ⌀⌀⌀ ✚

Rosa Dwarfking 78

(KORkönig)

see *Rosa* Zwergkönig 78®

Rosa Dynastie®

(MElpitac) Meilland (1990)

The outside of the flowers have a silvery, light pink color, whilst the inside are an intense pink. The full flowers cover the shrub the whole summer and have

Dynastie®

a mild fragrance. The shrubs grow upright and bear olive-green young leaves which darken with age. The leaves remain healthy. It's a mystery why this rose is not more widely available, particularly because of the hips it bears in the fall.

⚆ 40h 🌱🌱🌱 ☁☁ ✛

Rosa Easy Cover™ Towne & Country®

(POUleas) Poulsen (1996)

Beautiful compact bushes that bear small, glossy, medium green leaves. The abundant foliage hides the ground from view, which would equally be possible by the many semi-double, pink flowers, a little over an inch wide. The flowers clean moderately well. Despite this in 2000 Easy Cover™ won the golden certificate in the patio roses category at the International Rose Show in The Hague.

↔ 15h 🌱🌱🌱 ☁

Rosa Easy Going™

(HARflow) Harkness (1998)

This is a sport from another rose from Harkness: Rosa Livin' Easy, which is since no longer supplied

Easy Cover™ Towne & Country®

and has orange flowers. You can see this color occasionally with some flowers of the Rosa Easy Going™. This is called reversion (see Explanation of terms). However, the majority of flowers are yellow to apricot. They are grouped in trusses, are approximately three-and-a-half inches wide, full, cup-shaped and have a pleasant scent. The bush has vigorous growth, branches out wide and bears light green

Easy Going™

leaves, which become glossy dark green with age. They remain healthy.

✿✿ 30h 🌱🌱🌱 ☁☁ ✛

Rosa Eden Rose®85

(MEIviolin) Meilland (1987)

When buying this rose take care to look for the official cultivar name 'Meiviolin' as there is great confusion with the names. With the name Eden Rose you may actually end up with a rose-red flower. 'Meiviolin', which belongs to the Fleur Romantica® series of Meilland, is primarily white to cream with a salmon-pink heart. It can be used as a large bush or climber. The bushes grow three-and-a-half to five feet tall and bloom with very full, bi-colored flowers. Due to the natural spreading growth, training is recommended.

⚲ 60h 🌱🌱 ☁☁

Rosa Egeskov™ Castle®

(POUlrohill) Poulsen (1983)

One of the low floribunda roses that the Danish

Eden Rose®85

breeder Poulsen included in his Castle series. They are also included among the low shrub roses. The semi-double flowers are approximately three inches wide, soft pink and smell slightly of wild roses.

✻✻ 25h 🌹🌹🌹 ☁☁

Egeskov™ Castle®

Rosa eglanteria

see *Rosa rubiginosa*

Rosa Eglantyne

(AUSmak) Austin (1994)

This is one of the better English roses: rich blooms of very full, soft pink flowers. They have a delicious

Eglantyne

sweet fragrance. The wide flowers bloom beautifully above the light olive-green, later gray-green, foliage. The plant is bushy, which branches profusely and remains relatively low. Very suitable for bedding as well as for combinations with perennials in the border.

🌹GB 45h 🌹🌹🌹 ☁☁☁

Rosa Eglantyne Jebb

(AUSmak)

see *Rosa* Eglantyne

Rosa Egon Schiele™

see *Rosa* Astrid Lindgren™ Floribunda Poulsen®

Rosa Electron®

see *Rosa* Mullard Jubilee

Rosa Elegant Pearl®

(INTergant) Interplant (1984)

The semi-double, saucer-shaped flowers arranged in full trusses open out to an elegant wheel shape. They are cream, two-and-half inches wide with a mass of stamens and yellow pollen in the heart. The flowers have a light, fresh, fruity fragrance. The bushes exhibit good branching with glossy, bright green leaves, which, unfortunately, are susceptible to black spot. This low floribunda rose is suitable as patio rose for smaller gardens and can also be bred as a tree rose.

🔲 20h 🌹🌹🌹 ☁☁

Elegant Pearl® as a tree rose

Rosa Elektron

see *Rosa* Mullard Jubilee

Rosa Elena

(DICjana)
see *Rosa* Elina®

Rosa Elfe®

(TANcreif) Tantau (2000)
Earlier Tantau roses with the name Elfe are no longer available. This new climber is the replacement. The very full flowers have a special color: soft green on a base of ivory. Fantastic for romantic gardens. The flowers bloom the whole summer and have a mild fruity fragrance. The flowering shoots reach ten feet tall, but can also be trained along lower climbing supports, over which they would cascade under the weight of the flowers. Elfe® has shiny, dark green leaves that according to the breeder have good disease resistance.

🌱 80–120h 🌷🌷🌷 ☁☁

Elfe®

Rosa Elgin Festival

(AUSpoly)
see *Rosa* Charlotte

Rosa Elina®

(DICjana) Dickson (1984)
The flowers appear singly or in a truss with a few others. They are strikingly large – five inches – and

Elina®

sometimes bend under their own weight on the very robust stems. The soft, light yellow flowers fade eventually to ivory-white. They have a pleasant sweet, fruity fragrance. The flowers are badly affected by rain and clean poorly. The leaves are initially a lively yellow-green with burgundy and change to a mat, dark gray-green with age. The plant forms an attractive, high and dense bush with foliage that is very resistant to rose diseases.

☀ 45h 🌷🌷🌷 ☁☁☁ ✚ ADR TOP

Rosa Elka Gaarlandt

(-) Buisman (1965)
The bright red, semi-double flowers are cup-shaped, with yellow pollen displayed in the lighter colored heart. There is hardly any fragrance. The three-and-a-half-inch-wide flowers bloom on thin stems that bend under the weight of the trusses, making them look a little untidy.

Elka Gaarlandt

The bush itself grows rather irregularly.
✿✿ 30h 🌺🌺🌺 ☁

Rosa Elle®

(MEIbderos) Meilland

A seldom available rose from the Parfums de Provence® series of Meilland. The shrub Elle® is named after the women's magazine Elle. The flowers have a strong lime fragrance and are grouped in thick trusses (polyanthas type). The flowers are orange-yellow with soft pink.
⊛ 30h 🌺🌺🌺 ☁☁☁

Elle®

Rosa Elmshorn

(-) Kordes (1951)

The full, intense pink flowers of Elmshorn are pom-pon-shaped. They have hardly any fragrance and are

Elmshorn

not big, but appear throughout summer and fall in large trusses on the vigorous shrub. The shrub can reach six-and-a-half feet tall and five feet wide. The grass-green foliage is also rather small, but is strikingly resistant to fungal disease, particularly for a rose that was bred way back in 1951. No wonder that it has been granted the ADR award. Because of its positive characteristics, it is sold by many suppliers. Elmshorn is particularly suitable for the wilder garden.
⊛ 80h 🌺🌺🌺 ☁☁ ✚ ADR

Rosa Emera®

(NOAtraum)
see *Rosa* Heidetraum®

Rosa Emily Gray

(-) Williams (1918)

A vigorous rambler with glossy, dark green leaves, which can effectively cover a wall or fence. A sheltered location is recommended as the stems can be damaged by severe frost. From early to mid-summer trusses with large, semi-double flowers appear. They look rather messy and hang under their own weight. The yellow pollen is clearly visible. When they open the flowers are deep yellow but fade to a pale yellow with age. Emily Gray has a pleasant fragrance, but does not flower after its initial flush of blooms.
🍃 80–200h 🌺 ☁☁☁

Rosa Ena Harkness

(-) Norman/Harkness (1946)

The amateur breeder Albert Norman crossed the rose

Emily Gray

Rosa Crimson Glory with Rosa Southport to produce Ena Harkness. It turned out to be a golden crossing as this large-flowered rose is still being sold to this day. The full flowers have a perfect shape, are carmine red (which does not fade) and have the pleasant fragrance of Damask roses. These days there are better large-flowered roses: the large, heavy flowers of Ena Harkness are borne on relatively weak stems, causing them to tilt especially when wet. They also cannot withstand rain well. Feeding with potassium can help to strengthen the stems. Locate the rose in a well-ventilated spot. The upright bush bears relatively few, dark green leaves.

✳ 30h 🌹🌹🌹 ☁☁☁

Rosa Enchantment

(POUlskov)
see *Rosa* Dronning Margrethe™ Palace®

Ena Harkness

Rosa England's Rose

(AUSrace) Austin (2000)
This is a very special rose due to its soft colors. The oval pointed buds are soft yellow. On opening they change to the softest pink imaginable, with a very light apricot in the full heart. The very full, cup-shaped flowers lie close to one another. They have a fresh fragrance of tea roses. The bush is upright and bears gray-green leaves. For each rose sold, one English pound goes to the Royal National Rose Society for the establishment of a national rose garden.

🌹GB 45h 🌹🌹🌹 ☁☁☁

England's Rose

Rosa English Apricot

(AUSemi)
see *Rosa* Lucetta®

Rosa English Dawn

(AUSdapple)
see *Rosa* Dapple Dawn

Rosa English Yellow

(AUSmas)
see *Rosa* Graham Thomas®

Rosa Erfurt

(-) Kordes (1939)
The moderately full flowers almost appear single. They display a heart of yellow pollen and a light yellow spot surrounded by a ring of ivory-white. The rest of the flower is soft pink, which quickly

Erfurt

fades in the sun. This charming sight unfolds on a shrub with dark green leaves, reaching up to five feet tall. Erfurt is a very old shrub rose that is still very suitable for natural gardens, where bees can visit for the pollen.

🌐 40–60h 🌷🌷 ☁☁

Rosa Erica

(INTerop)
see Rosa Eyeopener®

Rosa Eroica

(Tantau)
see *Rosa* Erotika®

Rosa Eroika

(Tantau)
see *Rosa* Erotika®

Rosa Erotica

(Tantau)
see *Rosa* Erotika®

Rosa Erotika®

(-) Tantau (1969)
The large, full flowers have a perfect shape. They are deep red and velvety. They also have an intense, spicy perfume. As they are borne on long stems they are very suitable as cut roses. Since their introduction in 1969 they quickly became one of the most popular of roses. What's more, new flowers appear throughout the summer and fall. The bush grows vigorously and bears healthy, large leaves, which are initially red but then later turn a dark green.

🌟 30h 🌷🌷🌷 ☁☁☁ ADR

Rosa Escapade

(HARpade) Harkness (1967)
This is the oldest floribunda rose bred by Jack Harkness and is still one of the best. It has won many prizes, certificates and awards and still sells well (no longer by Harkness). The semi-double flowers unfold to reveal a bright florescent pink. They quickly change to an attractive, soft lilac-pink color. The open heart of the flower has a white eye, containing a striking tuft of golden pollen that attracts bees from afar. The fragrance is mild but pleasantly sweet and rosy. The abundant blooms appear in early summer. Subsequent blooms are less profuse, but continuous. The trusses are borne by long, thin, drooping stems about three-and-a-half feet high above the glossy, dark green leaves. The leaves remain very healthy.

✺✺ 30h 🌷🌷🌷 ☁☁ ✪ ADR TOP

Rosa Espéranza

(-) Delforge (1966)
The bright orange-red of this floribunda rose is striking even from a distance. Espéranza is often used as

Escapade

a bedding rose due to the rich blooms and masses of flowers on the healthy-looking bush.

The bush grows upright and bears many glossy, dark green leaves, which contrast wonderfully with the flowers. They are semi-double and cup-shaped with

Erotika®

an open heart. Hardly any fragrance is noticeable. Red hips are produced later in the season. The flower color is retained well, helping to win Espéranza several prizes.

✳✳ 40h 🌸🌸🌸 ☁

Rosa Esprit®

(KORholst)
see *Rosa* Holstein 87®

Espéranza

Rosa Essex

(POUlnoz)
see *Rosa* Pink Cover™ Towne & Country®

Rosa Euphoria®

(INTereup) Interplant (1995)
The flowers smell and look like sweet oranges. The base of the petals is golden as is the pollen. The edge of the single flowers is initially pure orange, later fading to salmon-pink. Insects are frequent visitors. This beautiful ground cover rose is unjustly not so well known and is sometimes even given the incorrect name of Rosa Euphorbia. Personally I am

Euphoria®

euphoric about this richly flowering rose with its wide-spreading branches and healthy shiny, dark green leaves.

↔ 25h 🌸🌸🌸 ☁☁☁ ✛

Rosa Eurostar

(POUlreb)
see *Rosa* Marselisborg™ Castle®

Rosa Evelyn

(AUSsaucer) Austin (1991)
For a long time Evelyn was one of the best-loved English roses, particularly because of the intense sweet fragrance of the flowers. The name of the rose was taken from the perfume manufacturer, Crabtree & Evelyn, that incorporated that fragrance in their rose perfume line. The flowers of Evelyn are very full, cup-shaped and approximately three-and-a-half inches wide. The flower color varies according to the flowering stage and season. Immediately after the beautiful round buds open the predominant color is apricot. In fall it is more pink, particularly the older flowers. These days there are English roses with better bush forms. Evelyn initially grows upright, but the stems are not strong enough to bear the weight of the flowers and end up drooping. This is only acceptable when the rose is planted amongst perennials or shrubs that provide support.

🌸GB 40h 🌸🌸🌸 ☁☁☁☁

Rosa Everblooming Dr. W. Van Fleet

(Somerset Rose Nursery)
see *Rosa* New Dawn

Evelyn

Rosa Everglades

(POUlege)
see *Rosa* Søren Kanne™ Floribunda Poulsen®

Rosa Evita

(TANlarpost)
see *Rosa* Polarstern®

Rosa Excelsa

(-) Walsh (1909)
This old hybrid can be used in many ways: as rambler, ground cover rose, low hedge and as a tree rose, producing the much loved weeping variety. The light green stems can be easily trained up to thirteen feet high. Rich trusses hang from the sideshoots. The flowers are full, bright pink, scentless and bloom rich and long. They eventually dry out in their trusses. This is quite unattractive and so should be cut off. The rose blooms just once in early summer, but for the rest of the season it continues bearing attractive, fresh, shiny, light green foliage.
↗/❀ 160h ♀ ⌀

Rosa Exception

(Baum)
see *Rosa* Rotes Meer

Excelsa

Rosa Exception

(Tantau)
see *Rosa* Märchenland

Rosa Exotic®

(FRYxotic)
see *Rosa* Warm Wishes

Rosa Exploit®

(MEllider) Meilland (1985)
After a stunning first flush of blooms of the large-flowered climber Exploit® less, impressive blooms follow for several months. The flowers have a bright, rose-red color, making it difficult to go with every wall. Very attractive on its own against a support, which is quickly overgrown by the vigorous, long stems bearing medium green, glossy leaves.
↗ 80h ♀♀♀ ⌀⌀

Rosa Eye Opener

(INterop)
see Rosa Eyeopener®

Exploit®

Rosa Eyeopener®

(INTerop) Interplant (1987)

Hundreds of single, bright red flowers of over one inch wide crowd this ground cover shrub. A small white eye is concealed behind the tuft of yellow stamens. Flowering starts at the height of summer and continues well into fall. Beautiful full trusses of flowers appear continually on a wide-spreading shrub, which bears many thorns and much foliage. The leaves remain healthy but are sometimes slightly affected by black spot.

↔ 15h ❦❦❦ ☁

Eyeopener®

Rosa F.K. Druschki

(Lambert)

see *Rosa* Frau Karl Druschki

Rosa Fair Play®

(INTerfair) Interplant (1977)

Full trusses of coral-red buds open to reveal cup-shaped, orange-red flowers with a white eye and golden pollen. They are single to semi-double and

Fair Play®

are slightly fragrant. The shrub has a spreading growth, but is actually too tall to be counted among the true ground cover roses. The attractive, bronze-green leaves are retained on the shrub for some time.

☽ 30h ❦❦❦ ☁☁

Rosa Fairy

(Bentall)

see *Rosa* The Fairy

Rosa Fairy Lights

(Poulmulti)

see *Rosa* Snow Cover™ Towne & Country®

Rosa Fairy Queen

(-) Vurens (-)

A polyantha rose that covers bedding well with its shiny foliage that remains very healthy. The young leaves are light grass-green, turning dark green with age. The semi-double, carmine-red flowers appear throughout summer in rich trusses. The rose is susceptible to mildew.

▣ 15h ❦❦❦ ☁ ✚

Fairy Queen

Rosa Fairy Tale Queen

(KORoyness)

see *Rosa* Märchenkönigin®

Rosa Fairyland

(HARlayalong) Harkness (1980)

The polyantha rose Fairyland produces profuse blooms of full flowers in July and August.

They are pure white or with hints of pink and are borne on spreading trusses. New trusses are formed throughout summer and fall. Fairyland is a crossing between the popular Rosa The Fairy and the pollen of Rosa Yesterday (also a rose from Harkness). The shrub grows particularly widthways, twice as wide as it is tall. It covers the ground well with healthy, glossy, medium green leaves. Also suitable for large pots or flower boxes.

↔ 15h 🌹🌹🌹 ☁ ✚

Fairyland

Rosa **Fairy-Tale**

(KElren) Keizer (1995)

There are quite a few roses called Fairy-Tale, so beware of any confusion. This patio rose from Keizer flowers with very full trusses of semi-double, pink flowers. They are only a little over one inch wide and have no scent. The bush develops new stems from one point. They have a spreading growth and so hang. The foliage is shiny and dark green.

🔲 20h 🌹🌹🌹 ☁

Fairy-Tale

Rosa **Falstaff**

(AUSverse) Austin (1999)

This recent English rose can be planted as a shrub in bedding or borders, but is also suitable as a low climber. The very full flowers are initially carmined-red, later turning to purple. They have a wonderful fragrance. The bush is upright and branches profusely. The medium-sized leaves are mat and dark green.

🌹GB/🖋 50–100h 🌹🌹🌹 ☁☁☁

Falstaff

Rosa **Fantin-Latour**

(-) unknown (± 1900)

It is no longer known who bred this rose, named after the French painter Henri Fantin-Latour. This Centifolia forms a high and wide shrub of five to six-and-a-half feet. It bears luxuriant, light gray-green leaves. At the height of summer the wonderful, full, pink flowers droop downwards.

Fantin-Latour

They have an intense yet mild fragrance. A marvelous rose for romantic gardens. Suitable as hedge.
🏵 70h ⚘ ✿✿✿✿

Rosa Fascination

(POUlmax)
see *Rosa* Fredensborg™ Castle®

Rosa Favori

(Lens)
see *Rosa* Favorite

Rosa Favorite

(LEN 3) Lens (1980)
Wonderfully formed, salmon-pink, full flowers bloom on a low bush of only twenty inches height. The flowers are saucer-shaped, which is quite unusual for a floribunda rose. The blooms continue throughout summer. There is little noticeable fragrance. The new stems and leaves are initially tinted red, later turning a mat medium green.
✳✳ 20h ⚘⚘⚘ ✿

Favorite

Rosa fedtschenkoana

(-) botanical rose (-)
A wild rose from the heart of Asia. Suitable for natural gardens of a wild character. The shrub can reach six-and-a-half feet and spreads out moderately wide through wild shoots (shoots from the roots). The stems are thin and bear few but viciously sharp thorns. The bluish gray-green leaves have up to nine

Rosa fedtschenkoana

leaflets. The single, small, white (sometimes light pink) flowers appear in trusses in early summer. They smell rather musty. In a favorable location they may repeat flower. The pear-shaped, orange-red hips are eaten by birds in the fall.
🏵 80h ⚘⚘ ✿ ✚

Rosa Fée des Neiges

(KORbin)
see *Rosa* Schneewittchen®

Rosa Feeling®

(-) Lens (1992)
A moschata hybrid (see also Rosa moschata) that can reach five feet tall. Trusses with butter-yellow buds develop on the drooping stems. They open out to reveal white flowers with large tufts of stamens and golden pollen.
🏵 60h ⚘⚘⚘ ✿✿

Feeling®

Rosa Felicitas®

(KORberis) Kordes (1998)

The drooping stems of Felicitas eventually grow to form a wide dome of over thirty inches tall and five feet wide. In the summer this dome is covered with medium-sized, single flowers. They are carmine with a lighter pink heart and yellow stamens. This broad shrub has a light rose fragrance. The long stems bear dark green leaves that are strikingly shiny. A splendid, healthy rose for public green areas and natural gardens.

🌹 30h 🍽🍽🍽 ☁☁ ✚ ADR

Felicitas®

Rosa Félicité Parmentier

(-) Parmentier (1834)

The Belgian amateur rose breeder Louis Parmentier should be posthumously congratulated with this old Alba rose, which is still very popular over one hundred and fifty years after its introduction. Its origins

Félicité Parmentier

are not known, but Félicité Parmentier has certainly characteristics of the Damask rose. The flowers, for example, eventually form a pompon by the outer petals bending backwards. The heart of the very full, wonderfully fragrant rose is soft pink. The petals become paler towards the outside. After flowering, which lasts several weeks in the summer, they clean poorly. On good soil the shrub grows to around five feet high and wide, and bears bluish green leaves that remain fairly healthy. The stems have few thorns.

🌹 45–60h 🍽 ☁☁☁☁

Rosa Fellowship

(HARwelcome) Harkness (1992)

An advantage of the Fellowship is the magnificent, compact form of the bush. It bears healthy, glossy leaves. The full flowers reach four inches wide, and have a light sweet fragrance with a fresh hint of lemon. They have an unusual red-orange color with apricot on the base of each petal. They hardly change color with age.

✦✦ 35h 🍽🍽🍽 ☁☁ TOP

Fellowship

Rosa Ferdy™

(KEItoli) Keisei (1984)

The long branches of Ferdy™ are very wide spreading and cover the ground with a mass of healthy foliage. In late spring the branches are covered with a great many semi-double pink flowers. This makes a marvelous site in spring and early summer. Unfortunately, it blooms only once and the flowers shrivel up quite unattractively on the plant. When planted on its own Ferdy™ behaves like a creeping ground

Ferdy™

cover plant, but if given support in the branches of shrubs or hedges, the shoots can reach five feet high. A very healthy rose that is hardly affected by black spot and mildew.

⊕ 30h ♀ ⌢ ✛

Rosa Fêtes des Mères

(Grootendorst)
see *Rosa* Mothersday

Rosa Feu d'Artifice

(Tantau)
see *Rosa* Feuerwerk®

Rosa Feuerwerk®

(-) Tantau (1962)
The orange flowers have a hint of salmon-pink, a color not often seen in roses and which is much

Feuerwerk®

more subtle than the name of the rose suggests. The semi-double, scentless flowers bloom in trusses. They appear the whole summer on the shrub, which grows up to five feet tall. The fairly healthy foliage is light green and contrasts beautifully with the flowers. The rose is becoming increasingly less widely available.

⊕ 60h ♀♀♀ ⌢ ✛

Rosa Feuerzauber®

(KORfeu) Kordes (1974)
The orange flowers with a hint of pink are full and have the classic form of large-flowered roses: tapered buds and a tapered heart in the flower. They are very suitable as cut rose, even though they are scarcely fragrant. In the garden it can be difficult to find flowers that combine with the rather overpowering color. That is why they are usually planted in beds. They bloom constantly, with several flowers together on the end of the upright shoots. The dark green foliage is glossy and is relatively healthy for a large-flowered rose. Despite this the rose is sold by increasingly fewer suppliers.

⚘ 40h ♀♀♀ ⌢

Feuerzauber®

Rosa Fiery™ Hit®

(POUlfiry) Poulsen (1998)
This patio rose blooms with orange to brick-red flowers of approximately two inches width. They bloom in trusses above the red-tinted green foliage. Suitable for large flower boxes and pots, as well as for low bedding.

▣ 15h ♀♀♀ ⌢

Fiery™ Hit®

Rosa filipes Kiftsgate

Rosa Fil d'Ariane®

(LENfil) Lens (1988)

A continuous-flowering shrub rose of which the forty-inch branches eventually bend and cover the ground. It bears semi-double, white flowers with a hint of pink and an open heart. This reveals a tuft of stamens with golden pollen.

↔ 25h ♀♀♀ ◌◌

Fil d'Ariane®

Rosa filipes Kiftsgate

(-) Murell (1954)

Take care with this seedling of the wild Rosa filipes from West China. It is phenomenally vigorous. Planted against a wall it can reach twenty-three feet high within three years. The record is an amazing one hundred and fifty feet! A tree would be completely overrun by the branches. It bears backward pointing hooked thorns, which makes pruning a tough chore

you would rather postpone. It is therefore best to plant the rose alone as a solitary shrub. It then grows to around thirteen feet tall and wide. In mid-summer full trusses appear with single, cream flowers. They have a pleasant fragrance and change in late summer to orange and later bright red hips.

⚶ 200h ♀ ◌◌ ✪

Rosa Fire Magic

(KORfeu)

see Rosa Feuerzauber®

Rosa Fire Pillar

see Rosa Bischofsstadt Paderborn

Rosa First Blush®

(MElzincaro) Meilland (2000)

First Blush® is a large-flowered rose with shapely carmine red flowers. It is not yet widely available.

⚹ 30h ♀♀♀ ◌

First Blush®

Rosa First Edition

(DELtep)

see *Rosa* Arnoud Delbard®

Rosa Fisherman

(AUSchild)

see *Rosa* Fisherman's Friend®

Rosa Fisherman's Friend®

(AUSchild) Austin (1987)

Round, red buds open slowly to reveal deep red flowers, which gradually acquire tints of pink But the overall impression of the very full, wide flowers is a rich red. They have a strong, old-fashioned fragrance. The robust branches bear many viciously sharp thorns. They first grow upright and then later outwards, as the thin ends of the shoots bend under the weight of the flowers, which can reach over six inches in width. Fisherman's Friend® is a little susceptible to mildew and very susceptible to black spot. The breeder David Austin believes that there are now better, comparable roses.

GB 30h 🌺🌺 ☁☁☁

Fisherman's Friend®

Rosa Flame Dance

(KORflata)

see *Rosa* Flammentanz®

Rosa Flamingo®

(KORflüg) Kordes (1979)

At the end of the impressively thorny branches open flamingo pink flowers. The orange-yellow buds unfold very slowly, the wonderfully formed flowers revealing themselves petal by petal. An excellent cut flower that keeps long. The flowers also last long in bedding, but once dead fall apart keeping the bush clean. The branches show upright growth, but are not very thick. They bear dark green, glossy leaves.

✻ 35h 🌺🌺🌺 ☁☁

Flamingo®

Rosa Flammentanz®

(KORflata) Kordes (1955)

The strikingly large, carmine-red flowers appear in mid-summer in vast numbers on the long stems of this large-flowered climbing rose. They have a moderate scent. The full flowers provide a fiery show, whether alone or against support, which can be a wall, a fence or a sturdy rose arch or pillar.

Flammentanz®

The vigorous shoots can reach up to seventeen feet, depending on the support. The young wood and foliage are grass-green and remain healthy, in part due to the vigorous growth of the climber.

ᔕ 80–200h ♀ ⬭⬭ ✚ ADR

Rosa Flash Meidiland

(MEIstocko) Meilland (1991)
In the heart of the single, dark red flowers of this shrub rose the yellow stamens contrast beautifully with the light heart. Despite the lack of fragrance, insects are frequent visitors to the flowers, and can remain so throughout the summer as this shrub blooms continuously. It is particularly suitable for informal settings, both in sections and between perennials. The young branches are tinted with the color of red cabbage and initially bear olive-green foliage, which darkens with age.

◍ 35h ♀♀♀ ⬭ TOP

Flash Meidiland

Rosa Flavia

(INTerette)
see *Rosa* Fleurette®

Rosa Fleurette®

(INTerette) Interplant (1977)
The shrubs send shoots diagonally upwards in all directions. At the ends they bear trusses of single

Fleurette®

flowers that hardly have any fragrance. They have a clear salmon-pink color with a light heart that during flowering gets increasingly bigger. Older flowers fade a great deal to a pale soft pink. The olive-green leaves contrast attractively with the color of the flowers, but are susceptible to black spot.

◍ 40h ♀♀♀ ⬭

Rosa Flirt®

(KORkopapp) Kordes (2000)
In these flowers you can still recognize the characteristics of the well-known rose The Fairy, the ancestor of this flower. The violet pink flowers of Flirt® are darker and less full.

Flirt®

Each petal appears strikingly serrated with round lobes on the outer edges. The yellow stamens are clearly visible in the lighter heart. The glossy, olive-green leaves cover the densely branched bushes of approximately twenty-five inches tall and thirty inches wide. Suitable for sections in bedding or a border with perennials.

@ 25h 🌹🌹🌹 ☁

Rosa **Flora Danica**™ **Paramount**®

(POUlrim) Poulsen (1996)

One of the lower large-flowered roses that Poulsen has included in the Paramount series. The full, apricot-colored flowers with traces of salmon-pink have a pleasant fragrance and grow to around three-and-a-half inches wide. They contrast wonderfully with the mahogany color of the young leaves, which later turn a glossy dark red green.

⚹ 30h 🌹🌹🌹 ☁☁☁

Flora Danica™ Paramount®

Rosa **Flora Romantica**®

(MElchavrin) Meilland (1998)

Rose breeder Meilland now includes the climbing rose that was previously called Rosa Mon Jardin et Maison in the Fleur Romantica® series, due to the romantic look of the soft yellow to white flowers. They are very full and have a sweet, fruity fragrance. Flora Romantica® is now recommended as a shrub but still has the tendency to climb.

🌱 35h 🌹🌹🌹 ☁☁

Flora Romantica®

Rosa **Floranje**

(-) RvS-Melle (1990)

The flowers are so close to one another on top of the stems that they together form a single round mass of bright orange-red. An impressive sight. However, the stems are particularly thick. They extend from a bush that is well clothed at the base with dark, gray-green leaves. The young leaves are light yellow-green. The semi-double flowers are cup-shaped. They have hardly any fragrance.

✹✹ 30h 🌹🌹🌹 ☁

Floranje

Rosa **Florentina**

(-) Kordes (1974)

The cylindrical buds open to reveal scarlet flowers with a perfect Hybrid Tea form. They are lightly fragrant but are still popular as a cut flower. Every vertical stem bears one flower. Florentina also thrives outside in beds. The bushes are upright, approximately thirty-five inches tall and twenty inches wide. They bear large leaves that are olive-green when young and turn dark green with age. For a large-flowered rose the foliage remains quite healthy.

⚹ 35h 🌹🌹🌹 ☁☁ ✚ ADR

Florentina

Flower Power

Rosa Flower Carpet® Red

(NOAre)
see *Rosa* Alcantara®

Rosa Flower Carpet® White

(NOAschnee)
see *Rosa* Schneeflocke®

Rosa Flower Carpet® Yellow

(NOAson)
see *Rosa* Celina®

Rosa Flower Carpet®

(NOAasa)
see *Rosa* Medusa®

Rosa Flower Carpet®

(NOAfeuer)
see *Rosa* Heidefeuer®

Rosa Flower Carpet® Pink

(NOAtraum)
see *Rosa* Heidetraum®

Rosa Flower Power

(FRYcassia) Fryer (1998)
This low shrub rose grows well in a large pot or container. The very full flowers bloom in trusses above healthy looking, dark green foliage. The light apricot petals curl. The flowers have no fragrance.
☻ 25h ♥♥♥ ⌣

Rosa Flower Power

(KORedan)
see *Rosa* Blühwunder®

Rosa Focus®

(NOAgut) Noack (1997)
The full, salmon-pink flowers of Focus® bloom wide open. They reach 4 inches wide, and have a light, sweet fruity fragrance. The bushes have rich, long-lasting blooms. They have vigorous upright growth and branch out fairly well. The stems are strong enough to bear the heavy flower trusses. They also bear strikingly many large amber-colored thorns. The dark gray-green leaves remain on the plant long into fall and provide good cover for bedding and borders. The plant is very resistant to rose diseases, for which it has been awarded. Focus® has, for example, received the Golden Rose, the highest distinction, of The Hague in 2000.
✻ 40h ♥♥♥ ⌣⌣ ✛

Focus®

Rosa Footloose™

(TANotax)
see *Rosa* Mirato®

Rosa Foxi Pavement

(UHLwa)
zie *Rosa rugosa* Foxi®

Rosa Foxy Pavement

(UHLwa)
see *Rosa rugosa* Foxi®

Rosa Fragrant Cloud

(Tanellis)
see *Rosa* Duftwolke®

Rosa Fragrant Delight®

(-) Wisbech Plant Co. (1978)
The name refers justifiably to the wonderful fruity
scent of the full flowers (22 petals). They are initially apricot to soft orange, later changing to salmon. In
very hot weather the flower fades and loses much of
its charm. However, it remains a very popular rose in
the cooler climates of North-West Europe and has
won many prizes. The bush branches well and is
dense with foliage, which is a combination of red,
olive-green and glossy, dark green. It has one big
disadvantage: Fragrant Delight® is very susceptible to
mildew.
✿✿ 40h ❦❦❦ ✿✿✿✿ TOP

Fragrant Delight®

Rosa Fragrant Gold

(TANdugoft)
see *Rosa* Duftgold®

Rosa Francine Austin

(AUSram) Austin (1988)
The low, spreading bush bears rich trusses of full
flowers, which hang like small pompons. They are
white, practically scentless and eventually open up to
reveal their pollen. The shrubs are often placed next
to one another in beds whereby its spreading growth
– a little wider than tall – acquires a ground cover
character. In contrast to other ground cover roses
this is not full with new branches and leaves. However, harder than normal pruning in spring
stimulates the formation of new shoots in the center.
The rose is also suitable as a low climber (when
supported) and in the weeping form. Francine Austin
is also a good cut flower.
↔/❦GB 40h ❦❦❦ ✿

Francine Austin

Rosa Francis E. Lester

(-) Lester (1946)
Those looking for a once-flowering rambler for
a natural garden will not find a better and healthi-
er plant. The vigorous branches and thorns find
support themselves, whether on an old tree, trellis,
rose pillar or arch. Some ties are necessary. In
early summer Francis E. Lester produces full
trusses of pleasantly scented, single flowers. They
have an ivory-white base with pink blotches,
resembling large apple blossom.

Francis E. Lester

After flowering they form small hips, which turn orange-red in September. They are eaten by blackbirds as of November when food gets scarce. Highly recommended.

🌿 160–200h 🌷 ◌◌◌ ✚

Rosa Françoise Drion®

(LENraba) Lens (1995)
This is one of the best moschata hybrids of Louis Lens (see also Rosa moschata). They bloom in long, tapering trusses. The breeder describes the color as mauve pink. The flowers have a white heart with yellow pollen. The color hardly fades and the flowers clean after a long flowering period without turning an unattractive brown. If you tie the strongest stems and cut away the weakest, a low rambler is formed.

☀/🌿 30–55h 🌷🌷🌷 ◌◌

Francoise Drion®

Rosa Frau Karl Druschki

(-) Lambert (1901)
Pink-tinted buds develop into magnificent, full, ivory-white flowers. They bloom in early summer and again in the fall. There is little fragrance. Although the rose is counted among the old remontant hybrids, it closely resembles modern large-flowered roses. It can be used as high shrub or low climber. Frau Karl Druschki is still regarded as one of the best white roses. The rose has attractive gray-green foliage.

❀ 60–80h 🌷🌷 ◌

Frau Karl Druschki

Rosa Fredensborg™ Castle®

(POUlmax) Poulsen (1996)
One of the low floribunda roses of Poulsen's Castle series, which is sometimes regarded as a low shrub

Fredensborg™ Castle®

rose. The semi-double, salmon-pink flowers appear in profusion on the low bush.

They have a wonderful shape and color that contrast well with the glossy, dark green leaves.

❋❋ 25h ✿✿✿ ☁

Rosa Frederic Mistral®

(MEltebros) Meilland (1998)

Not only are the flowers of Frederic Mistral® large, but the bushes can easily reach thirty inches tall and bear many large, usually healthy, medium green leaves. The soft pink flowers are over four inches wide and have an intense, fresh lemon fragrance.

❋ 30h ✿✿ ☁☁☁☁

Frederic Mistral®

Frederiksborg™ Castle®

Rosa Frederiksborg™ Castle®

(POUldrik) Poulsen (1998)

The salmon-pink petals reinforce the already feminine look of the flowers with their wavy edge. Unfortunately they are scentless. They are semi-double to full, almost four inches wide and flower in trusses. The bushy, branching shrub often grows to over three-and-a-half feet and bears shiny, dark green leaves.

❋❋ 50h ✿✿✿ ☁

Rosa Freisinger Morgenröte

(KORmarter) Kordes (1988)

The flowers, which primarily appear in the first half of the summer, have a basic orange color. From closer by apricot, yellow and pink can also be seen. They are semi-double, and eventually fully expose their heart of yellow stamens. The shrub grows to between three-and-a-half and five feet tall and at least as wide, making it particularly suitable for large, luxuriant gardens. It can also be used for hedging. The leaves are glossy, medium green.

Freisinger Morgenröte

◉ 50h ✿✿ ☁☁

Rosa Freude®

(DeKORat) Kordes (1975)

Freude® is one of the few large-flowered roses that has very good resistance to fungal diseases. The dark green leaves have a marvelous shine and remain healthy also in late summer. The shrub shows branching and upright growth. Several of the beautifully shaped, full flowers are borne together on the

Freude®

long stems. They are very suitable as cut flower, partly because they last well. I did not notice the so-called 'rich' fragrance. They have a peculiar color: like silvery moonlight on candy-pink with a golden undertone.

Freude® is also very good for outside, although the older flowers are sensitive to rain and the blooms come in waves. However, in summer the bush is never without flowers and it cleans well.

✱ 30h ♥♥♥ ◇ ✚ ADR

Rosa Friesia®

(KORresia) Kordes (1973)

It is because of its low growth and the glossy, fresh green leaves that Friesia® is one of the most popular yellow flowering roses. The bushes grow to only twenty-five inches height and approximately twenty inches wide. They have rich blooms throughout the summer with relatively large golden flowers. The flowers arise from pointed buds and open out wide

Friesia®

to a hemisphere shape. The yellow stamens are clearly visible in the center. With subsequent blooms the pleasantly fragrant flowers fade somewhat. Although Friesia® is classified as a disease-resistant rose it may still be affected by black spot, but growth continues undisturbed. Recommended.

✱✱ 25h ♥♥♥ ◇◇◇ ✚ ADR TOP

Rosa Frisson Frais®

(-) Lens (1990)

A moschata hybrid (see also Rosa moschata) with very full pyramidal flower trusses. The flowers are single and pink, with a wide white heart. We could also say: white flowers with a pink edge. They grow to over three inches and have a pleasant fragrance. From spring to early fall new, vigorous shoots appear on the highly branching shrub. Each new branch produces blooms, certainly if the old trusses are cut off before hips form. Frisson Frais® is highly

Frisson Frais®

suitable for natural gardens and fences in public green areas. The shrub reaches five feet tall.

◍ 60h ♥♥♥ ◇◇◇

Rosa Fritz Nobis

(-) Kordes (1940)

On looking at the shape of the buds and young leaves you would think that this is a large-flowered rose. But then the flowers open to a cup-shape, exposing their yellow heart of stamens. This is actually a descendant of the wild ramanas rose (Rosa rugosa) which can be seen from the growth and the sturdy, gray-green leaves. The flowers have a pleasant smell of apples. They are salmon-pink, which fades with age. Old flowers fall off after blooming. The only disadvantage

Fritz Nobis

Frühlingsduft

is the short duration of the bloom, which ends in early summer. Hips develop later in the season.

The shrub grows vigorously, up to six-and-a-half feet tall and wide, and is a true gem for a natural garden or park.

@ 80h ♀ ✿✿✿✿ ✚

The shrub bears bright green foliage, grows vigorously and reaches six-and-a-half feet tall and wide. This is the same immense size of the wild rose from Frühlingsduft originates: the tall, large-flowered form of the burnet rose (*Rosa pimpinellifolia* Grandiflora).

@ 80h ♀ ✿✿✿✿ ✚

Rosa Frohsinn® '82

(TANsinnroh) Tantau (1982)

This is not the floribunda rose 'Frohsinn' from Tantau from 1961, but a much younger large-flowered rose. The very large, full flowers are peach in color with a warm base of yellow. The flowers are wonderfully shaped and have a pleasant, fruity scent. The bush grows upright and bears glossy, dark green leaves.

✱ 30h ♀♀♀ ✿✿✿

Frohsinn® '82

Rosa Frühlingsduft

(-) Kordes (1949)

Large, semi-double, pink flowers unfold from golden buds. Their color fades with age, leaving a hint of pink in the cream and yellow that remains. The flowers are very fragrant, but unfortunately bloom primarily in early summer. Any subsequent blooms are quite scanty.

Rosa Frühlingsgold

(-) Kordes (1937)

The flowers of Frühlingsgold appear as early as May from reddish, tapered buds. They have a delicious fragrance and due to the profuse blooms can be smelled from a distance. The shrub is usually planted in parks and very large gardens, as it reaches eight feet tall and – due to the arching branches – at least as wide. Its ancestry can be seen from the moss-green leaves. It is a form of the burnet rose (*Rosa pimpinellifolia* Hispida). The other parental rose is Rosa Joanna Hill, a cultivar with creamy yellow, strongly fragrant flowers.

The only disadvantage of the rose are the short blooms, which only last three weeks.

@ 100h ♀ ✿✿✿✿ ✚

Frühlingsgold

Rosa Fuchsia Meidiland®

(MElpelta) Meilland (1994)
The long, drooping stems of Fuchsia Meidiland® form a cascade of shiny foliage. As of early summer they are covered with full trusses of semi-double, florescent pink flowers. The cream heart reveals the ochre-yellow pollen. After an initial exuberant bloom there follow a few less spectacular blooms throughout summer. The old flowers unfortunately do not fall off well, so the dry, brown flowers make an unattractive sight. Suitable for public areas and private gardens. The rose is a little susceptible to black spot.
● 30h 🌹🌹 ◌

Rosa Fuchsia Meillandecor

(MElpelta)
see *Rosa* Fuchsia Meidiland

Fuchsia Meidiland®

Rosa Fulton Mackay

(COCdana) Cocker (1988)
Long buds unfold to reveal shapely, full flowers. With age they become cup-shaped. The flowers appear orange, but contain subtle tints of apricot and salmon and sometimes rose-red. This large-flowered rose has a delicious spicy scent. Rich blooms appear in early summer. Subsequent flowering is continuous but less rich. The glossy, dark green foliage is a little susceptible to black spot. The vigorous bush con-

Fulton Mackay

stantly produces new foliage, keeping the shrub green for some time.
✳ 35h 🌹🌹🌹 ◌◌◌

Rosa Galaxy®

(MElhuterb) Meilland (1995)
A floribunda rose with the stature of a park or shrub rose. The bush grows primarily outwards and branches well. The full flowers of approximately two inches wide appear in trusses and shower the bush with flowers.
The color is subtle: cream to soft yellow with light pink tints. Do not confuse Galaxy® with Galaxy™ (MORgal), a miniature rose not included in this book.
✳✳ 25h 🌹🌹🌹 ◌

Galaxy®

Rosa gallica

(-) botanical rose (-)

The French rose grows in the wild in South and Central Europe up to Asia Minor. Before the arrival of Chinese roses it was the French rose that was used for crossing, from which the oldest cultivated roses have been bred.

Rosa gallica forms a relatively low bush, which grows in width through suckers. In early summer pink to carmine-red flowers appear. They are single and solitary or in small groups. The brick-red hips less noticeable.

❀ 40h ♀ ◌◌◌ ✛

Rosa Garden News

(POUlrim)

see Rosa Flora Danica™ Paramount®

Rosa gallica

Rosa Gartenarchitekt Günther Schulze

(AUSwalker)

see Rosa The Pilgrim™

Rosa Gärtnerfreude®

(KORstesgli) Kordes (1999)

This fresh looking bush has small, very shiny, dark green leaves. It grows to one-and-a-half feet tall and is therefore highly suitable for bedding as well as smaller gardens. Because of its size it just falls outside the category of patio roses, but does have the same compact growth with profusely branching stems, crowned by full flower trusses. The small, scentless,

very full flowers have a distinct raspberry color. They are resistant to rain and continue with attractive blooms after rainy periods. A polyantha rose of the same name (Kordes, 1965), but with orange-red flowers, is no longer sold, but you may come across it in rose gardens.

☺ 20h ♀♀♀ ◌

Rosa Gavnø™ Hybrid Tea Poulsen®

(POUlgav) Poulsen (1989)

The shape of the full flowers of Rosa Gavnø™ Hybrid Tea Poulsen® resembles that of large-flowered

Gärtnerfreude®

roses and the breeder has categorized it as such (Hybrid Tea). However, we could also call it a floribunda rose. The lightly fragrant flowers are three-and-a-

Gavnø™ Hybrid Tea Poulsen®

half inches wide. They are soft orange in color, which changes to salmon-pink with age. The leaves of the bushy plant are tinted red which can be clearly seen in the shiny dark green.

✳ 30h 🌼🌼🌼 ☁☁

Rosa Gelbe Dagmar Hastrup®

(MORyelrug) Meilland (1987)

We are particularly familiar with the ramanas rose or Japanese rose (Rosa rugosa) with pink and white flowers. This yellow variety is a welcome addition. The single flowers reach three inches wide. They start yellow, becoming paler with age. Unusually for a shrub of the rugosa type no hips are formed. Gelbe Dagmar Hastrup® consequently blooms for a longer period. The almost vertical stems bear large, dull, medium green leaves, which are susceptible to black spot and mildew. Despite this Gelbe Dagmar Hastrup® is a popular rose for public areas.

◑ 30h 🌼🌼🌼 ☁☁

Rosa Geoff Hamilton

(AUSham) Austin (1997)

The famous English garden journalist Geoff Hamilton was known for his great love of organic garden-

Gelbe Dagmar Hastrup®

ing (without the use of artificial fertilizers and pesticides). David Austin therefore selected a rose that was fairly resistant to known rose diseases. The bush grows vigorously and healthily. It bears soft pink flowers, the outer petals of which bend backwards and fade to white. The flowers have a light fragrance, with an old-fashioned rose perfume and the scent of apples. The flower stalks are actually too thin to bear

Geoff Hamilton

the weight of the flowers and so sometimes break in rainy weather.

🌷GB 50h 🌼🌼🌼 ☁☁ ✛

Rosa Georgette®

(KORacona) Kordes (1995)

A pink flowering miniature rose was already registered under the name Georgette® back in 1981. The Dutch company Interplant then later introduced a rose of the same name with white flowering trusses, which is no longer available. This new Georgette® from Kordes, a floribunda rose, has received the ADR award due to its good resistance to fungal diseases. The flowers unfold dark pink, changing quickly to a silvery light pink. They are semi-double, cup to saucer-shaped, with yellow stamens in the heart. The trusses appear already in early summer.

The bush is upright, vigorously branching, looking somewhat like a shrub. Flowers are produced the whole summer, but less than in early summer. The leaves are glossy green.

✳✳ 45h 🌼🌼🌼 ☁ ✛ ADR

Georgette®

Rosa Gertrude Jekyll®

(AUSbord) Austin (1986)

Both the shape and the fragrance of the flowers are reminiscent of the old roses that were the inspiration for David Austin Sr. to develop his own English roses. The pink flowers of Gertrude Jekyll® are very full, over three inches wide and smell wonderfully sweet. This rose is second only to Evelyn in terms of fragrance intensity of an English rose. Rose perfume is made from its petals. The bush has vigorous upright growth, but looks rather coarse so is best placed behind other plants in a border. In early summer, at the height of the blooms, the trusses become so heavy that the stems droop. In a border Gertrude Jekyll® will intertwine with the other plants. The large leaves change from burgundy to yellow-green then medium green. The same rose is sold under the name Rosa Gertrude Jekyll Climbing, which can grow to over seven feet when trained as a climber.

♀GB/↗ 45h/70h ♀♀♀ ◌◌◌◌

Gertrude Jekyll®

Gertrude Jekyll®

Rosa Ghislaine de Féligonde

(-) Turbat (1916)

This old rose is still very popular, particularly because it is one of the few multiflora hybrids that flowers for long periods. After the first flush in June-July it flowers again. The apricot-colored buds open out to semi-double flowers that are initially the same color, but then change to white to soft pink. The heart is later obscured by the curling petals. The light green foliage goes well with the fair flowers, which unfortunately scarcely have any fragrance. The profusely branching bush can be used as a high solitary plant or low rambler.

◍/↗ 40/100h ♀♀ ◌

Rosa Gilbert Becaud®

(MEIridorio) Meilland (1984)

This is one of the classics from Meilland. The perfectly formed bud opens to an equally perfectly formed flower that looks orange, but has subtle tints: orange-yellow with copper and charming light red venation. A typical Hybrid Tea or large-flowered rose, highly suitable for bouquets; certainly thanks to the copper-colored young leaves, which later turn mat green.

✳ 30h ♀♀ ◌

Ghislaine de Féligonde

Rosa Gina Lollobrigida®

(MEllivar) Meilland (1997)

The bush is nothing special: the medium-sized, medium green leaves are a little glossy and are borne on tall, vertical stems, but which are too short for a climbing rose. Only the intensely warm yellow

Gilbert Becaud®

Ginger Sylabub

flowers are of any note. They are beautifully formed and last the whole summer. Good as cut flower.
⚹ 40h 🌺🌺🌺 ☁☁

Rosa Ginger Sylabub

(HARjolly) Harkness (2000)
The flowers of Ginger Sylabub are so heavy that the stalks buckle or partially hang. For a bush rose this would be a disadvantage, but for a climbing rose this is actually a good thing. In this way we can see the hearts of the blooming flowers above us. And the heart of this new climbing rose from Harkness is extremely rich and full and frequently quartered in order to accommodate the many petals. The flowers

Gina Lollobrigida®

are fragrant and look romantic. The heart is apricot with the outer petals changing from a yellow-orange to a very pale light pink. This climber easily reaches heights of ten feet.
🌿 120h 🌺🌺🌺 ☁☁☁

Rosa Gioia

(Meilland)
see *Rosa* Peace®

Rosa Gisselfeld™ Hybrid Tea Poulsen®

(POUlgiss) Poulsen (1974)
The strength of this deep red, five-inch flower is that it is colorfast. The deep red color remains both outside under all weathers as well as in the vase, for which it is highly suitable. It has a light fragrance. The bush branches well and is compact.
⚹ 40h 🌺🌺🌺 ☁

Rosa Gîtes de France®

(MEIwaton) Meilland (1994)
An excellent rose to cover a fence. Gîtes de France grows to six-and-a-half feet tall and bears fragrant blooms. They have an unusual florescent carmine-

Gisselfeld™

pink color. The rose cleans moderately in wet weather. The mature leaves are dark green and remain healthy for a long time. The bush can also be grown as a solitary, reaching then chest height.

🌿 50–80h 🌷🌷🌷 ☁☁

Rosa Glacier™

(POUlfeld)
see *Rosa* Gråsten™ Floribunda Poulsen® (POUlfeld)

Rosa Glad Tidings

(TANtide)
see *Rosa* Lübecker Rotspon®

Rosa Glamis Castle

(AUSlevel) Austin (1992)
Glamis Castle produces globular, white flowers. In the center of the loose, full flowers you can often detect some cream or yellow. Trusses are borne

Gites de France®

throughout summer and fall. They have a strong myrrh fragrance. The plant has bushy upright growth, branches well and continues producing new trusses with flowers. A beautiful plant to combine in a border or to place together as bedding rose.

🌷GB 35h 🌷🌷🌷 ☁☁☁

Rosa glauca

(-) botanical rose (-)
The natural habitat of this rose is in the mountains of Central and Southern Europe. Its scientific name refers to the gray-blue color of the leaves.

This robust shrub bears flowers in early summer. The pink flowers with a white heart have no fragrance. After flowering, brown-red hips are formed in the course of summer which later turn purple.

An excellent shrub for public green areas and natural gardens

✽ 70h 🌷 ☁ ✚

Glamis Castle

Rosa Gletscherfee®

(KORdomal) Kordes (1991)
The white flowers of Gletscherfee® look impressive and are highly suitable for natural gardens. Bees fre-

Rosa glauca

Rosa glauca

quently visit these four-inch flowers. Their fragrance is a combination of roses and fresh apples. The shrub bears dense, glossy, olive to dark green foliage. It is sometimes affected by black spot, but usually remains very healthy. The shrub branches well. With a height and width of three-and-a-half to five feet it is very suitable for hedging.

🌢 40–60h 🌹🌹🌹 🗨🗨 ✚

Rosa Gloria Dei

(Meilland)
see *Rosa* Peace®

Rosa Glowing Achievement

(TANelliv)
see *Rosa* Stadt Eltville®

Rosa Glücksburg

(AUSren)
see *Rosa* Charles Rennie Mackintosh

Gletscherfee®

Rosa Godewind®

(KORbraufa) Kordes (1992)
The full trusses of cup-shaped, scarlet flowers contrast sharply with the glossy foliage. They unfold to reveal a red tint but change to dark green with age. The leaves have good disease resistance. Though cup-shaped the flowers are not very full, clearly displaying the yellow stamens in the heart. The shrub

branches well and reaches a little under four feet tall. This makes it suitable not only for low hedging, but also for bedding and as a solitary.

🌢 50h 🌹🌹🌹 🗨🗨 ✚

Rosa Godstowe Girl

(HARfurore) Harkness (2000)
The name of this large-flowered rose refers to the first public school for primary-aged girls in Great Britain. This school was established in 1900 and in 2000 celebrated its one-hundredth anniversary. The large, full red flowers are excellent cut flowers. They keep long in a vase, and outside they retain their color, even after periods of bright sunshine. They are not so resistant to rain. Therefore plant the bush in a sunny, airy location.

Godewind®

It has vigorous and branching growth, constantly producing new buds.

✳ 35h 🌹🌹🌹 🗨

Rosa Gold Bay®

(TANgoba) Tantau (1998)
The compact, sturdy stems bear red thorns, glossy dark leaves and full trusses with semi-double, yellow flowers. The flowers are wide, almost saucer-shaped, and reveal their orange stamens and golden pollen. Hips are formed later, though this low shrub rose continues to flower throughout the summer. It is

Godstowe Girl

used primarily in public green areas, but is also suitable for low bedding and border edges in private gardens. The rose belongs to the Stecktii® group and is propagated from cuttings.

🌀 20h 🌷🌷🌷 ⌣ ✛

Rosa Gold Glow

(-) Perry (1959)
The upright bushes sometimes reach shoulder height. They bear young bronze-tinted leaves, which later turn to a dark gray-green. The golden flowers are about four inches wide. They are very to extremely full, but eventually reveal their heart of red stamens. They are lightly fragrant and produce moderate blooms.

⚡ 60h 🌷🌷🌷 ⌣

Gold Bay®

Rosa Gold Magic Carpet

(Poulmulti)
see *Rosa* Snow Cover™ Towne & Country®

Rosa Gold Magic Carpet

(POUlurt)
see *Rosa* Sun Cover™ Towne & Country®

Rosa Gold Reef™ Towne & Country®

(POUldom) Poulsen (1998)
Stunning, deep golden flowers appear in trusses on the almost four-foot bush. The blooms of the semi-

Gold Glow

double to full flowers of three-and-a-half inches last the whole summer.
They have a light rose fragrance. They make excellent cut flowers, especially in biedermeier bouquets and other small bouquets. The bushy plant bears glossy, dark green leaves.

❂❂ 50h 🌷🌷🌷 ⌣⌣

Rosa Gold Star

(TANtern)
see *Rosa* Goldstern®

Rosa Gold Topaz

(KORtossgo)
see *Rosa* Goldtopas®

Rosa Goldelse®

(TANdolgnil) Tantau (1999)

Although Goldelse® is a floribunda rose the flowers often appear singly. They are also very large and extremely full. Particularly due to their copper-yellow color with a mild orange tint they have a classic look, making them very suitable for romantic gardens. They have a light, fruity fragrance. The flowers are so heavy that the stems bend under the weight. The bushes show good growth, and bear large, medium green leaves.

❁❁ 25h ❦❦❦ ◌◌

Rosa Golden Border

(HAVobog) Verschuren (1993)

The very full flowers seem to stick out like soft yellow balloons above the bush. They turn to a pretty pale yellow with age. New trusses continually reappear on this shrub with a polyanthas character. Its low, compact growth habit makes it excellent in bor-

ders. The light green foliage is a little susceptible to black spot.

◉ 25h ❦❦❦ ◌◌

Rosa Golden Celebration

(AUSgold) Austin (1992)

Golden Celebration is a rose that lives up to its name. The flowers shine golden amongst the mat, medium green leaves. They become very large and heavy, form very full cups and are intensely fragrant. The thin stems bend under the weight of the flowers and sometimes hang a little. This looks charming in a border with other plants. For the rest, the shrub is compact, bears abundant foliage and produces reliable blooms throughout summer and fall.

❁❁ 50h ❦❦❦ ◌ ⊕

Golden Border

Goldelse®

Golden Celebration

Rosa Golden Cover™ Towne & Country®

(POUlgode) Poulsen (1996)

The yellow flowers bloom in trusses. They are semi-double to full and cup-shaped. They have a light scent of wild roses. The glossy, medium green leaves are borne on a low shrub that is wide spreading.

⊛ 25h ♣♣♣ ⌒⌒

Rosa Golden Evolution

(-) CPRO/DLO (1997)

A very classic but somewhat dull, large-flowered rose. The full golden flowers hardly fade. They are approximately four inches wide and have a very light fragrance. Even though the moderate growth does not produce many new flowers, the bush is rarely without blooms. The bushes have a spreading growth with upright shoots. The young leaves are olive-green, changing dark green with age.

✳ 30h ♣♣♣ ⌒

Golden Cover™ Towne & Country®

Rosa Golden Flower Rain

(TANtern)
zie *Rosa* Goldstern®

Golden Evolution

Rosa Golden Fox

(-) Warner (1997)

The glossy, dark green bush branches well but has primarily upright growth.
At the top it bears trusses with semi-double, yellow flowers, which are almost scentless. They look fairly unexciting and are particularly suitable for bedding. Some exceptional plants can grow to around three-and-a-half feet.

▣ 20h ♣♣♣ ⌒

Rosa Golden Holstein®

(KORtikel) Kordes (1989)

The lightly full, wide open flowers would look quite natural if they were white or soft pink, but the bright

Golden Fox

golden color of Golden Holstein® is difficult to miss. The flowers go particularly well with the young leaves, which are a shiny light green, later turning dark green. The foliage remains healthy. The flowers are moderately full and resistant to rain. After flowering the flowers drop, keeping the plant clean.
�֍�֍ 30h 🌹🌹🌹 ☁ ✪

Rosa Golden Jet

(TANtasch)
see *Rosa* Goldschatz®

Rosa Golden Juwel

(TANledolg)
see *Rosa* Goldjuwel®

Golden Holstein®

Rosa Golden Monica®

(TANgolca) Tantau (1988)
The perfectly formed, full, deep golden flowers appear singly on the long, straight stalks. This makes Golden Monica® a beautiful cut flower, despite having little fragrance. If growth is maintained, it will flower throughout the summer, but – as is usual for large-flowered roses – not very richly. The rose has large, medium green leaves.
✶ 30h 🌹🌹🌹 ☁

Rosa Golden Plover

(Poulmulti)
see *Rosa* Snow Cover™ Towne & Country®

Golden Monica®

Rosa Golden Plover

(POUlurt)
see *Rosa* Sun Cover™ Towne & Country®

Rosa Golden Touch

(TANmirsch)
see *Rosa* Sonnenschirm®

Rosa Goldfinch®

(INTerbee) Interplant (1993)
Do not confuse this rose with the 1907 soft yellow rambler of the same name from Paul. The Goldfinch® from Interplant remains very low. The bushes bear thick foliage and full, golden flowers that do not fade. Cutting away old trusses will encourage further blooms.
▣ 20h 🌹🌹🌹 ☁

Goldfinch®

Goldmarie 82®

Rosa Goldjuwel®

(TANledolg) Tantau (1993)

This is a typical pot rose: small with dense branching, stocky growth. With good care – and that means not letting it dry out and feeding regularly – this rose can flower the whole summer. Better results are gained if planted in the garden. The very full golden flowers are scentless. They are perched above the medium green foliage, which remain strikingly healthy for a miniature rose.

🎴 15h 🌿🌿🌿 ✿ ✚

Goldjuwel®

Rosa Goldmarie 82®

(KORfalt) KORdes (1984)

The red ends of the broad egg-shaped buds predict what is to happen later: the large, full flowers begin

yellow but then eventually change to red. The open flowers look rather rumpled by then, in part due to the curved petals. Despite this they are fairly resistant to rain. The disease-resistant, leathery, dark green leaves are borne on upright branches that also bear very full flower trusses. A good bedding rose, which has the occasional pause in flowering.

✿✿ 25h 🌿🌿🌿 ✿ ✚

Rosa Goldquelle®

(TANellelog) Tantau (1988)

The rich trusses of full flowers bloom from mid-summer deep into fall. The dark green, glossy leaves also remain on the bush for some time, giving a calm setting for the golden flowers, which slowly reveal their yellow pollen with age. Even with rain the flowers remain beautiful and clean well. It has a light and plain fragrance. Goldquelle® grows vigorously up to 30 inches.

✿✿ 30h 🌿🌿🌿 ✿✿

Goldquelle®

Rosa Goldschatz®

(TANtasch) Tantau (1996)

The semi-double, subdued yellow flowers of Gold-schatz® open to four-inch-wide, saucer-shaped flowers, revealing their orange stamens. The color is bright but not too loud and does not fade in the sun. These rewarding flowers appear throughout the summer in trusses above the healthy, shiny, medium green leaves. This rose branches well and forms a full, wide bush, which keeps its foliage well into fall. A good addition to any garden, including natural gardens, and public green areas.

✿✿ 30h 🌺🌺🌺 ☁ ✚

Rosa Goldstern®

(TANtern) Tantau (1966)

Although Goldstern® dates back to 1966 it is still one of the best yellow climbing roses. The golden flow-

Goldschatz®

ers are extremely full, but eventually open to a cup-shape, revealing their hearts. The blooms begin early and rich. Further blooms can be enjoyed later in the summer. Without support, the plant forms a sturdy shrub of about five feet tall with deeply bending branches; with support it grows another four feet. The small leaves are covered by a blue sheen and are susceptible to mildew. Avoid confusing Goldstern® (TANtern) with Rosa Goldstar (CANdide) and the rose of the same name Rosa Gold Star (CANdide), a yellow flowering, large-flowered rose from 1983 from Cants of Colchester.

✐/↔ 60–100h 🌺🌺🌺 ☁

Goldstern®

Rosa Goldtopas®

(KORtossgo) Kordes (1963)

The apricot buds are borne singly or in trusses. Full flowers appear with a subtle color. The outer petals are a subdued orange with salmon. The inner petals become more yellow. They have a strong fragrance. Striking for the floribunda rose is the size of the bush. It grows vigorously and branches well but reaches only fifteen inches tall. The foliage is glossy dark green.

✿✿ 15h 🌺🌺🌺 ☁☁☁

Rosa Goldtopaz

(KORtossgo)

see *Rosa* Goldtopas®

Goldtopas®

Rosa **Goldy Meilove**®

(MEImarfey) Meilland (1998)

The pure yellow, full flowers are perched on top of a low bush with medium green leaves. The bush is sold in a pot and planted in a garden can grow up to twenty inches tall. The rose is also suitable for flower boxes and large pots. Ensure that they are watered and fed sufficiently to increase resistance to diseases.

▣ 20h ♣♣♣ ☁

Rosa **Golf**

(IVTagolf) CPRO-DLO (1993)

The extremely full flower trusses bear wonderfully formed, small, single, ivory-white flowers. They bloom throughout the summer and reach one-and-half feet tall, high above the glossy, light green foliage which later turns dark green. This is a ground cover rose. The flowers have a mild, fresh and fruity fragrance, and attract many insects.

◉ 20h ♣♣♣ ☁

Goldy Meilove®

Rosa **Gorgeous George**

(DELricos)

see *Rosa* Château de Versailles®

Rosa **Graaf Lennart**

(MEIsoyris)

see *Rosa* Matilda

Golf

Rosa **Grace**

(AUSkeppy) Austin (2001)

The very full flowers of Grace open cup-shaped from the oval buds, but quickly acquire the form of a rosette, whereby the petals on the edge arch back. They are pale yellow to cream-colored, whilst the heart of this richly full flower is apricot. The flower has a pleasant, sweet fragrance. The shrub branches well.

♣GB 50h ♣♣♣ ☁☁☁

Rosa **Grace Kelly**

see *Rosa* Princesse de Monaco®

Rosa **Graham Stuart Thomas**

(AUSmas)

see *Rosa* Graham Thomas®

Grace

Rosa Graham Thomas®

(AUSmas) Austin (1983)

In its time this rose was a sensation due to its golden color, combined with the form of an old-fashioned rose, which are never yellow. Rosa Graham Thomas was named after one of the leading authorities on old-fashioned roses. It is still one of the best English roses. The medium-sized flowers of over three inches width are very full and cup-shaped. They are subdued yellow with a lighter outer edge. They have a pleasant fragrance: fresh and sweet. The heart is only revealed once the flower falls apart. It cleans moderately well with rain. The young leaves are a yellowish green, later turning to a dull dark gray-green. The foliage stays remarkably healthy. The bush has fierce upright growth, sometimes with long stems, but never becomes very full (despite good branching). The same rose is also sold as a climbing variant under the name Rosa Graham Thomas Climbing.

♀GB/⚘ 50h/80h ♀♀♀ ⌁⌁⌁ ✚

Rosa Grand Canyon™

(POUlriber)
see *Rosa* Riberhus

Graham Thomas®

Rosa Grand Chateau

(TANelorak)
see *Rosa* Barkarole®

Rosa Grand Hotel®

(MACtel) McGredy (1972)

The full, red flowers reach five inches wide. They are borne in tight trusses of up to ten flowers and produce very rich blooms in mid-summer. Moderate though constant blooms follow. The velvety crimson color gets a bluish glow in sunny weather, turning the flower to carmine. With age the practically scentless flowers open to a cup-shape, revealing their yellow pollen. Old flowers clean well. The bush has vigorous vertical growth with relatively short branches. It bears large olive-green foliage that later turns glossy dark green. It is susceptible to mildew and black spot.

⚘ 60–120h ♀♀♀ ⌁ ADR

Grand Hotel®

Rosa Grand Nord®

(DELgord) Delbard (1974)

From the moment they open to when they fall the flowers of Grand Nord® retain their soft cream color. The petals are yellow at the base with a tinge of cherry-red sometimes at the edges. The full flowers eventually open cup-shaped, revealing a large tuft of golden pollen in the heart. They have a light, yet pleasantly fresh and sweet rosy fragrance. Grand Nord® makes a very good cut flower. It has vigorous upright growth in cold and particularly in warm climates, making it very suitable for combining with perennials at the background of borders.

Grand Nord®

The dark, gray-green foliage contrast wonderfully with the flowers.
✳ 50h ♣♣♣ ⌒⌒ TOP

Rosa Grand Siècle®

(DELegran) Delbard (1977)
The full flowers are primarily white, but have a bright pink heart. They have a fresh rosy and fruity fragrance. The attractive wide flowers open up from slender buds. The bush, with its gray-green foliage, grows and branches vigorously, and blooms the whole summer. Grand Siècle is also available as a tree rose
✳ 35h ♣♣♣ ⌒⌒

Grand Siècle®

Rosa Grandhotel

(MACtel)
see *Rosa* Grand Hotel®

Rosa Grand™ Palace®

(POUlgrad) Poulsen (1998)
A miniature rose for pots or flower boxes, as well as for bedding in smaller gardens. The three-inch-wide,

full flowers display a powerful, dark red color above the shiny, dark green leaves.
▣ 20h ♣♣♣ ⌒

Grand™ Palace®

Rosa Granny

(POUloma)
see *Rosa* Meine Oma™

Rosa Gråsten™ Floribunda Poulsen®

(POUlfeld) Poulsen (1996)
The shiny, dark green leaves contrast wonderfully with the semi-double flowers. They are cream with a hint of salmon, reach around four inches wide and have a light rose perfume. This is a bushy, well-branching shrub.
✳✳ 50h ♣♣♣ ⌒⌒

Gråsten™ Floribunda Poulsen®

Rosa Great Century

(DELegran)
see *Rosa* Grand Siècle®

Rosa Green Snake®

(LENwiga) Lens (1987)
The light green stems of Green Snake® make no attempt at upward growth. From a single point they grow outwards and cover the ground reaching out some five feet. The small leaves have a strikingly fresh, light green color. In early summer small, white flowers appear. They smell pleasant and attract many insects with their golden pollen. The blooms are never very rich and do not last long. It is particularly useful for public green areas and for private gardeners who want to cover a slope with fresh greenery. The foliage is highly resistant to rose diseases and is retained for some time.

↔ 10h 🌱 ☁☁ ✪

Green Snake®

Rosa Grimaldi®

(DELstror) Delbard (1997)
This is one of the spotted, blotched and striped roses in a series from the French breeder Delbard named after painters. The semi-double flowers of Grimaldi® have a basic cream color with spots and stripes of pink and cherry-red. They have a rose perfume with a hint of lemon. A fine cut rose.

※※ 35h 🌷🌷🌷 ☁☁

Grimaldi®

Rosa Gripsholm

(POUllug)
see *Rosa* Viborg™ Castle®

Rosa Grouse

(KORimro)
see *Rosa* Immensee®

Rosa Gruss an Bayern®

(KORmun) Kordes (1971)
The red flowers of this average looking rose appear the whole season in trusses. The flowers are semi-double and cup-shaped. The best feature of this floribunda rose is the healthy, glossy, dark green leaves. It branches well and reaches twenty-five to thirty-five inches tall.

※※ 30h 🌷🌷🌷 ☁ ✪

Gruss an Bayern®

Rosa Guiding Spirit

(HARwolave) Harkness (1989)

Guiding Spirit is a rose that grows equally wide as tall. The glossy, dark green leaves are quite graceful. The cup-shaped flowers appear in compact trusses and sometimes give the impression of a single form. They are semi-double, intense pink inside and a lighter pink on the outside. Golden pollen is revealed in the heart. Flowering continues well into fall. The rose is also suitable for pots and flower boxes.

🖼 20h 🌸🌸🌸 ☁

Guiding Spirit

Rosa Guirlande d'Amour®

(-) Lens (1993)

The buds are grouped in long, tapering trusses high above the shrub, which extend upwards from a single point. A typical moschata hybrid (see also Rosa moschata). A profusion of semi-double flowers crowd the trusses. They are pure white, and open into saucer-shaped flowers revealing a tuft of yellow

Guirlande d'Amour®

Guirlande d'Amour®

pollen in the heart, attracting many insects. It has a very light, but pleasant, musk fragrance. The shrub bears much foliage, also at the base. The leaves taper into points. The young foliage is light green, turning a mat medium green with age. The rose, which has won many prizes, can also be used as a rambler. Beautiful against a rose arch.

☀ / 🌿 50h 🌸🌸🌸 ☁☁

Rosa Guy de Maupassant®

(MEIsocrat) Meilland (1996)

A rose with an apple fragrance always makes an impression. And Guy de Maupassant® has a very fresh apple fragrance indeed. The very full, sometimes quartered, flowers are initially pink, later fading to a lovely subdued pink color. By that time the peony-type rose begins to droop under its own weight. Rose breeder Meilland very appropriately included this rose in the Fleur Romantica® series. Guy de Maupassant® is, however, susceptible to black spot.

✸✸ 30h 🌸🌸🌸 ☁☁

Guy de Maupassant®

Rosa Guy Laroche

(DELricos)
see *Rosa* Château de Versailles®

Rosa Gwent

(Poulmulti)
see *Rosa* Snow Cover™ Towne & Country®

Rosa Gwent

(POUlurt)
see *Rosa* Sun Cover™ Towne & Country®

Rosa H.C. Andersen™ Floribunda Poulsen®

(POUlander) Poulsen (1987)
The shrub grows remarkably vigorously and up-right, and on its long stalks bears full trusses of

H.C. Andersen™ Floribunda Poulsen®

H.C. Andersen™ Floribunda Poulsen®

bright red flowers with strikingly ruffled petals. They have a mild rose perfume. With age these semi-double flowers fade in color and fall off in their entirety, keeping the plant wonderfully clean. The foliage is initially reddish, later turning a glossy dark green.
✾✾ 50h ❦❦❦ ☁☁

Rosa Hallelujah

(DELatur)
see *Rosa* Alléluia®

Rosa Hampton™ Palace®

(POUlgret) Poulsen (1996)
A miniature from the Palace series of the Danish breeder Poulsen. The full, cream flowers of three inches width appear the whole summer above the glossy, medium green foliage. Suitable for small gardens, large pots and tubs.
▣ 20h ❦❦❦ ☁☁

Hampton™ Palace®

Rosa Hand in Hand

(HARaztec) Harkness (1984)
The semi-double flowers attract one's attention even from a distance, though they are only around two inches wide. It is the bright orange-pink that grabs the attention.

Hand in Hand

The scentless flowers bloom throughout the summer and fall in trusses on an upright shrub of only twenty-five inches tall. It grows round, reaching around twenty inches wide and bears many glossy, dark green leaves, which remain healthy.

🖼 25h 🌷🌷🌷 ✿ ✚

Rosa Händel

(MACha) McGredy (1965)

Händel is one of the stars of climbing roses, due to its wonderful shape and unique coloring of its flowers. The basic color is cream, with some yellow and rosy-pink edges. The scentless flowers grow in trusses on rather rigid branches that bear olive to medium green foliage. Mildew and black spot can be a problem.

🗲 80h 🌷🌷🌷 ✿

Händel

Rosa Hansa

(-) Schaum&Van Tol (1905)

Do not confuse this rose with Rosa Hansaland® from Kordes, as both descend from the ramanas rose (Rosa rugosa). The full flowers of Hansa are violet rose-red. They have a delicious scent of rose and cloves. The flowers change into large, bright red hips. This is a vigorous uprightly growing rose of up to six-and-a-half feet high and wide. Excellent as hedging.

🌼 80h 🌷🌷 ✿✿✿✿ ✚

Rosa Hansaland®

(KORhassi) Kordes (1993)

As is the case with Rosa Hansa, Rosa Hansaland® is a so-called rugosa hybrid (a descendent of the ramanas rose, Rosa rugosa). However, these semi-double flowers above the glossy, green foliage are crimson, and turn a wonderful orange and yellow in fall. The shrubs grow up to six-and-a-half feet tall and are excellent as hedging.

🌼 70h 🌷🌷 ✿ ✚

Hansaland®

Rosa Harlekin®

(KORlupo) Kordes (1986)

With an average height of six-and-a-half feet tall this climber can be used against walls as well as pillars and rose arches. The glossy, olive-green to dark green leaves look very decorative on the plant. Flowering is mainly in early summer, with sporadic blooms afterwards. The large, separate, full flowers have a unique color: basic cream color with rose-

Harlekin®

red on the edge of each petal, which slowly fades inwards.
Harlekin® has a pleasant rose perfume.
🌱 80h 🌷 ☁☁☁

Rosa Harry Wheatcroft

see *Rosa* Caribia®

Rosa Heart Throb

(HARqueterwife)
see *Rosa* Paul Shirville

Rosa Heartache

(KOReledas)
see *Rosa* NDR1 Radio Niedersachsen®

Rosa Heidefeuer®

(NOAfeuer) Noack (1995)
A ground cover rose from the Flower Carpet® series

Heidefeuer®

from the German breeder Noack. In contrast to Rosa Heidetraum® from the same series, this rose with crimson flowers grows upright. Despite this by the second year seventy per cent of the ground is already covered. This is primarily thanks to the extremely healthy foliage, which stays on the plant well into the fall. Highly recommended.
↔ 30h 🌷🌷🌷 ☁ ✚

Rosa Heidekind®

(KORiver) Kordes (1985)
This shrub rose originated from a crossing of the famous Rosa The Fairy with an unknown seedling. The full flowers are grouped in similarly full trusses on the low shrub, whereas with The Fairy they are pink and with Heidekind they are cherry-red. The profusely branching shrub reaches thirty inches tall and wide and bears dense, glossy, dark green foliage. The leaves are susceptible to mildew and a little to black spot.
🌐 30h 🌷🌷🌷 ☁

Heidekind®

Rosa Heidekönigin®

(KORdapt) Kordes (1985)
The up to six-and-a-half feet long stems bend and grow primarily outwards. Although this rose is known for its ground covering, when planted separately it can reach twenty-five inches tall, but then it does not cover the ground well. If the branches find support they grow vertically. Heidekönigin® is therefore particularly suitable for natural gardens. The semi-double pink flowers have an open heart. They appear in rich trusses on the end of the stems. After profuse first blooms in bursts some further flushes

Rosa Heideschnee®

(KORconta) Kordes (1990)

The usually single, white flowers appear in full trusses. They are saucer-shaped with yellow pollen in the center. Abundant blooms appear particularly in early summer, with mild blooms following the months after. The stems first grow upwards but eventually hang, resulting in a high, ground cover shrub. The glossy, dark green foliage can withstand shade fairly well.

↔ 25h ♀♀♀ ⌒⌒

Heideschnee®

Rosa Heidesommer®

(KORlirus) Kordes (1985)

The cream-colored buds develop into white, fairly full flowers with a natural look.

appear later. Heidekönigin® is lightly fragrant. The leaves stay on the shrub well into the fall and are very resistant to black spot and mildew.

↔ 25h ♀♀ ⌒⌒ ✛

Rosa Heidelinde®

(KORdehei) Kordes (1991)

The flowers have the color of blooming heather: old rose on opening then fading later. They combine splendidly with the shiny, dark green leaves. What's more, the small, semi-double flowers have a mild, sweet fragrance. Bees are attracted to the yellow pollen in the heart. The flowers bloom in rich trusses on the end of the stems that bend under their own weight on the side of the bush, giving a compact dome shape. Heidelinde® is resistant to mildew but black spot can sometimes be a problem.

✲✲ 20–35h ♀♀♀ ⌒⌒

Heidelinde®

They smell light and sweet, and bees are attracted to the pollen of the yellow stamens. They continue visiting the whole summer, despite the main flush being early in summer. The shrub grows upright, but the branches then hang to the side. The foliage is dark green and glossy.

🌀 30h ♀♀♀ ⌁⌁

Heidesommer®

Rosa Heidetraum®

(NOAtraum) Noack (1989)

This ground cover rose from the extremely healthy Flower Carpet® series produces from July very rich blooms of full trusses of semi-double flowers. They are pink and two-and-a-half inches wide, and totally cover the spreading branches. They have hardly any fragrance and clean badly, leaving many brown flowers on the trusses. The strikingly glossy, medium green leaves stay on the bush for some time, which

Heidetraum®

by the second year covers ninety per cent of the ground. The plant is very resistant to rose diseases and so is often planted in public areas.

↔ 30h ♀♀♀ ⌁ ✚ ADR

Rosa Heidi Kabel

(KORdiam)

see *Rosa* Holsteinperle®

Rosa Heimatmelodie®

(-) Tantau (2000)

Seldom do roses have such striking color patterns. The upper side of the petals of this full flower are carmine-red, with the underside practically chalk-white with a yellow tint. These eye-catching, scentless flowers appear the whole season in trusses on the profusely branching bushes, which when planted alongside one another form spectacular beds, both in private gardens and in public areas. The glossy, dark green leaves are resistant to fungal disease and remain attractive into the fall.

�֎�֎ 30h ♀♀♀ ⌁ ✚

Heimatmelodie®

Rosa Helena™ Renaissance®

(POUlna) Poulsen (1998)

The full ivory-white flowers (with a slight pink tinge) are open and spherical and reach over four inches wide.

Helena™ Renaissance®

Henri Matisse®

They have a delicious sweet rose fragrance, but unfortunately clean badly. The shrub has good regular branching and upright growth. Highly suited for bedding and mixed borders. The light olive-green color of the young leaves and the dark olive of the older leaves give the shrub a distinctive look.
ⓦ 45h 🌹🌹🌹 ☁☁☁☁

Rosa Henri Matisse®

(DELtisse) Delbard (1997)
The French breeder Delbard named his series of mottled and speckled roses after painters. Henri Matisse® is the deepest red rose from the series. The cream ba-

De bloem van Henri Matisse®

sis is all but drowned out by large splashes, stripes and blotches of dark carmine. The full flowers have a light rose and raspberry fragrance. They bloom throughout summer on a bush reaching almost four feet tall.
✳ 40h 🌹🌹🌹 ☁

Rosa Herbalist

(AUSsem)
see *Rosa* The Herbalist™

Rosa Heritage®

(AUSblush) Austin (1984)
The very full flowers of Heritage® are practically spherical. They eventually open out to around three inches wide. The medium-sized flowers have a deep cup-shape with a soft pink heart and a lighter edge, which eventually fades to mother-of-pearl white.

Heritage®

Heritage®

The long, almost thorn-free stems are too thin to bear the weight of the flower trusses and end up bending. It is therefore best to give this beautiful rose the support of perennials or other shrubs for an optimum and romantic result. The mild flower color goes well with many other colors, and the fragrance is not only strong, but also wonderfully sweet and fresh. The shrub branches out from the base and bears glossy, dark green leaves, which are susceptible to rust.
🌹GB 45h 🌹🌹🌹 ☁☁☁☁

Rosa Heroica

(-) Lens (1960)
In its day this was one of the best large-flowered roses. The bushes grow vigorously and in part due to this, bloom regularly from early summer to the fall. Despite the somewhat untidy look of the bushes, their large, medium green leaves make them good in

Heroica

bedding. The flower color is aptly described as cherry-red, but then velvety instead of glossy. With age the pink tint intensifies in the semi-double flower. There is very little fragrance.
✿ 30h 🌹🌹🌹 ☁

Rosa Herrenchiemsee

(POUlbella)
see *Rosa* Berleburg™ Castle®

Rosa Herz Ass®

(TANsaras) Tantau (1998)
The bushes of Herz Ass® are relatively small for a large-flowered rose. They continually form new shoots that bear pure red roses on the ends. The flowers are full and beautifully shaped. They retain their color and tolerate bad weather. They develop new flowers throughout summer and fall, which are mildly scented. The large, glossy, dark green leaves stay healthy for long. Highly recommended for bedding.
✿ 30h 🌹🌹🌹 ☁☁

Rosa Herz Dame

(Lens)
see *Rosa* Dame de Coeur

Herz Ass®

Rosa High Hopes

(HARyup) Harkness (1992)

With many climbing roses the flower shape is less perfect than the average large-flowered rose. High Hopes is an exception. The beautiful light to salmon-pink roses open from equally attractive buds. The mildly fragrant flowers bloom the whole summer. The plant reaches around ten feet, making it ideal for rose arches and pillars. Whether 'High Hopes' lives up to its name still remains to be answered as it has poor availability, despite its many awards.

⚘ 120h 🌹🌹🌹 ☁☁

Rosa Hidalgo

(MEltulandi) Meilland (1979)

A classic combination: mat, bronze to dark green leaves crowned with a dark red rose. Initially the

High Hopes

flower has the perfect form of a Hybrid Tea, later opening wide and cup-shaped. Hidalgo is a classic, long-stemmed cut rose, which has an intense rose fragrance. The bush has a vigorous but untidy growth habit. They are particularly suitable for bedding.

✾ 35h 🌹🌹🌹 ☁☁☁

Rosa Holstein 87®

(KORholst) Kordes (1987)

Take note of the number 87 behind the name of the rose, because Kordes introduced a Holstein

Hidalgo

in 1939 as well: a red richly blooming floribunda rose, which still seems to be popular in Switzerland. The new Holstein 87® is a low, continuous-flowering shrub rose with bright red flowers. The heart reveals both the stamens as well as some white stripes. They are resistant to bad weather and clean well as all petals fall off

Holstein 87®

the spent flower. The foliage is olive to dark green and glossy.

☺ 70h 🌹🌹🌹 ☁

Rosa Holsteinperle®

(KORdiam) Kordes (1987)

The full flowers of Holsteinperle reveal their bright coral-red color particularly in the sun. They open slowly from the bud and keep well as a cut rose. They are unfortunately scentless. The leaves are initially wine-red and change quickly to deep 'spruce'-green. The rose grows vigorously and upright.

✻ 35h 🌹🌹🌹 ☁

Rosa Honeycup®

(-) Pouw (1990)

The 'honey yellow' of the very full flowers appear somewhat apricot in color. The flowers are lightly fragrant and are borne by a vigorously growing, upright bush with large foliage, which is initially reddish, turning later to dark green.

✻ 30h 🌹🌹🌹 ☁☁

Rosa Honoré de Balzac®

(MEIparnin) Meilland (1998)

The carmine-like pink petals of this very full rose seem to be bleached apart from the edges. The globular flowers comprise up to one hundred petals and grow to over five inches wide. They have a mild peach perfume. A disadvantage of this rose is that it is susceptible to rain, after which it looks

Holsteinperle®

Honoré de Balzac®

unattractive. The rose is, however, resistant to fungal diseases.

✻ 35h 🌹🌹🌹 ☁☁ ✛

House Beautiful

Honeycup®

Rosa House Beautiful

(HARbingo) Harkness (1995)

A less well-known patio rose with soft yellow flowers. They are full, mildly scented and appear throughout the summer in trusses on the low bush.

▣ 25h 🌷🌷🌷 ☁

Rosa Humanity

(HARcross) Harkness (1995)

The bush is too large to be regarded as a patio rose but it does have the characteristics of one. The rose blooms even in a pot. The trusses with their deep red flowers are raised over thirty inches above the ground. They bloom the whole summer deep into

Humanity

fall, and are lightly fragrant. Also suitable as low hedge.

✸✸ 30h 🌷🌷🌷 ☁☁

Huques Aufray

Rosa Huques Aufray

(DORastri) Dorieux (1996)

The branches first grow upwards. Under the weight of the full trusses they droop to form a vase-shaped shrub approximately five feet tall. Each flower is about three inches wide. They have a cream heart with yellow stamens and pollen, which attract many insects. The flowers are covered by bright pink stripes and blotches on a subdued pink background. They have a light, pleasant rose fragrance. The shrub has a vigorous growth habit with healthy-looking light green leaves, which later turn a gray to medium green.

◍ 60h 🌷🌷🌷 ☁☁

Rosa Ice Cream

(KORzuri)

see *Rosa* Memoire®

Rosa Ice Meidiland®

(MEIvahyn) Meilland (1996)

The semi-double flowers of Ice Meidiland® are white with tinges of pink. They bloom on a healthy bush that grows no more than twenty inches tall but reaches twice the width. Ice Meidiland® is therefore rec-

Ice Meidiland®

ommended as a ground cover rose and looks particularly spectacular against a slope. The dark green foliage has good resistance to the usual rose diseases.

◍ 15h 🌷🌷🌷 ☁ ✛

Rosa Iceberg

(KORbin)

see *Rosa* Schneewittchen®

Rosa Iceberg, Climbing

see *Rosa* Climbing Iceberg

Rosa Iga®'83 München

(MEIbalbika) Meilland (1984)

Although Iga®'83 München is among the strongest roses and is seldom affected by black spot or mildew, it seems to be slowly disappearing from the cata-

Iga®'83 München

logues. This is a shame, because it is the disease-resistant varieties that have a future. What's more, the floribunda rose grows in a shrub-like manner and

Ilse Krohn Superior®

has rich and long-lasting blooms of semi-double florescent pink flowers.

✿✿ 30h ❦❦❦ ↝ ✚ ADR

Rosa Ilse Krohn Superior®

(-) Kordes (1964)

Rosa Ilse Krohn is a white flowering climbing rose from Kordes from 1957. The same breeder brought out a repeat flowering variety in 1964 and added Superior to the name. The flowers are very full and pure white, with star-shaped pointed petals. Whilst Ilse Krohn only blooms in early summer, the superior version also produce some smaller blooms afterwards. The wonderfully fragrant flowers hang from the dark green foliage.

✣ 80–120h ❦❦ ↝↝↝ ✚

Rosa Imagination

(POUldron)

see *Rosa* Schackenborg™ Castle®

Rosa Immensee®

(KORimro) Kordes (1982)

With this plant in the garden the bees do not seem interested in anything else. In a German dialect 'Imme' means 'bee', and bees are indeed crazy for the pollen of the single, mother-of-pearl white to soft pink flowers, which smell mild and fresh. Unfortunately, they only bloom for a few weeks in June. The stems become weak and long, though strong, covering a large area with their light green leaves, thereby complete-

Immensee®

Impératrice Farah®

Imperial™ Palace®

ly obscuring the ground. The shrub is resistant to fungal disease and retains its foliage well into fall. Highly recommended for large, natural gardens and public areas. Very suitable for slopes.

↔ 20h ♀ ⌒⌒ ✚

Rosa Impératrice Farah®

(DELivour) Delbard (1992)

This is more a rose for the collections of experienced rose enthusiasts. The bush has large, light green leaves and grows very much upright. In summer it produces beau-

Impératrice Farah®

Rosa Imperial™ Palace®

(POUlchris) Poulsen (1996)

This miniature rose can be used in bedding as well as large flower pots and boxes. The bright, crimson flowers are full and bloom wide open (about three inches).

▣ 20h ♀♀♀ ⌒⌒

Ingrid Bergman®

Rosa Ingrid Bergman® Hybrid Tea Poulsen®

(POUlman) Poulsen (1986)

The clear, dark red of this large-flowered rose is very eye-catching, particularly as the rose is almost five inches wide. They are full and have a light, sweet, fruity fragrance. Unfortunately, the rose does not

tiful, star-shaped flowers with an ivory-white to creamy yellow basic tint. The ends of the petals are cherry-red, particularly in warm weather. They have a light fruity scent. Impératrice Farah® is also available as a tree rose.

⚹ 50h ♀♀♀ ⌒⌒

clean well. The bush grows upright with much foliage at the base. The foliage is remarkably resistant to rose diseases.

✷ 35h ❦❦❦ ☁☁ ✚

Rosa **Ingrid Weibull**®

(TANweieke) Tantau (1981)

This floribunda rose produces very rich blooms. The semi-double red flowers appear in their dozens on a single truss. They are borne on sturdy stalks that manage to withstand the great weight. The scentless flowers are very resistant to rain. A truss lasts weeks before it is spent. It is then best to cut it off to stimulate further growth and blooms. The

Ingrid Weibull®

bushes are compact and are wider than they are tall. They bear medium green, glossy leaves. Highly recommended for bedding in natural gardens and public areas.

✷✷ 35h ❦❦❦ ☁

Rosa **Integrity**

(HARvintage)

see *Rosa* Savoy Hotel

Rosa **Intrigue**

(KORlech)

see *Rosa* Lavaglut®

Irish Hope

Rosa **Irish Hope**

(HARexclaim) Harkness (1998)

Very full flowers become even more romantic when the petals have a ruffled edge, as is the case with Irish Hope. They have a sweet and lemon fragrance. The petals in the heart of the flowers are apricot. The outermost petals fade to cream with a pink tinge. They bloom in trusses on a robust shrub with dark green leaves.

✷✷ 50h ❦❦❦ ☁☁☁

Rosa **Isabel**™ **Renaissance**®

(POUlisab) Poulsen (1998)

The deep red, full flowers are cupped when open and reach four inches wide. They have a light fragrance for a rose from the Renaissance group, which the

Isabel™ Renaissance®

Danish breeder Poulsen created to produce fragrant crossings between old and modern roses. Isabel™ is a fine cut rose, although it does not last long.

◍ 45h ❦❦❦ ☁☁

162

Rosa Isis

(POUlari)

see *Rosa* Karen Blixen™ Hybrid Tea Poulsen®

Rosa Isobel Champion

(DELgeot)

see *Rosa* La Marseillaise®

Rosa Jacqueline du Pré®

(HARwanna) Harkness (1988)

This is a wonderfully formed shrub with a perfect dome shape. The numerous, dark green leaves stay attractive for quite some time. From early May until well into fall trusses of white flowers appear above the plant, giving the effect of snow on the dome-shaped bush. On closer inspection you can see the pink tinge of the young flowers. They are semi-double and open to reveal white, almost saucer-shaped flowers, up to four inches wide. The heart contains striking orange stamens with yellow pollen, which at-

Jacqueline du Pré®

tracts bees and other insects. The young flowers are particularly fragrant: light, sweet with a hint of musk and a little more lemon. Highly recommended.
⊛ 60h 💐💐💐 ☁☁

Rosa James Galway

(AUScrystal) Austin (2000)

One of the more recent English roses is named after the flutist James Galway. The full flowers have a wonderful fragrance of old roses. In the heart they are a warm soft pink, fading to a light pink towards the edges. The shrub has vigorous growth with practically thorn-free stems that bend under the weight of the leaves and flowers. The rose is particularly suitable for combining

James Galway

with perennials at the back of a border, but can also be used as a climber. In that case the rose is sold under the name Rosa James Galway Climbing.
💐GB/⚘ 55h/100h 💐💐💐 ☁☁☁

Rosa Jardins de Bagatelle®

(MEImafris) Meilland (1986)

A pink glow sometimes shines through the cream color of this long-stemmed, large-flowered rose. The full flowers smell wonderful, making them extra suit-

Jardins de Bagatelle®

able as cut flower. This variety won golden medals at the rose inspections in Genoa and Geneva. The mat, dark green leaves are relatively large. The healthy bush has vigorous upright growth.
✳ 35h 💐💐💐 ☁☁☁

Rosa Jardins de l'Essonne®

(DELchame) Delbard (2000)

This is one of the latest roses of the French breeding family Delbard. The trusses do not bear many flowers, yet the full, cup-shaped flowers form a complete bouquet.

They also have a pleasant spicy fragrance. The upright bush with its sturdy stems bears light gray-

Jardins de l'Essonne®

green (later deep gray-green) foliage, which contrasts wonderfully with the cream flowers with a yellow heart.

�֎✿ 35h 🌹🌹🌹 ☁☁

Rosa Jasper

(POUlbella)

see *Rosa* Berleburg™ Castle®

Rosa Jazz

(POUlnorm)

see *Rosa* That's Jazz™ Courtyard®

Joey's™ Palace®

Rosa Joey's™ Palace®

(POUljoey) Poulsen (1998)

A miniature rose with full flowers three inches wide. They have a fashionable color, apricot with salmon-pink, and have a light wild rose perfume. Suitable for small gardens as well as for large pots and flower boxes.

▣ 20h 🌹🌹🌹 ☁☁

Rosa Johann Strauss®

(MEloffic) Meilland (1994)

On opening the flowers have the softest pink color imaginable, which fades with age. The heart glows yellow. The flowers appear in trusses of a few per stalk. They are lightly fragrant and due to their light color can combine very well with other plants. The

Johann Strauss®

relatively low bush bears abundant mat, dark green foliage.

✿ 25h 🌹🌹🌹 ☁☁

Rosa Johannisfeuer®

(TANreufis) Tantau (1988)

The vigorous upright shrub bears large, healthy, glossy, dark green foliage. Trusses with bright red flowers are produced throughout summer. The semi-

Johannisfeuer®

double flowers are saucer-shaped and display a modest tuft of stamens. They are unfortunately scentless.
◍ 40–60h 🌹🌹🌹 ☁ ✪

Rosa John Clare

(AUScent) Austin (1994)
For an English rose John Clare remains remarkably low and produces strikingly rich and long blooms. The shrub has spreading growth. New trusses of

John Clare

loose, full, bright red flowers appear throughout summer and autumn. They are rather untidy with a shallow cup-shape. They have a light fragrance, but clean well.
🌹GB 35h 🌹🌹🌹 ☁

Rosa John Leese

(POUlrise)
see *Rosa* Kong Frederik den IX™ Hybrid Tea Poulsen®

Rosa John Waterer®

(-) McGredy (1970)
Pointed buds open to reveal wonderfully formed, carmine-red flowers with a mild rose fragrance. The flower stalks are just about unable to support the

John Waterer®

weight of the large, full flowers and so bend a little. Apart from that, the bush has vigorous upright growth. The stems and young leaves have a reddish hue, but later turn dark gray-green.
✿ 30h 🌹🌹🌹 ☁☁☁

Rosa Josie Whitney

(HARfacey) Harkness (2000)
Josie Whitney is neither a well-known rose enthu-

Josie Whitney

siast nor the wife of one. Together with her husband Bill Whitney she won a television quiz in which couples had to show how well they knew one another. The star prize was to have a rose named after the wife. And this particular rose looks almost as bizarre as the way in which it got its name. The flower is a collection of color splashes: dark yellow, orange with carmine-pink to salmon-pink on the edges. They bloom in trusses of the densely covered bush.

✿✿ 40h ♀♀♀ ◌

Rosa José Carreras™ Hybrid Tea Poulsen®

(POUlnew) Poulsen (1998)
The full, cream flowers reach six inches wide when open fully. They are lightly fragrant and the cream

José Carreras™ Hybrid Tea Poulsen®

color goes well with that of the foliage: mahogany when young, glossy, dark green with age. Particularly suited to climates with dry summers.

✿ 40h ♀♀♀ ◌◌

Rosa Joyfulness

(TANsinnroh)
see *Rosa* Frohsinn® '82

Jude the Obscure

Rosa Jude the Obscure

(AUSjo) Austin (1995)
In a rainy summer we would not see the full glory of the flowers of Jude the Obscure. They would suffer from balling and the still closed buds would turn brown and drop off. But in a dry climate the flowers develop beautifully: large, very full and cup-shaped with petals curling inwards. The inner petals are yellow, and the outer ones a very pale yellow. It has a strong, fruity fragrance. The shrub has a bushy habit and is often wider than it is tall.

♀GB 45h ♀♀♀ ◌◌◌◌

Julia™ Renaissance®

Rosa Julia™ Renaissance®

(POUlheart) Poulsen (1997)

The round buds open to reveal very full flowers with a creamy pink color. They have a light but pleasant fragrance and are suitable as cut rose, even though they do not last long. The shrub grows vigorously, under very favorable conditions growing to five feet tall.

🌐 45h 🌹🌹🌹 ☁☁

Rosa Just Joey

(-) Cants of Colchester (1972)

This is one of the most popular roses amongst enthusiasts at the moment. The full flowers bloom in trusses. They are very wide (five-and-a-half inches), and have a 'contemporary' color – amber to soft orange – and have an intense, sweet fragrance. The bush has a loose growth habit and branches well

Just Joey

Just Joey

but rather irregularly. The blooms are also quite irregular resulting in occasional pauses. The large

leaves have a reddish hue and change to a wonderful gray-green.

✳ 30h 🌹🌹🌹–🌹🌹 ☁☁☁☁ ✚

Rosa Kaj Munk™ Paramount®

(POUldunk) Poulsen (1999)

One of the lower growing, large-flowered roses that Poulsen included in the Paramount series. The full, golden flowers reach around three inches wide. They have a pleasant fragrance and are also suitable as cut rose.

✳ 30h 🌹🌹🌹 ☁☁☁

Rosa Kalmar™ Castle®

(POUlkalm) Poulsen (1999)

The full, scentless flowers bloom above the glossy, dark green foliage of this relatively low floribunda rose. The flower color is very light: apricot with very soft salmon-pink.

✿✿ 25h ❀❀❀ ⌒

Rosa Karen Blixen™ Hybrid Tea Poulsen®

(POUlari) Poulsen (1996)

Beautifully formed, white flowers of five inches wide on long stalks. Because of their limited longevity they are not so suitable as cut rose. However, that is the only minus point. They have a light but pleasant fragrance and are very resistant to dis-

Karen Blixen™ Hybrid Tea Poulsen®

ease. In fact, this is one of the few large-flowered roses that has such a low susceptibility to black spot and mildew.

✽ 30h ❀❀❀ ⌒⌒ ✚

Rosa Kassel

(-) Kordes (1957)

Although Kassel is no longer in the catalogue of breeder Kordes, this old, but strong climbing rose can still be found in many places. The pointed buds are deep red. They open to reveal wonderfully formed, full flowers. They are first bright red. When fully open they are cup-shaped. They reach four

Kassel

Kassel

inches wide and fade to old rose. They sometimes reveal their pollen and have a mild rose fragrance. The young stems are initially rhubarb red; later green. They are quite sturdy and planted separately can grow to become a large shrub, or tied to form a climber. The large leaves are light green, later medium green. Kassel is somewhat susceptible to black spot.

✎ 80–120h ❀❀ ⌒⌒

Katharina Zeimet

Kathryn McGredy

Rosa **Katharina Zeimet**

(-) Lambert (1901)

A profusely branching bush with young foliage that is reddish later turning mat, dark green.

This rose is susceptible to black spot. Katharina Zeimet has trusses with semi-double cream flowers approximately one-and-a-half inches wide, which appear throughout the summer.

They have a light rose perfume. The variety belongs to the polyantha roses, remains low and has thin stems.

▣ 20h ♀♀♀ ∽∽

Rosa **Katherine Mansfield**

see *Rosa* Charles de Gaulle

Rosa **Kathryn McGredy**

(MACauclad) McGredy (1996)

This is a rose that prefers dry climates as the flowers clean badly after rain and often form a fungus affected mass. Apart from this, Kathryn McGredy is a superb rose: very full, pink flowers that change to salmon-pink with age. They keep their attractive form for long and have a light fruity fragrance. The upright bush, which has moderate growth, has plenty of foliage at the base, thereby quickly covering a bed. The young leaves are initially red, later turning glossy, dark gray-green, and are healthy.

✳ 40h ♀♀♀ ∽∽ ✛

Kathryn McGredy

Kathryn Morley

Rosa **Kathryn Morley**

(AUSclub) Austin (1990)

The inward curling petals of the large flowers appear serrated. They are soft pink. A light, spicy scent comes from the mysterious heart. The much lighter surrounding petals form an irregular high cup on the long stalks of the upright shrub.

❀GB 40h ❀❀❀ ☁☁

Rosa **Keep in Touch**

(HARdrama) Harkness (1999)

This recent floribunda rose grows equally wide as tall and bears many glossy, medium green leaves. The bright red flowers open cup-shaped. The heart, which occasionally has white stripes, reveals a large

Keep in Touch

tuft with golden pollen. The older flowers retain the strong red color.

✿✿ 30h ❀❀❀ ☁

Rosa **Kent**

(POUlcov)

see *Rosa* White Cover™ Towne & Country®

Rosa **Key West**

(POUlerry)

see *Rosa* Cherry Cover™ Towne & Country®

Rosa **Kiftsgate**

(Murell)

see *Rosa filipes* Kiftsgate

Kir Royal®

Rosa **Kir Royal**®

(MEInibur) Meilland (1995)

The semi-double flowers of Kir Royal® have the color of almond blossom, but then with cherry-red venation. They have little fragrance, but are very fresh. They remind one of spring amid the medium green leaves. The climber reaches ten feet tall and grows vigorously even if affected by disease.

↗ 80–120h ❀❀❀ ☁☁

Rosa **Kirsten Poulsen**

(-) Poulsen (1924)

This is an old-fashioned rose that, thanks to its vigorous growth, is still available, though increasing-

Kirsten Poulsen

ly less so. Kirsten Poulsen bears single, carmine-red flowers which fully open out in good weather, when insects are attracted to the pollen. As is typical for a polyantha rose the buds appear in trusses. Once spent the flowers develop into hips. These do little for the look of the plant, so are best removed: only then will the bush continue to bloom.
✳✳ 40h 🌷🌷🌷 ☁

Kong Frederik den IX™

Knirps®

Kong Frederik den IX™

Rosa Knirps®

(KORverlandus) Kordes (1997)

This rose could also easily be classified with the patio and miniature roses. However, Kordes wanted to emphasize the ground cover characteristic of this compact bush. The shrub does not produce long shoots, but does grow primarily widthways. The dark green, shiny leaves are sometimes obscured by the rich blooms: trusses with small but very full, pink flowers.
↔ 10h 🌷🌷🌷 ☁

Rosa Kong Frederik den IX™ Hybrid Tea Poulsen®

(POUlrise) Poulsen (1998)

The almost five-inch flowers of this large-flowered rose appear in trusses, sometimes more than ten per truss. They are full and display a whole pallet of colors: from light yellow via apricot to salmon-pink. The fragrance is mild and fruity. Unfortunately, they clean badly with rain and the bush grows rather irregularly.
✳ 40h 🌷🌷🌷 ☁☁

Rosa Königin der Rosen®

(KORbico) Kordes (1964)

Above the bronze-tinted foliage bloom very full flowers that appear orange but on closer inspection have subtle hues: salmon-pink and on the back an orange-yellow tint. The flowers are borne singly on long, very thorny stalks. They are highly suited as cut roses, as they last long and have a light but pleasant fragrance. The bush has branching and upright growth, and is reasonably resistant to disease.
✳ 30h 🌷🌷🌷 ☁☁ ✚ ADR

171

Königin der Rosen®

Rosa Königin Margrethe

(POUlskov)
see *Rosa* Dronning Margrethe™ Palace®

Rosa Konrad Adenauer Rose®

(TANedauk) Tantau (1954)
This rose from days gone by is still available, probably due to its wonderful fragrance; after all there are many other roses with beautifully formed full, dark red flowers. Those of Konrad Adenauer Rose® reach four inches wide. The light green, glossy leaves of the upright bush provide a sharp contrast to the red of the flowers. The rose is particularly suitable for those that like such contrasts.

✻ 30h 🌹🌹🌹 ☁☁☁☁

Konrad Adenauer Rose®

Rosa Kookaburra

(KORlomet)
see *Rosa* Vogelpark Walsrode®

Rosa Kordes' Brillant®

(KORbisch) Kordes (1983)
The shape and the fresh green foliage of Kordes' Brillant® are reminiscent of Rosa Schneewittchen®, but here the flowers are not white but bright orange to a striking red. Several flowers together are borne in trusses at the ends of the branches. The flowers are cup-shaped and loosely full. They have a light fragrance of wild roses. The shrub has a bushy, upright growth habit and reaches five feet tall.
☻ 40–60h 🌹🌹🌹 ☁☁

Kordes' Brillant®

Rosa Kordes' Brilliant

(KORbisch)
see *Rosa* Kordes' Brillant®

Rosa Kordes' Rose Bella Rosa

See *Rosa* Bella Rosa. For all other names that begin with Kordes' Rose, you can find them in this encyclopedia using the name that follows Kordes' Rose.

Rosa Korwondis

(KORwonder)
see *Rosa* Bella Rosa®

Rosa Kronborg™ Castle®

(POUltry) Poulsen (1996)

A wonderful rose for beds in small gardens, or even in large flower boxes or pots. The three-inch-wide flowers are very full and crimson. They have no fragrance.
✲✲ 25h ♀♀♀ ☁

Rosa Kupferkönigin®

(KORanderer) Kordes (1996)

The caramel-colored buds open to reveal the perfectly formed, full flowers of Kupferkönigin®. They

Kupferkönigin®

have the color of brass (yellow-copper) and are paler at the edges. The weather has little effect on their color and form: they hardly fade in the sun and stay in shape after rain. Each rose blooms on its own stalk. Although the fragrance is very light it makes a good a cut rose that lasts long. The bush grows upright and bears glossy, dark green leaves.
✲ 30h ♀♀♀ ☁☁

Rosa L.D. Braithwaite

(AUScrim) Austin (1988)

This English rose is an impressive looking plant. The sturdy branches grow diagonally. At the ends are trusses bearing very full, bright crimson flowers that are four inches wide. The velvety, deep red buds open to reveal rosette-shaped flowers that have the sweet and fresh fragrance of old roses. The young shoots bear numerous, bright red thorns, which later turn brown. The large, dull, dark gray-green foliage is unfortunately susceptible to black spot. The rose, which grows equally wide as tall, is named after the father-in-law of David Austin Sr.
♀GB 40h ♀♀♀ ☁☁☁☁

L.D. Braithwaite

L.D. Braithwaite

Rosa L'Aimant

(HARzola) Harkness (1994)

The pointed buds unfold to reveal the full flowers with their wavy edges. They are fresh and clear pink in color with sometimes apricot in the heart. They bloom in trusses on a vigorous bush. L'Aimant makes a very good cut flower. As bonus it has a delicious fragrance.

✿✿ 35h 🌺🌺🌺 ☁☁☁☁

L'Aimant

Rosa La Grande Parade

(HAVal) Verschuren (1986)

This upright floribunda rose with a shrub rose habit will completely cover a bed or border with its medium green leaves. Towering above the foliage are the trusses of single flowers. The flowers are two inches wide, cherry-red with a large greenish white eye. Insects can easily visit the flowers, but would not be attracted by any fragrance as they hardly have any. The shrub looks impressive, shows vigorous growth and also has good resistance to rose diseases.

✿✿ 45h 🌺🌺🌺 ☁ ✚ TOP

La Grande Parade

Rosa La Marseillaise®

(DELgeot) Delbard (1976)

The sturdy stems of this large-flowered rose each bear one or just a few oval buds.

La Marseillaise®

They develop into perfectly formed full, crimson flowers. They have a light fragrance, but nonetheless make a good cut rose. They are sensitive to bad weather. The bush grows vigorously and branches well. La Marseillaise® has glossy, medium green leaves.

✳ 35h 🌹🌹🌹 ⌣⌣

Rosa La Paloma® 85

(TANamola 85) Tantau (1985)

The pointed buds open to reveal the very full, cream flowers. They have little fragrance but are quite resistant to bad weather. They appear the whole summer and fall in trusses above the striking grass-green foliage. The plant has good resistance to disease and so is often used in public areas. It is also suitable for filling beds, particularly because the upright, low bush branches well and retains its foliage into fall.

✳✳ 25h 🌹🌹🌹 ⌣ ✛

La Paloma® 85

Rosa La Reine Victoria

(Schwarz)
see *Rosa* Reine Victoria

Rosa La Sevillana®

(MEIgekanu) Meilland (1978)

The first blooms of La Sevillana® are very impressive, after which many other blooms follow deep into fall. The bouquets of partially full, vermilion flowers extend above the bronze-tinted foliage. The plant has a fairly untidy growth habit. La Sevillana® is used in beds, but if it is not pruned in spring it develops into a shrub of around four feet tall and wide. Also very suitable for hedging. The flowers have a light apple fragrance. Hips are formed in fall. In part due to its excellent resistance to black spot and mildew La Sevillana® has received the ADR award.

✳✳ 30h 🌹🌹🌹 ⌣ ✛ ADR

La Sevillana®

Rosa La Tour d'Argent

(DELricos)
see *Rosa* Château de Versailles®

Rosa La Ville de Bruxelles

(-) Vibert (1849)

The very full and quartered, pink roses have an intense and delightful fragrance. The three-inch-wide, flat flowers hang gracefully to the side of the five-feet-tall shrub, which can grow equally wide.

La Ville de Bruxelles

The very thorny branches bear large, mat medium green leaves. This is rightly one of the most popular Damask roses. It blooms in the first half of summer. The flowers cannot withstand rain. Place the shrub therefore in a ventilated and sunny spot.

◉ 60h ❦ ☁☁☁☁ ✛

Rosa Lac Blanc

(KORweirim)
see *Rosa* Weisse Immensee®

Rosa Lac Rose

(KORimro)
see *Rosa* Immensee®

Rosa Lady Di®

(-) Huber (1982)
The globular, pink flowers are borne singly, or in small trusses. They are full and excellent for display in a vase. They are therefore primarily grown as cut rose. It has a light and pleasant fragrance. A disad-

Lady Di®

vantage of Lady Di® is that it is sensitive to bad weather. With lengthy periods of rain the buds will not even open. The bush grows moderately, upright and regularly, but remains quite small. This rose has large olive-green foliage, which later turns dark green.

✳ 30h ❦❦❦ ☁☁

Rosa Lady Diana

(Huber)
see *Rosa* Lady Di®

Rosa Lady Like®

(TANekily) Tantau (1989)
This is one of the strongest large-flowered roses, with an excellent resistance to the fungal diseases that normally affect the leaves of other Hybrid Teas. After a rich start the large, full flowers appear during the rest of the summer in small numbers. They have a strong pink color with a silvery hue. Lady Like® is very suitable as cut rose, although not everyone may enjoy the intensely sharp fragrance. The bush grows upright and branches well. The foliage is glossy and dark green.

✳ 30h ❦❦❦ ☁☁☁ ✛

Lady Like®

Lady Meillandina®

Rosa **Lady Meillandina**®

(MEllarco) Meilland (1986)

Lady Meillandina® is a typical miniature rose with full, soft pink flowers above the dark green foliage. Recommended for in pots or flower boxes. Keeping it from drying out and giving enough feed will help it continue growing and blooming.

▣ 15h ❦❦❦ ☁

Rosa **Lady of the Dawn**®

(INTerlada) Interplant (1985)

A very richly blooming floribunda rose. The semi-double flowers of around three inches wide are soft pink with a yellow tinge. They are saucer-shaped with a golden tuft of stamens in the heart. It gives off hardly any perfume. The bush blooms throughout summer and fall. It has vigorous, though irregular, growth. The sturdy leaves change from a reddish to olive green.

✲✲ 35h ❦❦❦ ☁

Rosa **Lady Sunblaze**

(MEllarco)

see *Rosa* Lady Meillandina

Rosa **Lancashire**

(KORstesgli)

see *Rosa* Gärtnerfreude®

Rosa **Lancôme**®

(DELboip) Delbard (1977)

The long, sturdy stems make Lancôme® an ideal cut rose, despite its lack of fragrance. The full carmine-pink flowers stay good for long.

Lady of the Dawn®

Lancôme®

You can pick bouquets the whole summer, because though the rose doesn't produce large blooms they are continuous. The bush has good branching growth and bears glossy, dark green leaves.

✳ 35h 🌷🌷🌷 ☁

Rosa Land Brandenburg

(POUloma)
see *Rosa* Meine Oma™

Rosa Landora®

(SUNblest) Tantau (1970)
The fact that this rose sells well is not so much to do with the flowers. These, incidentally, are beautifully formed and hold their pure yellow color well. However, they do not stand out against the background of the bush. Its great popularity is largely thanks to the flowers' ability to withstand bad weather and the

Landora®

leaves' excellent resistance to fungal disease, though black spot may occur occasionally. The dark green, glossy leaves are borne on an upright bush with good branching growth.

✳ 30h 🌷🌷🌷 ☁☁ ✚

Rosa Landrover

(-) Van den Berg (1995)
Stronger even than the normal ramanas rose this rugosa hybrid spreads through suckers. This shrub therefore has a more or less ground cover habit. Rich blooms of carmine-tinted pink flowers appear in early summer. Moderate blooms are produced during the rest of summer, along with decorative orange-red hips. The healthy leaves are well shaped and turn a wonderful fall color.

☺ 10–25h 🌷🌷🌷 ☁☁ ✚

Landrover

Rosa Lapponia®

(TANnipola) Tantau (1978)
The full, salmon-pink flowers are saucer-shaped. They appear the whole summer and fall in trusses on the low bush. The fragrance is mild but pleasant. The flowers last long, also with bad weather. The light green, glossy foliage remains quite healthy into fall. Lapponia® has a bushy habit.

✳✳ 20h 🌷🌷🌷 ☁☁

Rosa Latina

(POUlcov)
see *Rosa* White Cover™ Towne & Country

Rosa Lavaglow

(KORlech)

see *Rosa* Lavaglut®

Rosa Lavaglut®

(KORlech) Kordes (1979)

The very full flowers have an eye-catching deep red color, that even approaches black. This against a background of dark green, glossy leaves, which when young are tinted bronze and olive-green! The flowers, like flattened balls, bloom the entire summer and early fall. They develop in full trusses from wide buds. The plant has bushy growth and grows equally wide as tall.

�֎֎ 25h ♈♈♈ ☁☁

Lavaglut®

Rosa Lavender Cover™ Towne & Country®

(POUlrust) Poulsen (1997)

Trusses with pink to mauve-colored flowers bloom on a low shrub with shiny, dark green leaves, which are light green when young. The semi-double flowers reach only a little more than an inch wide, but appear in large numbers. They have light fragrance of wild roses.

֎ 25h ♈♈♈ ☁☁

Lavender Cover™ Towne & Country®

Rosa Lavender Dream®

(INTerlav) Interplant (1984)

The semi-double flowers bloom like lilac pink clouds on top of the stalks. In the garden around the pond of the Arcen Castle Gardens in the Netherlands they are combined with blue flowers and white begonias. The bust of an important rose breeder looks on: Francis Meilland. Lavender Dream® has rich blooms that continue into fall. There is no fragrance.

֎ 30h ♈♈♈ ☁ ✚ ADR

Lavender Dream®

Rosa Lavender Friendship®

(HAVeuship) Verschuren

In the growing season this ground cover shrub continuously produces new shoots up to three-and-half feet tall. They bear very full trusses with buds that develop into single, purple-pink flowers. In the heart some white can be seen behind the yellow pollen. The flowers fade with age turning to what you could call, with a little imagination, lavender blue. They are a little sensitive to bad weather. The flowers are scentless, but are still frequently visited by insects.

↔ 30h 🌹🌹🌹 ☁

Lavender Friendship®

Rosa Lavender Pinocchio

(-) Boerner (1948)

Few roses have such a striking color as Lavender Pinocchio. The old rose color changes with age, to the brown of a used coffee filter! This may not sound

Lavender Pinocchio

Lavender Pinocchio

flattering but the color is superb. The flowers open from red-brown buds grouped in trusses on long, bending stems. The flowers bloom throughout summer and fall. The spreading shrubs reach one-and-a-half meters tall. They bear light green foliage.

✹✹ 20h 🌹🌹🌹 ☁☁

Rosa Lavnia

(TANklewi)
see *Rosa* Lawinia®

Rosa Lawinia®

(TANklewi) Tantau (1980)

The full, pink flowers of Lawinia® are cup-shaped and become so heavy that they hang. But this is an advantage for a climbing rose as you can better see the flowers. Despite their large size the flowers can

Lavender Pinocchio

withstand bad weather well and have a pleasant fruity fragrance. After an initial rich bloom, some repeat flowering occurs throughout summer and early fall. Depending on good care and support, the climber can reach ten feet tall. If planted against a tree the sturdy branches can grow even higher. They bear medium green, glossy leaves.

⚘ 80–120h 🌺🌺 ❀❀❀

Rosa Lazy Days

(POUlkalm)
see *Rosa* Kalmar™ Castle®

Rosa Le Rouge et Le Noir®

(DELcart) Delbard (1973)
The scarlet, velvety flowers of Le Rouge et Le Noir® seem to be powdered with black soot, particularly along the veins of the outer petals. They are full and have a magnificent cup-shape. They have a pleasant rose fragrance with a hint of vanilla. The vigorous bush bears glossy, dark green leaves. Le Rouge et Le Noir® is also available as a tree rose.

✳ 30h 🌺🌺🌺 ❀❀❀

well-formed flowers, which have a pleasant fruity fragrance. The very full flowers are apricot-colored with soft pink tints. Although the flowers are relatively small, they are heavy enough to bend under their own weight on their stalks. They clean badly, with the petals not turning brown but ochre-yellow. After the initial blooms in early summer scanty blooms appear in fall, but only on the new shoots. These grow primarily upwards, forming a small shrub that is suitable for the back of a border. Leander® has large, dull, medium green leaves. The same rose is sold as a climbing rose under the name Rosa Leander climbing®. With its vigorous upright growth it easily reaches over ten feet.

🌺GB/⚘ 70h–140h 🌺🌺 ❀❀❀

Leander®

Leander®

Le Rouge et Le Noir®

Rosa Leander®

(AUSlea) Austin (1982)
Leander® is older than numerous other English roses. David Austin used this rose particularly because of its

Rosa LeAnn Rimes

(HARzippee)
see *Rosa* Perception

Rosa Leeds Castle

(TANrupeza)
see *Rosa* Purple Haze®

Rosa Leersum 700®

(INTerleer) Interplant (1979)
Those looking for a floribunda rose that is not very susceptible to black spot and mildew, look no further than Leersum 700®. The bush blooms with four-inch-wide, single flowers. They are initially cup-shaped, later turning saucer-shaped. First apricot-colored with salmon-pink, fading considerably with age. They have no detectable fragrance. Nonetheless

Leersum 700®

Leersum 700®

insects frequently visit the golden pollen. The bush grows upright and has fairly branching growth with large, mat, dark green leaves. Leersum 700® is also highly suitable for public areas.
✿✿ 35h ❦❦❦ ⌣ ✚ TOP

Rosa Leonard Dudley Braithwaite

(AUScrim)
see *Rosa* L.D. Braithwaite

Rosa Leonardo da Vinci®

(MEIdeauri) Meilland (1994)
The ball-shaped buds of Leonardo da Vinci® (officially: Leonardo de Vinci) open to reveal the extremely full flowers that can have up to eighty petals. Once open they hang to the side under their own weight, resembling the flowers of a peony rose. Also their deep pink color is reminiscent of this. The

Leonardo da Vinci®

color is soft enough for the flower to be combined with other flowering plants in a romantic border. The plant is fairly healthy and has vigorous growth, but unfortunately little fragrance.
✿✿ 30h ❦❦❦ ⌣⌣ TOP

Rosa Les Amoureux de Peynet®

(MEItobla) Meilland (1992)
Due to the fairly long and rather thin stems the trusses of semi-double, pink flowers hang gracefully to the side. A group of bushes will quickly resemble a shrub

rose, with their low growth and rich blooms in trusses. The bushes are also richly covered with mat, dark bronze-tinted leaves, which can be affected by black spot.

✿✿ 25h 🌳🌳🌳 ☁

Rosa Letizia

(KORzuri)
see *Rosa* Memoire®

Les Amoureux de Peynet®

Rosa Leverkusen®

(-) Kordes (1954)
The continuous-flowering climbing rose spreads out its blooms over many months, whereby pauses in flowering occur. The light yellow flowers are often in small groups on the ends of the stems. They are semi-double, eventually revealing their heart and have a light, sweet fragrance. The bush has healthy though not vigorous growth, and reaches on average

Leverkusen®

just over six feet tall. Very suitable, therefore, for a rose arch, pillar or fence. It can tolerate partial shade.

✗ 70–95h 🌳🌳 ☁☁

Rosa Lexington

(POUlgode)
Rosa Golden Cover™ Towne & Country®

Rosa Lichtkönigin Lucia®

(KORlilub) Kordes (1966)
This shrub with strikingly healthy, dark green leaves has vigorous upright growth, so can be used as a solitary plant as well as a hedge plant and climber. Although the variety was introduced way back in 1966 it still seems to be one of the healthiest of roses. The full flowers are initially buttercup yellow, fading with age to sulfur-yellow. They are lightly fragrant. It blooms throughout summer and early fall, with many flowers particularly after warm weather. They can be romantically arranged in a vase.

☀ / ✗ 80h 🌳🌳🌳 ☁☁ ✚ ADR

Rosa Liesbeth Canneman

(INTernetuv) Interplant (1997)
The golden, semi-double flowers are cup-shaped. They are over three inches wide and have a light,

Lichtkönigin Lucia®

fresh rose fragrance. The upright bushes reach three-and-a-half feet tall. They have very regular growth and are densely clothed by dark green foliage.

✿✿ 45h 🌳🌳🌳 ☁☁

Liesbeth Canneman

Rosa Lilac Charm

(-) Le Grice (1961)

This is a very charming rose. The single flowers have an unusual soft mauve color, with orange-red stamens and yellow pollen, zealously collected by bees. The flowers reach three inches wide and bloom in trusses on a low bush; they are therefore relatively large. They have a distinctive rose fragrance: light but pleasantly sweet and fresh. The bush has an attractive regular form and branches well. The young leaves are mahogany, later turning deep green, which goes wonderfully with the color of the flower.

✿✿ 25h 🌹🌹🌹 ☁☁

Rosa Lilac Mystery

(-) unknown (1994)

The semi-double flowers are first pink when they bloom, but fade with age turning to lilac-blue. They bloom throughout the summer in trusses on long,

Lilac Charm

drooping stems with shiny, medium green leaves. The shrub covers the ground partially.

↔ 15h 🌹🌹🌹 ☁

Rosa Lili Marlene

(KOlima)

see *Rosa* Lilli Marleen®

Lilac Mystery

Rosa Lilian Baylis

(HARdeluxe) Harkness (1996)

From a distance they look like blooming dahlias. But when close by you will see that the full flowers have a pleasant rose fragrance. The older petals begin to curl backwards and together form a pompon. The flower heart is a soft yellow; the outer edge cream. The flowers appear throughout the summer and fall in trusses. Each blooming branch forms a complete bouquet. Lilian Baylis keeps long as a cut rose.

✿✿ 70h 🌹🌹🌹 ☁☁

Lilian Baylis

Rosa Liliana

(POUlsyng)
see *Rosa* Clair™ Renaissance®

Rosa Lill Lindfors

(POUlrohill)
zie *Rosa* Egeskov™ Castle®

Rosa Lilli Marleen®

(KOlima) Kordes (1959)
Lilli Marleen® has scarlet flowers that appear from velvety, deep red buds. The three-inch flowers are semi-double and cup-shaped. Only when close by can you smell the light, fresh rose fragrance. The flowers appear throughout the summer in trusses on the over one-and-a-half feet tall bushes. The leaves are reddish, later turning a mat medium green. It can withstand fungal disease very well, which is probably why it used often in public green areas. Also suitable for low hedging. A popular rose that has won several awards.
✸✸ 20–30h 🌷🌷🌷 ☁☁ ✚

Rosa Lilli Marlene

(KOlima)
see*Rosa* Lilli Marleen®

Rosa Linderhof®

(KORelasting) Kordes (1999)
The densely branched, upright shrubs are ideal for

Lilli Marleen®

planting in a row to form a bushy hedge. The higher stems bend somewhat showing their natural flowers at eye level. They are single and pink; white towards the heart with yellow stamens. Bees are frequent visitors even though the flowers scarcely have any fragrance. The blooms last the whole summer. The glossy leaves are olive to dark green
🌐 60–70h 🌷🌷🌷 ☁

Rosa Litakor

(KORlita)
see *Rosa* Lolita®

Rosa Little White Pet

see *Rosa* White Pet

Linderhof®

Rosa Livin' Easy™

(HARwelcome)
see *Rosa* Fellowship

Rosa Lolita®

(KORlita) Kordes (1972)
The orange-red buds open to reveal the large, full flowers. From a distance they appear orange-yellow, but from close by they have a subtle combination of colors: copper, apricot and salmon-pink. They have a heavy rose fragrance and are suitable as cut rose. The young leaves are reddish, later becoming fern-green. They are borne on an upright bush of approximately thirty inches high and twenty inches wide.
✱ 30h 🌷🌷🌷 ☁☁☁ ADR

Lolita®

Rosa Lord Byron

(MEltosier)
see *Rosa* Polka®91

Rosa Louis de Funes®

(MEIrestif) Meilland (1987)
The full flowers of Louis de Funes® display warm tints: copper, orange and orange-yellow. They are borne on short stalks on the upright bushes, which can reach three-and-a-half feet. Louis de Funes® grows vigorously, but the glossy, dark green leaves are susceptible to black spot.
✿ 40h ♀♀♀ ✑✑

Rosa Louis' Double Rush®

(LENna) Lens (2000)
With this floribunda rose the breeder Louis Lens tried to improve his own - very popular - Rosa Rush®. The flower color is much the same, but with Double Rush® the flowers are full. They develop from red buds. Surprisingly, a pink rose appears of

Louis de Funes®

approximately two-and-a-half inches wide with much white, particularly in the heart. The young leaves have a brown hue, later turning a glossy dark green. A good rose for bedding and even for low hedging.
✾✾ 50h ♀♀♀ ✑

Rosa Louis' Rambler®

(-) Lens (1997)
When this rambler has sufficient space it can grow to almost thirty-five feet. In June yellow buds with a pink tint appear in very full trusses. The buds have glands which points to a moss rose ancestry. The fact

Louis' Double Rush®

that the multiflorous rose (Rosa multiflora) is in the family can be seen in the overwhelmingly full blooms. Late June and early July the climber is overladen with relatively large, white flowers, which have a pleasant fragrance.
⚘ 80–400h ♀ ✑✑✑

Rosa Louisa Stone

(HARbadge) Harkness (1997)
The name 'English rose' is actually only used for the creations of David Austin, but suits Louisa Stone well. Here we also see the bushy shrub form

Louis' Rambler®

and delicate, full flowers that have the character and fragrance of old roses. Louisa Stone has an apricot to salmon-pink heart with ivory-white towards the outside. It has a light, but pleasant fragrance. The shrub reaches thirty inches tall and branches out in a fan-like manner to twenty-five inches wide.

⚘ 30h 🌹🌹🌹 ☁☁

Rosa **Louise Gardner**

(MACerupt) McGredy (1987)

Although the full flowers appear in multiflorous

Louisa Stone

trusts, this rose is regarded as a large-flowered rose. With a width of over three inches the cup-shaped flowers are indeed large when they are fully open.

Louise Gardner

The color is subtle: first yellow with orange blotches on the side of the petals, later increasingly coral-red and eventually salmon-pink. It is very slightly fragrant and the blooms are not very rich. The upright bush bears large, mat, gray-green leaves.

✻ 30h 🌹🌹🌹 ☁

Rosa **Louise Odier**

(-) Margottin (1851)

In good summers this old Bourbon rose will bloom continuously throughout summer. The very full and often quartered pink flowers tilt gracefully to the side. They appear in trusses on the man-sized shrub that produces spreading, drooping branches. The large leaves are mat, medium green. The flowers have an intense fragrance. On opening they smell of acid drops. The older flowers have a wonderful rose fragrance.

❀ 70h 🌹🌹🌹-🌹🌹 ☁☁☁☁

Rosa **Love Letter**®

(-) Lens (1980)

A wonderful floribunda to combine with perennials. Ideal in a 'silver' or 'golden' border with white or yellow flowers. The scarcely fragrant flowers are

Louise Odier

semi-double. They appear on an irregularly growing bush throughout the summer and fall.

✻✻ 25h 🌹🌹🌹 ☁

Rosa **Lovely Fairy**

(SPEvu) Vurens-Spek (1990)

It is only in the color of its deep pink flowers that this sport differs from its famous parent Rosa The Fairy, which blooms light pink. Lovely Fairy, too, is highly

Love Letter®

suitable as a weeping tree rose, due to its drooping branches. As a low shrub the thin branches of this polyanthas bend under the weight of the full trusses of semi-double flowers. The flowers are cup-shaped, only one-and-a-half inches wide and have no fragrance. The shiny, dark green leaves contrast well with the flowers and remain healthy.
🖼 15h 🌷🌷🌷 ⬤ TOP

Rosa Lübecker Rotspon®

(TANtide) Tantau (1988)
The splendidly rich blooms in full trusses, the beautifully formed flowers with their burgundy color and

Lovely Fairy

Lovely Fairy

the attractive, dark green foliage have given this rose its excellent reputation. In 1989 it won 'Rose of the Year' in Great Britain. The bush stays relatively low, and has branched, bushy growth. The glossy, dark green leaves go well with the flower trusses and stay attractive well into fall. Highly suitable for bedding, but can also be used as hedging and even in large pots.
�֎ 60h 🌷🌷🌷 ⌣

Rosa Luberon

(UHLater)
see *Rosa rugosa* Pierette®

Lübecker Rotspon®

Rosa Lucetta®

(AUSemi) Austin (1983)
The semi-double flowers of Lucetta® are initially salmon-pink, but as they open further they become increasingly paler, eventually turning practically white. They are saucer-shaped with golden pollen in the open heart. They have a strong fragrance and

Lucetta®

rich and long-lasting blooms on a shrub that has a loose form. The branches have a spreading habit and bear large, mat gray-green leaves.
🌹GB 50h 🌹🌹🌹 ✿✿✿

Rosa Macabo™

see *Rosa* Astrid Lindgren™ Floribunda Poulsen®

Rosa Machana

(-) McGredy (1983)

Although this rose is regarded as a miniature, the flowers are far from small. They reach three inches wide, which is quite something for a bush of around fifteen inches tall. Its small size and large flowers make it very suitable as a tree rose. The semi-double

Machana as tree rose

Machana

flowers are pure yellow and cup-shaped when fully open, and display golden pollen.
🔲 15h 🌹🌹🌹 ✿

Rosa Madame Antoine Meilland

(Meilland)

see *Rosa* Peace®

Rosa Madame Figaro®

(DELrona) Delbard (2000)

To celebrate the twentieth anniversary of the French magazine for young women 'Madame Figaro' fair flowers with a pink hue were looked for. The French breeder Delbard had precisely such a rose, with rich and lengthy blooms and a very fresh lemon and aniseed fragrance; and voila, Madame Figaro®.
✳✳ 40h 🌹🌹🌹 ✿✿✿

Rosa Madison

(POUlrijk)

see *Rosa* Bayernland Cover™ Towne & Country®

Madame Figaro®

Rosa Magic Carpet

(JAClover) Jackson & Perkins (1977)

In summer this ground cover rose is overladen with semi-double flowers. They are pink with a lavender hue, and have a white heart containing yellow pollen. They have a pleasant, spicy fragrance and are visited by many insects. The healthy, glossy, dark green leaves appear to be quite resistant to rose diseases and stay on the branches until early winter. The shrub grows to twenty inches tall and at least twice as wide.

Magic Carpet

Magic Meidiland®

Magic Carpet

Due to its durable health, prize winner Magic Carpet is frequently used in public areas.
↔ 20h 🌸🌸🌸 ◌◌◌ ✚

Rosa Magic de Feu

(KORfeu)
see *Rosa* Feuerzauber®

Rosa Magic Meidiland®

(MEIbonrib) Meilland (1994)
This is one of the strongest roses: very resistant to black spot and mildew, vigorous growth and rich blooms. The shrub reaches around thirty inches tall and grows so vigorously widthways that the entire ground is covered by its small, glossy, dark green leaves. The leaves stay attractive up to late fall. This highly recommended rose is also often sold as a tree rose. The single, pink flowers have a charming white heart. They are scarcely fragrant.
🌐 30h 🌸🌸🌸 ◌ ✚ ADR

Rosa Magic Meillandecor

(MEIbonrib)
see *Rosa* Magic Meidiland

Rosa Magneet

(Tantau)
see *Rosa* Feuerwerk®

Rosa Maidy®

(KORwalbe) Kordes (1984)
The rich blooms of Maidy® continue throughout the summer. For a miniature rose the flowers, which appear in trusses, are relatively large. They are scarlet, but the underside of the petals is strikingly silver. This silver color has a rose red hue, apart from the edges, which are also pure red. The bush branches profusely and bears many moss-green leaves.
▣ 35h 🌸🌸🌸 ◌

Maidy®

Rosa Maigold

(-) Kordes (1953)

Maigold produces rich blooms as early as May. The four-inch-wide flowers appear in large numbers on the tall shrub or low climbing rose. They have a wonderful fragrance, are loosely semi-double and have a bronze-yellow color. However, the blooms are of short duration, particularly in very warm weather. After three weeks the blooms of Maigold are fully spent, although it tries to produce some flowers in fall. The shrub grows upright, with the older branches eventually bending to the side. Maigold can also be used as a climber.

� /âŒ˜ 60–100h ❀ ✿✿✿

Rosa Mainaufeuer®

(KORtemma) Kordes (1990)

The stems of Mainaufeuer® first grow vertically, but quickly bend under the weight of the numerous flowers and then completely cover the ground with

Maigold

glossy, medium green leaves. The whole summer and fall the rose blooms with multiflorous trusses of semi-double, scarlet flowers. The heart displays a lighter blotch with yellow stamens. Although Mainaufeuer® is known for its disease resistance, the bush is often attacked by black spot, however, this does not affect its growth.

↔ 20h ❀❀❀ ✿

Rosa Mainzer Fastnacht®

(TANnacht) Tantau (1964)

The light lavender-blue with a hint of pink of this large-flowered rose is very popular among rose

Mainaufeuer®

enthusiasts. This rose enjoys international fame as one of the best blue roses. This is due not only to the color and the perfect form of the full flowers, but also the delicious fragrance and the long-lasting blooms well into fall. The blooms, however, are never very rich. The fully open flowers are cup-shaped. The colors develop the best at sunny locations.

✳ 30h ❀❀❀ ✿✿✿

Rosa Make Up®

(MElxetal) Meilland (1988)

The official name of this rose is Rosa Denise Grey, but these days it's sold more often under the name

Mainzer Fastnacht®

Make Up®. It is perhaps because of this change of name that the rose is not so well known, which is a shame, as it deserves greater recognition. The shrub grows vigorously outwards. It is well covered with mat, light then later dark, green leaves. The foliage contrasts well with the soft pink, semi-double flowers, which appear throughout the summer in attractively branched plumes. They have hardly any

Make Up®

fragrance. Although the leaves look healthy for a long time they are sensitive to black spot. They are hardly affected by mildew.

◎/✿✿ 35h 🌺🌺🌺 ☁ TOP

Rosa Malcolm Sargent

(HARwharry) Harkness (1988)
Few large-flowered roses can be used for hedging, as they only bloom on top of the bushes. Malcolm Sargent is an exception to this. The full, scarlet flowers also bloom lower down, on the side of the bush. The bush has regular growth, both high and wide. When planted side by side the bushes, with their dark green foliage, make quite a good hedge. When planted in groups (twenty-five inches from one another) they can fill a bed well. As a solitary Malcolm Sargent is a wonderful, round bush with flowers on all sides. The flowers have a light and spicy fragrance.

Malcolm Sargent

They form green hips, which do not look particularly attractive so are best removed.

✿ 50h 🌺🌺🌺 ☁☁

Rosa Malverns

(KORdehei)
see *Rosa* Heidelinde®

Rosa Mamy Blue®

(DELblue) Delbard (1991)
The large, mauve-colored flowers of Mamy Blue® can, with a little imagination, be called blue. Especially on a cloudy day they appear so. They are very full and have an attractive form. The fragrance is pleasantly fresh and sweet and quite strong. The bushy plant bears medium green leaves.

✿ 35h 🌺🌺🌺 ☁☁☁

Rosa Manhattan

(POUlharmu)
see *Rosa* Charming Cover™ Towne & Country®

Mamy Blue®

Rosa Manita®

(KORberuhig) Kordes (1996)
Due to its rich blooms of large, semi-double pink flowers, when mature this climbing rose will fully cover a fence or wall with a pink curtain. The flowers have a light, pleasant fragrance. They have a white heart with yellow stamens. The glossy, dark green leaves remain healthy. They are borne on a robust climber, which is seldom taller than ten feet.

⚘ 200–300h 🌺🌺🌺 ☁☁ ✪ ADR

Rosa **Manou Meilland**®

(MEltulimon) Meilland (1979)

The bright reddish pink flowers make a wonderful sight above the dark green foliage. The flower color is described as mauve, or cyclamen pink - a difficult color to describe with silver highlights. This unusual color contributes to this rose's popularity. The flowers are large and have the form of a Hybrid Tea, but are grouped in trusses. It has a rose fragrance and a healthy upright growth habit. Manou Meilland® is very suitable for bedding. The leaves are a little susceptible to black spot.

✻/✻✻ 30h ♀♀♀ ⌒⌒

Rosa **Many Happy Returns**

(HARwanted) Harkness (1991)

At the height of the blooms the bush is practically

Manou Meilland®

covered by the rich trusses of light pink flowers. The flowers are full and have a light, fruity fragrance. The bush flowers throughout the summer, later producing red hips. The bush has a branching habit, is bushy and grows almost as wide as it is tall. It has glossy, medium green leaves.

✻✻ 30h ♀♀♀ ⌒⌒

Many Happy Returns

Rosa **Marcel Pagnol**

(MEIsoyris)

see *Rosa* Matilda

Märchenkönigin®

Rosa Märchenkönigin®

(KORoyness) Kordes (1986)

Strikingly pointed buds open to reveal slender flowers that even so can reach five inches wide. They are usually borne singly on the long stems. It therefore makes a good cut rose with a pleasant but light fragrance. The color is the softest pink imaginable. Wonderful in combination with the mat, dark green foliage.

❋ 30h 🌹🌹🌹 ☁☁

Rosa Märchenland

(-) Tantau (1946)

Märchenland, which was bred in 1946, sometimes has trusses bearing up to forty flowers. The attractive, semi-double flowers are large and open, revealing the yellow stamens. The inside of the petals are light pink and the underside a salmon-pink, giving the flower an overall pale impression. Märchenland has a light and pleasant fragrance and blooms continuously. This floribunda has the growth habit of a shrub rose. The vigorous branches can reach five feet high. They bear fairly healthy, glossy, dark green leaves.

❋❋ 60h 🌹🌹🌹 ☁☁

Märchenland

Rosa Marco Polo®

(MEIpaleo) Meilland (1994)

Take care that you do not confuse this rose with the pink, large-flowered rose called Rosa Marco Polo. That pink Marco Polo was registered back in 1971. So always look at the official cultivar name that is often - but not always - stated next to the trade name. The Marc Polo® here is a yellow blooming, full,

Marco Polo®

large-flowered rose. It has a wonderful lemon aroma, for which it has already received an award.

❋ 30h 🌹🌹🌹 ☁☁☁

Rosa Margaret Merril®

(HARkuly) Harkness (1978)

This floribunda has won numerous prizes, in particular due to the wonderful fragrance of the full flowers. The newly opened flowers are tapered, but later open to a cup-shape. They are pearl-white, but later have a salmon-pink hue, particularly in the heart of the as yet not fully opened flowers. The upright bush has good branching growth and bears fresh, green leaves.

❋❋ 35h 🌹🌹🌹 ☁☁☁☁

Margaret Merril®

Rosa Margaret Roberts

(AUSpale)

see *Rosa* Redouté

Rosa Margaret Thatcher

(KORflüg)
see *Rosa* Flamingo®

Rosa Maria

(-) Gregory (1965)
During blooming the single flowers change from orange-red to scarlet, often with a lighter heart. They bloom in large trusses above the large leaves, which due to the extremely dark green color contrast sharply with the color of the flowers.
✿✿ ☀ 25h 🌷🌷🌷 ◌

Maria

Rosa Maria Hofker®

(INTerhof) Interplant (1992)
Orange-red-tinged buds open to form full, medium-sized flowers with a soft yellow color. The flowers are cup-shaped and have hardly any fragrance. The flowers are borne singly or in small trusses. The bush never produces rich blooms and there are pauses

Maria Hofker®

between the flushes. The shiny, dark green leaves go very well with the soft color of the flowers.
✿ 30h 🌷🌷 ◌

Rosa x *mariae-graebneriae* 'Hannover'

(-) botanical rose (-)
Rosa x *mariae-graebneriae* is a crossing that originated in a garden, with the probable parents *Rosa virginiana* and *Rosa palustris*. The bush reaches five feet tall. Although some people regard 'Hannover' as typical for the crossing, this cultivar is clearly smaller. The branches are less rigid, have greater spreading growth and as a result cover the ground more or less completely. The flowers are single and have a light pink color with a blue hue. They never appear in large numbers, but bloom constantly throughout summer. They have a good fragrance and attract many insects. The leaves turn a splendid orange-red color in fall.
✿ 30h 🌷🌷🌷 ◌◌◌ ⊕

Rosa x *mariae-graebneriae* 'Hannover'

Rosa Maria Mathilda®

(LENmar) Lens (1980)
There is a pink haze in the white, semi-double flowers of this floribunda. Ruffled petals surround the heart of golden pollen. The rose became immensely popular and won numerous prizes, partly because of the good growth of the bushes and the attractive contrast between the flower color and the extremely dark green, mat leaves. The flowers, however, cannot withstand long periods of bad weather.
✿✿ ☀ 30h 🌷🌷🌷 ◌ TOP

Maria Mathilda®

Rosa Mariandel®

(KORpeahn) Kordes (1985)

Mariandel® has won many medals and citations despite the fact that there are many other red floribundas. The flowers of Mariandel®, however, bloom on a compact, bushy plant with glossy, dark green leaves. The young leaves are a wonderful burgundy. The blooms of full flowers continue throughout

Mariandel®

Mariandel®

summer and fall. The flowers are a dark, velvety red and do not discolor; they remain attractive even after rainy periods. They are scarcely fragrant.
✿✿ 25h ❦❦❦ ☁

Rosa Marie Curie®

(MEllomit) Meilland (1996)

The trusses of cherry-red buds open to reveal beautiful, cup-shaped flowers with a strikingly wide heart of golden pollen. They are full, peach-colored with tinges of yellow and salmon, and have a delicious, sweet fragrance. Unfortunately, they clean badly after rain. The bushy shrub goes well among perennials, for example in an orange-yellow border, but is also suitable in combination with soft blue delphiniums or other cut flowers in a vase. The leaves are glossy dark green and susceptible to black spot.
✿✿ 30h ❦❦❦ ☁☁☁

Marie Curie®

Rosa Marie Pavic

(Allégatière)
see *Rosa* Marie Pavié

Rosa Marie Pavié

(-) Allégatière (1888)

The knee-high bushes bear grass-green leaves that unfold to reveal a reddish tinge. An impressive sight when contrasted against the very full, creamy white to soft pink flowers. The intensity of the pink can vary

Marie Pavié

according to the weather, but the heart of the flowers is always strongly colored. They have a pleasant fragrance. This fragrance as well as the fact that it blooms throughout the summer is the reason why this very old polyantha rose is still extremely popular.
✻✻ 25h ♀♀♀ ⌒⌒⌒

Rosa Marie-Louise Marjan®

(KORfinger) Kordes (1999)
The buds and young flowers are soft apricot with a pink hue. They fade with age, eventually becoming pure white. The large flowers are borne singly on the end of the long stems. They have a spicy, sweet fragrance. Marie-Louise Marjan® is a good cut rose. The upright shrub reaches over forty inches tall. The burgundy young leaves are glossy and change to medium green.
✻ 50h ♀♀♀ ⌒⌒

Marie-Louise Marjan®

Rosa Marinette

(AUScam) Austin (1995)
The buds of Marinette have a striking, small cylinder shape. They open out to light, clear pink flowers with a butter-colored heart. As the flowers continue to open they fade even more. Creamy tints finally predominate the semi-double, saucer-shaped flowers. The over three-inch-wide flowers appear to float between the medium green foliage on top of their thin stems. The shrub has a very loose growth habit and becomes equally wide as tall.
♀GB 50h ♀♀♀ ⌒⌒

Marinette

Rosa Marjorie Marshall

(HARdenier) Harkness (1996)
Only the fragrance disappoints with this shrub rose. For the rest it is a very appealing rose. The large, full,

Marjorie Marshall

flat open flowers are apricot-colored in the heart with very light pink outer edges. This healthy-looking shrub is also characterized by good repeat blooms and dark green foliage. The shrub grows almost as wide as it is tall and produces attractive flowers for both the garden and the vase.

🌀 50h 🌷🌷🌷 ☁

Rosa Marondo®

(KORtitut) Kordes (1991)

The height of Marondo® is very much up to you. The branches creep out in all directions, but if they find support can grow upwards. Against a fence, wall or trellis they can reach almost seven feet. Luxuriant blooms of semi-double pink flowers are produced in early summer. They are lighter in the heart and display the yellow stamens. The fresh, shiny green foliage remains fairly healthy, even though black spot and mildew will occasionally affect the plant.

↔ 25–80h 🌷 ☁ ✚ ADR

Marondo®

Rosa Marselisborg™ Castle®

(POUlreb) Poulsen (1996)

The full, golden flowers of this floribunda bloom on a low bush. This variety is sometimes regarded as

Marselisborg™ Castle®

a low shrub rose. The four-inch-wide flowers have a light fragrance of wild roses.

✺✺ 25h 🌷🌷🌷 ☁☁

Rosa Mary Magdalene

(AUSjolly) Austin (1998)

The tapered buds open to reveal beautiful, rosette-shaped flowers, with petals that are shorter in the heart than outside. They have a very refined, light apricot color with a hint of the softest pink. And the fragrance is just as old-fashioned: Mary Magdalene

Mary Magdalene

smells of tea roses. The shrub has a spreading habit with large, mat, medium green leaves.

❀GB 35h ❀❀❀ ᗡᗡᗡ

Rosa **Mary Rose**®

(AUSmary) Austin (1983)

Although not everyone is won over by the flower shape of Mary Rose, the qualities of this shrub are undisputed. It has excellent branching and forms many mat, medium green leaves that remain healthy. The long flower stems branch out at the top and each bear a truss of light pink flowers. According to breeder David Austin they are only slightly fragrant, but I find them rather strong, wonderfully fresh and sweet. The flowers have a loose form and look a little messy. The advantage: once spent the flowers clean very well. The almost four-inch-wide flowers appear throughout the summer and fall in large numbers. The stems are strong enough to remain upright.

❀GB 45h ❀❀❀ ᗡᗡᗡ ✚

Mary Rose®

Rosa **Mary Webb**®

(AUSwebb) Austin (1984)

The wide buds of Mary Webb® swell up and turn yellow with red streaks. Nothing to lead you to think that the flowers will turn out practically white with a hint of lemon yellow. The flowers are full, cup-shaped, concealing their pollen, and have a fresh and sweet fruity fragrance. The very full flowers reach almost four inches wide and bloom in trusses of around nine per truss. Despite their

Mary Webb®

large weight they hardly hang. Unfortunately, they cannot withstand bad weather and clean badly. They therefore appear better suited to drier climates than the oceanic climates of North-West Europe. The bush branches well and bears medium to dark green leaves.

❀GB 90h ❀❀❀ ᗡᗡᗡ

Rosa **Matilda**™

(MEIsoyris) Meilland (1994)

Rose breeder Meilland has brought out two roses with practically the same name: Matilda™ and Matilda®. The latter has creamy white flowers, which

Matilda™

turn pink toward the edges. Matilda™ in the photo is a large-flowered rose of the grandiflora type. The large flowers have a wonderful fruity fragrance and are very suitable as cut rose. The glossy, green foliage is dark red when young. In France the bush is sold under the name Marcel Pagnol®, in the Netherlands as Graaf Lennart®.

☀ 35h 🌹🌹🌹 ☁☁☁

Rosa Max Closup

(-) McGredy (1995)

Each stem of Max Closup bears only a few wide buds, but these develop into four-inch, full flowers that have a light rose perfume. They are first apricot-colored, then later salmon-pink; in time they become an increasingly lighter pink, but they never lose their color. The bush grows upright and bears large leaves, which are initially reddish, becoming dark green with age. The leaves are borne by remarkably thick stems that reinforce the robust character of this rose.

☀ 35h 🌹🌹🌹 ☁☁

Max Closup

Rosa Maxim®

(TANmixa) Tantau (1993)

This large-flowered rose has not really 'broken through' yet. It is available in only a few places, which is surprising considering its unusual color composition, which resembles ice cream with cherry sauce: a creamy white basis with areas and streaks of cherry-red. As the flower ages the creamy white gets the upper hand. Maxim® is lightly fragrant. The

Maxim®

bush grows vigorously, with long stalks, making it ideal for bouquets.

☀ 30h 🌹🌹🌹 ☁☁

Rosa May Gold

(Kordes)

see *Rosa* Maigold

Mayor of Casterbridge

Rosa Mayor of Casterbridge

(AUSbrid) Austin (1996)

The petals of Mayor of Casterbridge lie folded in the heart of the flower. Some pollen can often be seen, though the flower is very full. A ring of petals surround these inner ones, together forming a shallow cup. The heart of the flower is soft pink, the outside even lighter. It has a light and fruity fragrance. The upright shrub has large, medium green leaves.

🌷GB 40h 🌷🌷🌷 ⌇⌇

Rosa Mazurka

(MEItune) Meilland (1995)
Once spent the flowers clean wonderfully. The petals fall off without having faded and form a light rose pink blanket under the bush. The flowers have a light and fruity fragrance. A beautiful rose for bedding. The bush reaches thirty to forty inches tall and bears medium green leaves. Its resistance to rose disease is rather variable. It is not always resistant to mildew

Mazurka

and black spot. Though the rose is found less frequently in catalogues these days it can often be ordered with some persistence.

✸✸ 35h 🌷🌷🌷 ⌇⌇ ADR

Rosa McCartney Rose

(MEIzeli)
see *Rosa* The McCartney Rose

Rosa Medima

(POUlvue)
see *Rosa* Victor Borge™ Hybrid Tea Poulsen®

Rosa Medusa®

(NOAsa) Noack (1996)
The numerous, full, pink flowers of Medusa® bloom

Medusa®

cup-shaped and eventually display their heart with yellow pollen. They appear in trusses that can contain up to thirty flowers. They bloom throughout summer and early fall. This shrub with its shiny, dark green leaves reaches around thirty-five feet tall and hides the ground from view. It has excellent resistance to rose diseases.

↔ 35h 🌷🌷🌷 ⌇ ✚ ADR

Rosa Meilland's Rose Amstelveen

(MEIpopul)
see *Rosa* Amstelveen®

Rosa Meine Oma™ Floribunda Poulsen®

(POUloma) Poulsen (1996)
Thin stems reach upwards, later bending under the weight of the trusses of very full (sometimes quartered) soft pink flowers. They have no fragrance, which may be a little surprising. Despite this they would do well in a romantic border or bed.

Meine Oma™ Floribunda Poulsen®

The bush with its loose growing habit not only bears tilted flowers of two-and-a-half inches wide, but also beautiful shiny olive-green leaves (later medium green).
☼☼ 25–60h ✿✿✿ ☁

Rosa Melrose

(-) RvS-Melle (1990)
The initially pointed flowers soon open fully to a cup-shaped. The color is a bright fluorescent pink, but this fades substantially so that the old flowers are a pale pink, giving the flowering bush a bi-colored look. The just about full flowers have a light fruity fragrance. They reach around three inches wide and clean moderately well in rainy weather. The

Melrose

bush grows upright, but also has strong sideways growth through excellent branching at the base. The relatively thin stems are strong enough to bear the flower trusses. The few thorns are small and red. The young leaves are yellow-green, later dull gray-green.
☼☼ 35h ✿✿✿ ☁☁ TOP

Memoire®

Rosa Memoire®

(KORzuri) Kordes (1992)
From a distance the flowers appear pure white, but on closer inspection reveal a creamy white nuance with a pink hue in warm weather. During the entire flowering period they retain their perfect Hybrid Tea form and have the typical fragrance of these large-flowered roses. The bushy, branched plant bears large, glossy, strikingly dark green leaves.
☼ 35h ✿✿✿ ☁☁☁

Rosa Memory Lane

(POUlbella)
see *Rosa* Berleburg™ Castle®

Metro

Metro

Rosa Metro

(MACbucpal) McGredy (1987)

The bush is clothed well in glossy, dark green leaves. Above the foliage are large, full flowers that have a pleasant fragrance. They are cream-colored with a pink hue that intensifies towards the heart. They bloom throughout the summer and early fall and - for a New Zealand rose - can withstand wetter climates well.

30h

Rosa Michael Crawford

(POUlvue)

see *Rosa* Victor Borge™ Hybrid Tea Poulsen®

Rosa Michel Hidalgo

(MEltulandi)

see *Rosa* Hidalgo

Rosa Michelangelo®

(MEltelov) Meilland (1997)

The full, yellow roses have a globular form, though they develop from thin buds. With age the outer petals fade to a creamy white. They have a wonderful perfume, and justly won the Fragrance Prize in 2001 during the Rose Show in the Dutch city of The Hague. The leaves are a glossy, dark green. Do not confuse this rose with Rosa Michelangelo (MACtemaik) from McGredy.

25h

Michelangelo®

Michka®

Rosa Michka®

(MElvaleir) Meilland (1998)

This is a large-flowered golden rose with some peach tinges and dark venation. As climber it can reach seven feet, so is suitable for fences and plant pillars. Without support it can reach five feet tall.

80h

Midget Gem®

Midget Gem®

Rosa Midget Gem®

(-) Dickson (1994)

Apricot-colored buds open to reveal full trusses of single, yellow flowers of almost two inches width. On opening the transparent light yellow fades even further: first only on the edges, later everywhere. The flowers are pleasantly fragrant. The shrub grows slowly outwards, with an almost ground cover habit. The shrub bears tapered, shiny, dark green leaves that have a bronze tinge.

25h

Rosa Mignon

(Pernet-Ducher)

see *Rosa* Cécile Brünner

Rosa Milky Way®

(INTerway) Interplant (1991)

The pink-tinged buds are borne in small trusses. They develop into milky white flowers that can reach five inches wide and have a wonderful, fruity rose perfume. Periods of rich blooms are interspersed with periods when the shrub produces new buds. The young leaves are a light olive-green, turning a glossy dark green with age. The shrub bears dense foliage at the base. The thick, heavily thorned stems grow upright. Its sideward branching growth is less attractive.

Milky Way®

30h

Rosa Milrose®

(DELbir) Delbard (1965)

Milrose® is an attractive bedding rose. Throughout the summer semi-double flowers appear in luscious trusses above the glossy, light green foliage that is bronze-tinged and seems quite resistant to rose diseases. The practically fragrantless flowers fade with age to white with a pink hue. They are cup-shaped and display their yellow pollen in the heart. A recommended rose that is still very much worthwhile.

Milrose®

30h

Rosa Mirabel

(COCdana)

see *Rosa* Fulton Mackay

Rosa Mirato®

(TANotax) Tantau (1998)

This is certainly one of the best roses for public areas and natural gardens: rich and long-lasting, continuous blooms, very resistant to rose diseases and with a wide growth habit, making it suitable for low bedding and as ground cover rose. However, with long periods of bad weather the brown flowers stay on the bush, even though it is often claimed to clean well. The full, bright pink flowers with an

Mirato®

orange tint finally open saucer-shaped, revealing the lighter heart and pollen. Mirato® is slightly fragrant. The bush reaches twenty-five inches tall and so wide that you only need four bushes to effectively cover ten square feet of ground. The foliage remains on the bush well into fall.

↔ 25h 🌺🌺🌺 ⌒ ✛ ADR

Rosa **Mirato Dream**®

(TANrostax)
see *Rosa* Pearl Mirato®

Rosa **Miss Pam Ayres**

(KORmarie)
see *Rosa* Bonanza®

Rosa **Miss Schweiz**

(TANziewsim) Tantau (1995)
There are so many scarlet, large-flowered roses, why did breeder Tantau add yet another in 1995? Because of the enormously rich blooms, says the North German breeder. The blooms are not only abundant but also long lasting. New flowers appear throughout summer and fall. They are full and beautifully formed and are borne on strong, straight stems. The leaves have a red tinge and change to a glossy dark green.

⚘ 30h 🌺🌺🌺 ⌒

Miss Schweiz

Rosa **Mister Lincoln**

(-) Swim&Weeks (1964)
The attractive, deep red flowers later turn a carmine-red color. They are full, pleasantly fragrant and as

Mister Lincoln

they are borne on long stems, they are suitable as cut rose. In the garden the bush appears to be rather poorly clothed in dark green foliage.

⚘ 30h 🌺🌺🌺 ⌒⌒⌒

Rosa **Mistress Quickly**

(AUSky) Austin (1995)
The flowers of Mistress Quickly bear a strong resemblance to those of old roses, but then in miniature. The full lilac pink flowers may be small, but appear in large numbers on the bush, creating a mass of color. They are very slightly fragrant. The shrub has upright growth so is best at the back of a border. It also makes a good low climber. The leaves seem to be quite resistant to fungal diseases.

🌺GB 120h 🌺🌺🌺 ⌒ ✛

Mistress Quickly

Rosa Mlle Cécile Brünner

(Pernet-Ducher)
see *Rosa* Cécile Brünner

Rosa Mme A. Meilland

(Meilland)
see *Rosa* Peace®

Rosa Mme Cécile Brünner

(Pernet-Ducher)
see *Rosa* Cécile Brünner

Rosa Mme de Stella

(Margottin)
see *Rosa* Louise Odier

Rosa Mme Giscard d'Estaing

(-) Dorieux (1993)
For a single-flowered rose the white flowers are remarkably large. They reach around five inches wide and bloom in trusses on the upright stems. The color is a creamy white, and contrast sharply with the leathery, mat, dark green leaves, that are tinged with red. Insects visit the yellow pollen in the flower, which has a light, sweet rose perfume.
✻ 30h ❀❀❀ ☁☁

Mme Giscard d'Estaing

Rosa Molineux

(AUSmol) Austin (1994)
Molineux is particularly suitable for bedding. Plant the small, upright bushes close to one another for an

Molineux

optimal result. The very full, deep yellow flowers appear throughout the summer in trusses. Their tea rose fragrance with a hint of musk has won them many fragrance prizes. Molineux is also a healthy rose, as fungal diseases rarely take hold of the dark green leaves.
❀GB 35h ❀❀❀ ☁☁☁☁

Rosa Mon Jardin et Ma Maison

see *Rosa* Flora Romantica

Rosa Mondiale®

(KORozon) Kordes (1993)
The fragrantless flowers of Mondiale® are popular as cut rose. This is in part due to their longevity, but also their beautiful form and typical rose color. Mondiale® has intensely pink flowers, particularly in the heart and the edges of the petals. Tints of salmon and creamy white can also be seen. The bush grows to around four feet and is suitable for gardens as well. It bears glossy, dark green leaves.
✻ 45h ❀❀❀ ☁

Mondiale®

Rosa Monica®

(TANakinom) Tantau (1986)

Strikingly slender buds open to reveal wonderfully formed, full flowers with an extraordinary color. The color appears orange, but on closer inspection subtle nuances can be seen: golden with dashes of red-orange, often beautifully venated. The flowers are usually borne on long, straight stems. Monica® is therefore very suitable as cut rose, although they are mildly fragrant. The bush has vigorous upright growth with large, glossy, dark green leaves.

✱ 35h ♀♀♀ ◌◌

Rosa Monika

(TANakinom)

see *Rosa* Monica®

Monica®

Rosa Montana®

(Royal Occasion) Tantau (1974)

The bright red flowers of Montana® contrast strikingly with the light green leaves. The full, slightly fragrant flowers are cup-shaped when open, eventually revealing their heart with yellow pollen. They appear in rich trusses, which are spread out over the season. They can withstand rain very well. The bushes have upright growth, branch profusely and are strong enough for public areas. They are also suitable for adding color to private gardens. The

Montana®

leaves are hardly affected by diseases and remain on the bush for some time.

✱✱ 30h ♀♀♀ ◌ ✚ ADR

Rosa Moon River™

(KORconta)

see *Rosa* Heideschnee®

Rosa Morgenrot®

(KORheim) Kordes (1985)

In spring Morgenrot® is practically covered by its single flowers. They are large, saucer-shaped, bright red and fragrantless. Insects have easy access to the yellow stamens. The main flush of blooms is in spring, but flowers can be seen on the bush

Morgenrot®

throughout the summer. The bush branches profusely, more wide than high. The mat leaves are initially light green, later turning darker.
🌐 30h 🌷🌷🌷-🌷🌷 ☁

Rosa Morgensonne 88®

(KORhoro) Kordes (1988)
Full, light yellow flowers appear on this climbing rose, which can reach six to ten feet tall. The flowers bloom in early summer in large numbers amid the shiny, medium green leaves. Further flushes are produced later in the season. Unfortunately the flowers are fragrantless.
🌱 80–120h 🌷🌷 ☁

Rosa Morning Jewel

(-) Cocker (1968)
At the height of its blooming period in early summer

Morgensonne 88®

Morning Jewel is laden with semi-double, pink flowers. They are slightly fragrant and provide an attractive contrast amid the fresh, light green leaves. The climber even blooms in places where other roses are less successful: against walls that are largely in the shade or in windy sites. Further modest blooms can only be expected if located more favorably.
🌱 120h 🌷🌷 ☁ ✚ ADR

Rosa Morsdag

(Grootendorst)
see *Rosa* Mothersday

Morning Jewel

Rosa Mothers Day

(Grootendorst)
see *Rosa* Mothersday

Rosa Mothersday

(-) Grootendorst (1949)
The semi-double, cherry-red flowers have an unusual ball shape. This is because the petals lay closely on top of one another, usually completely covering the heart. They are fragrantless. The bush of this polyantha rose is wide spreading with good branching growth. The blooming shoots extend upwards some twenty-five inches. The leaves are long, initially olive-green, later shiny, dark green. The variety is also suitable as a tree rose.
📷 20h 🌷🌷🌷 ☁

Rosa Mountbatten®

(HARmantelle) Harkness (1982)
This is one of the best yellow flowering floribundas

Mothersday

from the 1980's. This rose has received numerous awards due its beautifully formed three-inch-wide flowers and their layered distribution across the bush. The canary-yellow, full flowers sometime display a hint of pink on the edges. They are slightly fragrant. The upright bush is sturdy, and bears strong thorns and many exceptionally healthy, dark, green leaves. You can even use Mountbatten® for hedging.

✿✿ 45h 🌹🌹🌹 ☁☁ ✚

Mountbatten®

Rosa Mozart

(-) Lambert (1937)

Plume-shaped trusses with bright pink flowers bloom on the long stems of Mozart. The flowers have a prominent white eye with yellow pollen, and have a light lemon fragrance. Older flowers fade almost completely, which does not help the look of the rose. This musk hybrid is quite a messy shrub. It is fairly well covered in foliage. It appears to be susceptible to black spot.

☺ 100h 🌹🌹🌹 ☁☁

Mozart

Rosa Mr. J.B.C.

(-) DICkson (1993)

The upright and profusely branching bush is well covered in healthy foliage. The branches bear full trusses with cup to saucer-shaped flowers of around two inches wide. The rich blooms of yellow flowers make an attractive color spectacle. The older flowers turn a little orange. The flowers comprise of around ten petals and a heart full of golden pollen. They have a light and fruity fragrance. Bees are frequent visitors. Mr. J.B.C. bears glossy, olive-green leaves.

✿✿ 30h 🌹🌹🌹 ☁☁

Mr. J.B.C.

Rosa Mr. Lincoln

(Swim&Weeks)
see *Rosa* Mister Lincoln

Rosa Mrs Doreen Pike

(AUSdor) Austin (1993)

Although it was David Austin Sr. who bred this rose, Mrs Doreen Pike is first and foremost a rugosa hybrid. In these descendants of the ramanas rose Austin crossed the characteristics of the English rose group that he had developed. And the pink flowers are indeed very full, forming a rosette. What's more, they have a strong, sweet fragrance. The shrub, however, grows more wide than tall and bears faded green, wrinkled leaves on the upright branches.

@ 35h ♀♀♀ ◌◌◌◌

Mrs Doreen Pike

Rosa Mrs. Jones

(DELge)

see *Rosa* Centenaire de Lourdes® Rose

Rosa Mullard Jubilee

(Electron) McGredy (1970)

Wide, red buds open to reveal the six-inch, full, deep pink flowers. These are held in trusses above the foliage on sturdy, thorny stems. They have an attractive form, bloom wide open and have a delicious, sweet rose perfume. The bush grows upright and is well covered in leaves right down to the base. The young leaves are olive-green with a red tint, later turning

Mullard Jubilee

Mullard Jubilee

gray-green. This excellent rose has won numerous awards.

☀ 30h ♀♀♀ ◌◌◌

Rosa multiflora

(-) botanical rose (-)

This multiflorous rose grows in the wild in Japan, China and Korea. Here it is particularly suited to natural gardens. The shrub has long, drooping branches. If trained they can reach thirteen feet tall; as a shrub approximately seven feet. It bears few thorns, which are not particularly sharp. The creamy white flowers bloom in trusses in early summer. They have a light fruity fragrance. The flowers eventually fade to pure white. Red hips appear in fall. The rosa multiflora is one of the ancestors of the numerous cultivated roses that are described as multifora hybrids. They can be recognized by the serrated stipules at the base of each leaf. The polyantha rose is an example of a crossing between the rosa multiflora and continuous-flowering Chinese roses. With modern roses the multiflorous habit of the floribundas

Rosa multiflora

is derived from the rosa multiflora. The trusses of rich blooms as well as its few thorns makes this multiflorous rose very popular.
❀ 200h ⚘ ෴෴ ✚

Rosa München 83

(MElbalbika)
see *Rosa* Iga®'83 München

Rosa Muttertag

(Grootendorst)
see *Rosa* Mothersday

Rosa My Granny

(POUloma)
see *Rosa* Meine Oma™

Rosa Mystic

(POUlor)
see *Rosa* Supreme Cover™ Towne & Country®

Rosa Naheglut

(POUlnorm)
see *Rosa* That's Jazz™ Courtyard®

Rosa Naheglut™ Courtyard®

(POUlnorm)
see *Rosa* That's Jazz™ Courtyard® (POUlnorm)

Rosa Nahema®

(DELéri) Delbard (1998)
The flowers of this climbing rose have the romantic look of old roses. They are very full, soft pink and open to a globular form. They have an intense but fresh rose perfume with a hint of fruit. A beautiful climber for areas with warm and dry summers.
↗ 70h ⚘⚘⚘ ෴෴෴

Nahema®

Rosa Nashville

(POUlbico)
see *Rosa* Candy Cover™ Towne & Country®

Rosa Natascha

(HARwharry)
see *Rosa* Malcolm Sargent

Rosa NDR1 Radio Niedersachsen®

(KOReledas) Kordes (1996)
A spectacular new addition: fantastically rich blooms and shiny, deep olive-green leaves that remain extremely healthy, and single flowers that fall apart once spent, thereby effectively cleaning the bush. The medium, saucer-shaped flowers appear in trusses from pink buds. The flowers are an old rose color, which fades further with age. The fragrance is light and fresh, and bees are frequent visitors to the golden pollen. Due to its vigorous growth the bush is sometimes classified as a shrub rose. Highly recommended.
✿✿/↔ 120h ⚘⚘⚘ ෴ ✚

NDR1 Radio Niedersachsen®

Rosa Neige d'Eté®

(-) Lens (1991)

This is actually no more than a white version of Rosa Bouquet Parfait®. Both roses of Louis Lens produce rich trusses of buds on top of the shoots. The flowers in a truss open up almost simultaneously, thereby producing a complete bouquet of roses. Here they are semi-double, deep cup-shaped and snow-white. The heart bears golden pollen. The flowers are very suitable as cut rose, are long lasting and can withstand bad weather.

⚘ 50h 🌹🌹🌹 ☁☁

Neige d'Eté®

Rosa New Daily Mail

(Tantau)
see *Rosa* Pussta®

Rosa New Dawn

(-) Somerset Rose Nursery (1930)

There is no other rose that has been planted more frequently in the last ten years than New Dawn. It has been proclaimed as 'world rose': the most popular rose in the world. And although you might get fed up with seeing New Dawn in practically every kind of garden, its fame is well deserved. New Dawn is usually sold as a climbing rose - or better still - as a rambler. However, you can also use this rose in all sorts of other ways. As a solitary they can reach almost seven feet tall, growing with long threadlike stems branching off in every direction. If they find support they can reach around seventeen feet tall, with the blooming shoots hanging downwards. Tying is recommended. The full flowers have the lightest pink imaginable. With very sunny weather they appear almost pure white. When the nights become colder, then the pink returns. The flowers have a pleasant, spicy fragrance. The great advantage of New Dawn is the long-lasting blooms, which continue from early summer till deep into fall. There are periods of more modest blooms but the bush is never without flowers. Unfortunately, these days there are New Dawn roses on the market that are not continuous-flowering. These were the result of people budding the eyes on the long, fast-growing branches (according to a supplier who did this himself, without being aware of the disastrous results). So if you have a once-flowering New Dawn there is only one thing to do to increase the length of blooms: buy a new one.

🌿 80–200h 🌹🌹🌹 ☁☁☁ ✚

New Dawn

New Dawn

Rosa New Face®

(INTerclem) Interplant (1977)

The shrub grows wide and reaches almost seven feet tall. This size can be curtailed with more severe pruning. Very full, loose trusses of single flowers appear throughout summer and fall above the arched-shaped branches. The flowers are creamy white with old rose blotches, which fade with age. Due to its lengthy blooms and bright, green leaves this is a superb shrub for those with enough space.

🌼 50–80h 🌹🌹🌹 ☁

Rosa New Rouge Meilland

(MEImalyna)
see *Rosa* Rouge Meilland®

New Face®

Rosa New Valencia

(KOReklia)
see *Rosa* Valencia®

Rosa New Zealand

(MACgenev) McGredy (1989)

The full flowers have an intense and deliciously sweet fragrance, as heavy as honeysuckle. The flowers have an attractive form and color, also when older, with tints of apricot and salmon. It thrives in sunny climates, as both the buds and flowers cannot withstand rain and clean badly. The medium green leaves are prone to fungal disease. The bush has vigorous upright growth and a fairly irregular form. Due to the slow regrowth the flushes occur in waves rather than continuously.

✳ 35h 🌹🌹 ☁☁☁☁

Rosa Night Life

(POUllight)
see *Rosa* Night Light™ Courtyard®

New Zealand

Rosa Night Light™ Courtyard®

(POUllight) Poulsen (1981)

The red buds open to reveal surprising yellow flowers that can reach four inches wide. They bloom in small groups at the end of this shrub-like rambler. The young leaves are reddish, but change quickly to glossy medium green.

🌿 70h 🌹🌹🌹 ☁☁

Rosa Nil Bleu®

(DELnible) Delbard (1976)

The buds of the Nil Bleu® don't give anything away yet. It is only once the large, full flowers unfold from

Night Light™ Courtyard®

the buds that you see the mauve to lavender-colored petals. They curl backwards and the flower often tilts under its weight. You may think that this is not a rose for windy or rainy climates, but the petals appear thick enough to withstand bad weather quite well. It is therefore surprising that this rose has disappeared from the catalogue of breeder Delbard. However, it

Nil Bleu®

can be obtained from other suppliers. The pleasantly fragrant flowers appear the whole summer on a well-branching, upright bush with gray-green leaves.

✳ 40h 🌹🌹🌹 ☁☁☁

Rosa Nirvana®

(MEIrisouru) Meilland (1977)

Apricot-colored buds open to reveal bright pink flowers. They are semi-double, cup-shaped and display a wide heart with pollen. The flowers have a slight and unpleasant fragrance. They are borne singly or in small trusses. The foliage is olive-green, later turning to glossy gray-green. The bush has good branching growth, blooms moderately well and the flowers clean badly after rain.

✳✳ 30h 🌹🌹🌹 ☁

Rosa Noack's Blühendes Barock®

(NOAbell) Noack (1997)

As of July trusses of dozens of fruity smelling, pink flowers are raised above the foliage. The flowers of this richly blooming floribunda are only just over two inches wide. However, they are so full and there are

Nirvana®

so many on a single truss that the stems bend under the weight, keeping the bush relatively low. Noack's Blühendes Barock® bears many glossy, olive to dark green leaves, which have excellent resistance to black spot and reasonably so to mildew.

✳✳ 70h 🌹🌹🌹 ☁☁ ✚

Noack's Blühendes Barock®

Rosa Noble Anthony

(AUSway)
see *Rosa* Noble Antony

Rosa Noble Antony

(AUSway) Austin (1995)
The carmine petals of the full flower bend backwards, forming a dome-shaped rosette. It has a delightful fragrance of old roses, which has earned Noble Antony a fragrance prize during tests in Glasgow, Scotland. The shrub grows upright, though still remains rather low. It is suitable for planting in the foreground of a shrub border, but can also be combined with perennials. It is best to locate it away from other roses due to its susceptibility to black spot.
⚘GB 35h ⚘⚘⚘ ☁☁☁☁

Noble Antony

Rosa Nordina™ Courtyard®

(POUlskab) Poulsen (2000)
One of the latest additions to the Courtyard series of the Danish breeder Poulsen. This is a relatively low rambler with a shrub-like growth habit and large flowers that appear throughout the summer. The semi-double flowers of Nordina are pink with a little yellow in the open heart. The reddish green leaves have an attractive shine.
⚲ 70h ⚘⚘⚘ ☁☁

Rosa Nostalgie®

(TANeiglat) Tantau (1995)
This is one of the most remarkable roses of the last few years. The globular flowers are bi-colored with a creamy white heart and cherry-red outer petals (primarily on the top of the petals). They are known to be fragrant but in practice that is a little disappointing. With bad weather the flowers hang unattractively on the bush, but when the weather

Nordina™ Courtyard®

improves they clean up well. The variety belongs to the 'nostalgic roses' group created by the breeder Tantau. They are both strong and charming and are the answer to the popular English roses. The upright bush bears red-tinged leaves that change to dark green. It is large and remains healthy.
✻ 35h ⚘⚘⚘ ☁☁ ⊕

Nostalgie®

Rosa Nuage Parfume

(Tanellis)
see *Rosa* Duftwolke®

Rosa Octavia Hill

(HARzeal) Harkness (1995)

The soft pink flowers are very full and often quartered, giving a romantic impression. The pleasant, sweet-fresh rose fragrance adds to this. With age the flowers open cup-shaped and fade charmingly. But after a week of rainy weather Octavia shows its shortcomings. The buds no longer open due to balling and the spent flowers hang rotting on the bush. The bush incidentally has excellent growth. It produces rich and long-lasting blooms, branches regularly, thereby filling a border or bed well with foliage, which is first olive then later shiny, dark green.

✲✲ 30h ✿✿✿ ☁☁☁

Rosa Oh La La

(Tantau)
see *Rosa* Olala®

Octavia Hill

Rosa Ohlala

(Tantau)
see *Rosa* Olala®

Rosa Olala®

(-) Tantau (1956)

The semi-double flowers of almost four inches wide begin bright red, later fading to a dark pink. They bloom in trusses and open cup to saucer-shaped. In part because the stems grow diagonally, the bush remains extremely low, although there are exceptions. The advantage of this growth habit is that it covers its area well. Olala® has medium-sized, dark green leaves.

✲✲ 30h ✿✿✿ ☁

Rosa Old Fragrance

(TANschaubud)
see *Rosa* Duftrausch®

Rosa Old Velvet Moss

(Laffay)
see *Rosa* William Lobb

Olala®

Rosa Olympic Fire

(TANeuschip 92)
see *Rosa* Olympisches Feuer®

Rosa Olympisches Feuer® 92

(TANeuschip 92) Tantau (1992)

This is the successor to Rosa Olympisches Feuer from the same breeder. This new version is more disease hardy and grows more compact with greater sideways branching. The three-inch-wide, full flowers are slightly fragrant but are very much present through their bright fluorescent orange-red color. The young leaves are tinged with mahogany, changing later to a mat gray-green.

✿✿ 30h ♟♟♟ ◌ ✚

Rosa Omi Oswald®

(-) Lens (1988)

It is for good reason that this is one of the best-loved moschata hybrids of Louis Lens (see also Rosa moschata). The orange-tinged yellow buds open to reveal soft yellow flowers, which slowly fade to white. The flowers are almost two inches wide, which is very large for a moschata hybrid, making them very popular as cut rose. Just a few stems full

Olympisches Feuer® 92

with these semi-double flowers and you will quickly fill a vase. The bush grows upright without the branches hanging.

✺ 30h ♟♟♟ ◌

Rosa Opalia®

(NOAschnee)

see Rosa Schneeflocke®

Rosa Orange Babyflor®

(TANegnaro) Tantau (1994)

The bright orange-red of the full flowers of this

Omi Oswald®

miniature rose will tempt you to buy them straight-away. The breeders ensure that this miniature rose blooms in the pot early on. You can enjoy them first in the house, but you will eventually have to put them in a container or large pot outside with good fertile soil, otherwise growth and the blooms will stop. The young foliage has a red tinge, later becoming a shiny dark green.

▦ 10h ♟♟♟ ◌

Rosa Orange Fire®

(INTerfire) Interplant (1987)

The trusses of the orange three-inch flowers shine

Orange Babyflor®

bright high above the foliage, like lighthouses amid the green bedding. They sometimes bend under the weight of the trusses. The semi-double flowers are slightly fragrant: at the most a light fruity perfume. Due to their pronounced color they are more suitable for bedding than borders. The color contrasts well with the dark burgundy-tinged leaves and stems, which eventually turn a dark gray-green. This upright bush is dense with foliage. It is well known for its good resistance to black spot and mildew.

⚇ 40–60h 🌷🌷🌷 ⌁ ✪ TOP

Rosa **Orange Meillandina**®

(MEIjikatar) Meilland (1982)

A miniature rose with orange-red flowers that retain their color well even with age. The bush is compact and grows wider than its full height. It can bloom in a pot, but grows better planted in the garden, for example on the edge of a border.

▣ 10h 🌷🌷🌷 ⌁

Orange Fire®

Rosa **Orange Morsdag**

(-) Grootendorst (1956)

This sport of Rosa Mothersday differs only in terms of flower color, which is light and somewhat orange. The globular flowers of this polyantha rose reach over an inch wide. They appear in trusses. The almost thorn-free stems bear olive-green (later dark

Orange Meillandina®

green) leaves. Orange Morsdag is also available as tree rose.

▣ 20h 🌷🌷🌷 ⌁

Rosa **Orange Sunblaze**

(MEIjikatar)

see *Rosa* Orange Meillandina

Orange Morsdag

Rosa **Orange Symphonie**®

(MEIninrut) Meilland (1994)

When a rose is a little too big to be called a miniature, it is called a patio rose. And this is the case for Orange Symphonie®, with its height of fifteen inches. The bush still manages to fit in a large pot. It bears many vermilion-orange flowers, which are usually borne singly on the stems.

▣ 15h 🌷🌷🌷 ⌁

Orange Symphonie®

end of each stem is a very full, cup-shaped flower. The color can vary somewhat, from carmine-red to a purple hue, but is usually a striking red. Although the flower is supposed to be very fragrant, I found it moderate, though pleasantly sweet and with a typical aroma of old roses. The flowers quickly become unattractive particularly after bad weather, and because moderate blooms are produced that are interrupted with pauses, this English rose makes little impression.

⚘GB 150h ⚘⚘ ⌒⌒

Rosa Osiana

(-) Tantau (1989)

The long buds open to reveal beautiful, ivory-white flowers with a pink tinge. Each full flower is borne singly on a sturdy stem. Osiana makes a very good cut flower and has a wonderful fragrance of fruit and roses. The large leaves are mat, gray-green. The rose is rarely for sale.

✳ 30h ⚘⚘⚘ ⌒⌒⌒

Rosa Othello

(AUSlo) Austin (1986)

Othello produces long, sturdy vertical stems that bear reddish thorns and mat, dark green leaves. At the

Othello

Rosa Our Molly

(DICreason) Dickson (1994)

The bright red of these single flowers contrast sharply with the white eyes. They are only slightly fragrant

Osiana

Our Molly

and bloom in large trusses. Orange hips appear in the fall. The mat gray-green leaves tone down the overall color somewhat. These leaves are borne in great numbers on the regularly branching shrub.

🌐 80h 🌹🌹🌹 ☁

Rosa Pallisade Rose®

(KORdapt)
see *Rosa* Heidekönigin®

Rosa Palmengarten Frankfurt®

(KORsilan) Kordes (1988)
This is an extremely rich and long-blooming rose. The flowers appear in full trusses. They have a baroque look, but appear to be susceptible to heavy rain. They have a light apple fragrance. The shrub reaches some thirty inches tall and is heavily covered by attractively shiny, light green leaves. After three years the ground underneath is completely obscured. And because the shrub grows particularly outwards it is also used for ground cover by planting two shrubs per ten square feet and light pruning. A highly recommended, extremely healthy rose that is seldom affected by fungal disease.

🌐/↔ 30h ☁☁ ✚ ADR

Palmengarten Frankfurt®

Rosa Panache

(POUltop)
see *Rosa* Top™ Hit®

Rosa Paola®

(TANaloap) Tantau (1981)
One of the many perfectly formed, bright red tea roses. The full, velvety red flowers open out from long buds. They are borne singly on sturdy stems. They have a light and pleasant fragrance. Paola® makes a good cut rose. The large, mat, dark green leaves are borne on the upright bush, which remains reasonably healthy. This and the continuous-flowering habit ensure that the bush looks attractive for some time.

✳ 30h 🌹🌹🌹 ☁☁

Paola®

Rosa Papa Meilland®

(MEIcesar) Meilland (1963)
Papa Meilland® has velvety red flowers in the perfect shape of a Hybrid Tea. The deep olive-green leaves

Papa Meilland®

provide a beautiful contrast. And the fragrance - delicious! But now to the shortcomings of Papa Meilland®: it does not bloom throughout the summer, but repeatedly; it grows in bursts; and it is prone to rose diseases. However popular this rose used to be, those days are gone.

⚘ 30h 🌼🌼 ⌘⌘⌘⌘

Rosa Papi Delbard®

(DELaby) Delbard (1995)

Not a bad rose to name after your father, as this is very similar to the romantic old roses of the past. The cup-shaped flowers are extremely full and tilt under their own weight on the stalks, causing them eventually to hang. For a climbing rose this is more of an advantage than a problem. The flowers display all sorts of nuances of colors: apricot, mild orange, amber and salmon-pink. What's more, they have a wonderful fresh and fruity fragrance.

🗲 80h 🌼🌼🌼 ⌘⌘⌘

Papi Delbard®

Rosa Pariser Charme

(-) Tantau (1965)

The pointed buds of Pariser Charme open to reveal wide, full flowers with a pure pink color. They reach over four inches wide and hang under their own weight. They have a delicious, sweet fragrance.

Pariser Charme

The rather old-fashioned looking rose has dense, olive-green foliage, which remains quite healthy.

⚘ 30h 🌼🌼🌼 ⌘⌘⌘

Rosa Parkdirektor Riggers®

(-) Kordes (1957)

A vigorous and healthy climbing rose that, depending on the support, can grow to over thirteen feet. Amid the striking, dark green leaves appear semi-double, bright crimson roses. They are fragrantless. After the initial rich bloom a few repeat flushes appear. The climber grows to around five feet wide and is also very suitable for growing against shady walls.

🗲 80–160h 🌼🌼 ⌘ ✚ ADR

Parkdirektor Riggers®

Rosa Parkjuwel

(-) Kordes (1950)

If Parkjuwel were to bloom throughout the summer it would be very popular. After all, the full, pink flowers are large, beautifully shaped and have a wonderful fragrance. The rose also has attractive, leathery, light gray-green leaves. The shrub branches profusely, reaching man-height and is very thorny.

🌸 60h 💈 ☁☁☁☁

Parkjuwel

Rosa Parkzauber

(-) Kordes (1956)

A once-flowering moss rose with fuchsia pink flowers. They bloom only in early summer. The flowers are cup-shaped, round and semi-double. They have a pleasant fragrance. Parkzauber reaches five feet tall

Parkzauber

and branches profusely, producing a wide shrub. It bears dark green leaves.

🌸 60h 💈 ☁☁☁

Rosa Partridge

(KORweirim)

see *Rosa* Weisse Immensee®

Rosa Parure d'Or®

(DELmir) Delbir (1968)

The basic color of the semi-double flowers of Parure d'Or® is golden, with a sharply contrasting orange to salmon-pink color on the edges. Flowers bloom throughout the summer on this vigorous climbing rose with glossy, dark green leaves.

🌿 80h 💈💈💈 ☁☁

Parure d'Or®

Rosa Pas de Deux™ Courtyard®

(POUlhult) Poulsen (2000)

The flowers are initially ochre-yellow on opening, becoming lighter yellow with a pink tinge as the flowers open further. The heart with pollen is revealed in these cup to saucer-shaped, semi-double flowers. They are lightly fragrant. The bushy branched shrub is sold as a rambler.

🌿 80h 💈💈💈 ☁☁

Pas de Deux™ Courtyard®

They have a tea rose fragrance. The mat, medium green leaves are borne on a bushy shrub, which grows as wide as its full height.

🌹GB 50h 🌹🌹🌹 ☁☁

Rosa Paul Noël

(-) Tanne (1913)
A modern rambler that was already around back in 1913 and is still valued today for its full, flesh-colored flowers that have a fresh, fruity fragrance. They tilt sideways on their short stalks. The climbing branches are long and can be trained over ten feet upwards. The dense foliage is light green. After the first rich blooms further more modest ones follow.

🍃 120h 🌹🌹 ☁☁☁

Paul Noël

Rosa Pat Austin™

(AUSmum) Austin (1995)
From the moment the buds open the flowers of Pat Austin™ steal the show. They are then spherical. They open further to a deep cup-shape with somewhat ruffled petals. They are orange inside and copper-yellow outside, giving a bi-colored effect.

Pat Austin™

Rosa Paul Ricard®

(MEInivoz) Meilland (1994)
The amber-colored flowers fade during hot summers in the bright sun, but they do retain their spectacular form. They are perched stately on long stalks and are highly suited as a cut rose, in part due to their delicious, spicy fragrance. The large leaves are mat, medium green and are borne on an upright bush, which often reaches three-and-a-half feet.

⚜ 40h 🌹🌹🌹 ☁☁☁

Rosa Paul Shirville

(HARqueterwife) Harkness (1983)

Beautifully formed buds open slowly to reveal the full, salmon-pink flowers. The outer petals are lighter, with the rest fading with age. The flowers give off a delicious, sweet fragrance, and seem made for display in a vase. They bloom throughout the summer (the richest in July) on a healthy looking bush. The leaves have a purple-red hue and eventually turn a glossy dark green.

⚘ 35h ♀♀♀ ◌◌◌

Paul Shirville

Rosa Paul's Himalayan Musk Rambler

(-) Paul (± 1900)

This musk hybrid has frighteningly vigorous growth. If guided by a tree the thin branches of this rambler

can completely engulf the tree, which in turn may sometimes need support to keep it standing. In the middle of summer a cascade of slightly fragrant, semi-double, light pink flowers appear on the branches. Oval hips form later. If planted at the right location, therefore where its vigorous growth does not lead to any problems, this rose can develop into a complete 'blooming landscape'.

⚘ 80–400h ♀ ◌◌ ✦

Rosa Peace®

(-) Meilland (1945)

The Second World War gave this legendary rose its names. Breeder Francis Meilland had already bred it in 1935 and named it after his mother: 'Mme A. Meilland'. However, just before the war the plant began to drift and in Germany was given the name 'Gloria Dei' and in Italy 'Gioia'. In 1945, on the day that Berlin fell, an American company introduced the rose under the name 'Peace'. The rose is sometimes called the rose of the twentieth century, so

Peace®

much approval has it gained in all sorts of inspections and shows. What's more, nineteen sports have been derived from Peace and the rose served as parent plant for 157 other cultivars. No wonder: the fragrant flowers are large, have subtle colors with creamy, soft yellow and light pink tints and can withstand rain. The bush grows vigorously with large, very healthy, dark green leaves. Peace® is currently among the most disease-resistant roses around, although it is not always free from black spot.

☀ 30h 🌹🌹🌹 ◌◌ ✛

Rosa Peacekeeper

(HARbella) Harkness (1995)

The name of this floribunda is in honor of the work of the United Nations. The bushes are highly suited for bedding. Vast numbers of buds appear in early summer, which open to reveal beautiful flowers. They are initially pure orange, but change gradually via salmon-pink and apricot to golden yellow, and then eventually end up pale yellow. The spicy scented flowers clean well when spent. It has bushy growth and is almost equally wide as tall. It bears mat, light green leaves.

✳✳ 30h 🌹🌹🌹 ◌◌

Peacekeeper

Rosa Peach Surprise

(POUlrise)

see *Rosa* Kong Frederik den IX™ Hybrid Tea Poulsen®

Rosa Peachy Pink Magic Carpet

(POUlor)

see *Rosa* Supreme Cover™ Towne & Country®

Rosa Pearl Drift®

(LEGgab) Le Grice (1981)

The semi-double flowers of Pearl Drift bloom cup-shaped, revealing their yellow pollen. They are slightly fragrant. The pink flowers are so light that they appear white. They open throughout the summer from pink buds on a sturdy shrub with shiny, dark green leaves.

◍ 40h 🌹🌹🌹 ◌

Pearl Drift®

Rosa Pearl Mirato®

(TANrostax) Tantau (2001)

Pearl Mirato® only differs from the very robust rose Mirato® (see Mirato®) in terms of color. The semi-

Pearl Mirato®

double flowers of Pearl Mirato® are light pink with pearl-white on the outside. The shrub reaches almost two feet tall and wide and blooms throughout the summer and into fall.

↔ 60h ❦❦❦ ⌀ ⊕

Rosa Pearl Meidiland

(MEIplatin) Meilland (1989)

The semi-double flowers are initially the softest pink imaginable, but quickly fade to a pearl-white. Though they appear in trusses the flowers reach three inches wide. During the flushes the rose is completely covered with flowers. The shrub has a spreading growth from a single point, with knee-high drooping branches, which nonetheless do not fully cover the ground. Red hips are usually formed in fall. The shrub is resistant to mildew but can be affected by black spot.

◉ 20h ❦❦ ⌀

Pearl Meidiland

Rosa Peaudouce

(DICjana)
see *Rosa* Elina®

Rosa Pebble Beach

(POUleas)
see *Rosa* Easy Cover™ Towne & Country®

Rosa Peer Gynt®

(-) Kordes (1968)

The very full flowers of this large-flowered rose have a golden basic color, which does not fade in the sun

Peer Gynt®

but actually becomes more intense. The edges of the petals have rose-red tinges. The strong stems, the durability of the flowers and their wonderful fragrance make Peer Gynt® very suitable as cut rose. It is also a success in the garden: it can withstand the rain well. The upright shrub grows vigorously, with glossy, olive-green leaves.

✲ 30h ❦❦❦ ⌀⌀⌀

Rosa Pegasus

(Ausmoon) Austin (1995)

With its very drooping branches on a low shrub Pegasus is quite different from what we expect from an English rose. The flowers don't even look that much like a rose. The flowers are so full, with the edges bending back, that they seem more like a camelia flower. In the heart the flowers are apricot, turning lighter outwards. The light fragrance, however, is

Pegasus

typical for a tea rose and the leaves are shiny as is the case for most modern Hybrid Teas.
🌹GB 35h 🌹🌹🌹 ☁☁

Rosa Penelope

(-) Pemberton (1924)

The full trusses of orange-red buds open to reveal semi-double, pleasantly sweet smelling flowers. Initially in addition to the creamy white there is also a hint of soft pink to be seen, which gradually fades. Although this rose is said to bloom throughout summer, its blooms are interrupted by pauses. However, this musk hybrid remains popular with those keen on romantic gardens. The bush grows upright and branches well. It bears mat, dark, gray-green leaves with strikingly serrated edges. Do not confuse this Penelope with - at least - two other roses of the same name. When buying look out for the breeder and year.
✳✳ 40h 🌹🌹 ☁☁☁

Penelope

Rosa Penny Coelen

(MEInimo)
see *Rosa* Regatta®

Rosa Penny Lane

(HARdwell) Harkness (1998)

A rambler with supple branches. The shiny, dark green foliage appears healthy. The flowers open mainly in early summer. They are very light apricot

Penny Lane

in color and very full. They are lightly fragrant. With good growth repeat blooms can be expected.
🌹 120h 🌹🌹 ☁☁

Rosa Penthouse

(MACsatur) McGredy (1988)

The four-inch-wide flowers are very full with scalloped petals in soft pink. This popular rose has a pleasant fragrance: a sweet and yet fresh rose perfume. The bush grows upright vigorously but can look messy through irregular growth. The leaves are large, initially red for a short time, then mat, medium green. It remains remarkably healthy.
✳ 40h 🌹🌹🌹 ☁☁☁ ✛ TOP

Penthouse

Rosa Perception

(HARzippee) Harkness (1997)

The full flowers can reach five inches wide, when grown for shows. The edges are pink, whilst the basic color is ivory-white, often with some yellow. They

Perception

have a delicious rose fragrance with a hint of lemon. The flowers are usually borne singly on sturdy stems and so make good cut roses. This upright bush becomes relatively tall, so is best at the back of a border. It bears large, dark green leaves.
✿ 50h ♀♀♀ ◌◌◌

Rosa **Perdita**®

(AUSperd) Austin (1983)
The flowers of Perdita® do not yet have a stable color. Sometimes they are creamy white, other times apricot and - particularly later in the season - they appear soft pink. However, they are always deep cup-shaped and very full. The stems are no longer able to hold the heavy flowers (especially after rain), and so they hang. And this while the wonderfully fragrant flowers develop from slender, pointed buds. The upright shrub bears glossy, dark green leaves.
♀GB 40h ♀♀♀ ◌◌◌◌

Perdita®

Rosa **Perle Meillandecor**

(MEIplatin)
see *Rosa* Pearl Meidiland

Rosa **Perpetually Yours**

(HARfable) Harkness (1999)
The flowers of this modern climbing rose are very full. Sometimes more than seventy petals crowd around the heart, often forming a quartered rose. The flower is lemon yellow to cream, sometimes with tints of apricot in the heart. They have a light fragrance, which is the only difference it has with the popular English roses of David Austin. The heavy flowers tilt sideways on this climber with mat, dark green leaves.
🌱 120h ♀♀♀ ◌◌

Rosa **Peter Cottrell**

(HARentente) Harkness (1999)
The red buds of this fairly recent floribunda open up wide. The flowers are full and soft yellow with a light pink edge. They have a light fragrance. The bush has a globular form, reaches thirty-five inches tall and

Perpetually Yours

twenty-five inches wide. It bears strikingly shiny, red-tinged leaves that change to dark green.
✿✿ 35h ♀♀♀ ◌◌

Rosa **Peter Wessel**

(TANtide)
see *Rosa* Lübecker Rotspon®

Peter Cottrell

Rosa Petit Four®

(INTerfour) Interplant (1981)
A very richly blooming miniature rose with one-and-a-half-inch-wide, semi-double, pink flowers in subtle shades of dark to light pink. The flowers appear into fall on a compact bush with glossy, fresh green leaves.
🔲 15h 🌸🌸🌸 ♻

Rosa Petit Maquis

(KORholst)
see *Rosa* Holstein 87®

Petit Four®

Rosa Pheasant

(KORdapt)
see *Rosa* Heidekönigin®

Rosa Phillipa

(POUlheart)
see *Rosa* Julia™ Renaissance®

Rosa Piccola

(TANolokip)
see *Rosa* Piccolo®

Rosa Piccolo®

(TANolokip) Tantau (1984)
This is a rose of remarkable proportions. The full, bright orange-red flowers have the form of a tea rose and are very large in relation to the bush, which grows to around one-and-a-half feet tall. The flowers appear in trusses just above the foliage. It blooms throughout summer and fall and are very rain hardy. In short, an exceptional bedding rose, but also suitable for low hedging. The leaves have tints of burgundy and change to shiny medium green.
✹✹ 20h 🌸🌸🌸 ♻

Rosa Pierette Pavement

(UHLater)
see *Rosa rugosa* Pierette®

Rosa Pierre de Ronsard

see *Rosa* Eden Rose®85

Piccolo®

Rosa Pigalle®84

(MEIcloux) Meilland (1985)

Describing the color of this rose as orange does not do justice to its cream, yellow and orange to fluorescent red tints. The flowers are grouped in small trusses and are quite large for a floribunda rose. The bush branches profusely and bears dull, medium green foliage.

✲✲ 30h ✿✿✿ ☁

Rosa Pilgrim™

(AUSwalker)

see *Rosa* The Pilgrim™

Rosa Pimpernelle

(DELdog)

see *Rosa* Pimprenelle®

Pigalle®84

Rosa pimpinellifolia

(-) botanical rose (-)

The burnet rose thrives in poor soil. In dune areas and other places with loose, sandy soil the shrub prefers places where humus and nutrients collect, but also grows well in poorer soils. Their natural habitat covers a wide area: from North-West Europe all the way to the Eurasian continent up to Korea. In gardens it looks its best in poor soil, where the shrub grows compact and rich. The single flowers bloom in mid-summer. They are an inch wide, creamy white, and form hips as of August. Very suitable for cultivating in pots.

✲ 40h ✿ ☁ ✚

Rosa pimpinellifolia

Rosa Pimprenelle®

(DELdog) Delbard (1997)

What you first notice about this shrub is the thickness of the branches. They are very robust for a plant of some thirty inches tall. They bear large, glossy, dark green leaves and trusses with golden flowers of almost four inches wide. The flowers are single with a striking heart full of yellow stamens. The typical rose perfume is both fresh and intensely sweet. The flowers fade to light yellow with age. Large hips are formed.

✲ 25h ✿✿✿ ☁☁☁

Rosa Pink Abundance

(HARfrothy) Harkness (1999)

New flower trusses appear throughout the summer and fall on this very richly blooming floribunda. The

Pimprenelle®

flowers are salmon-pink with a little orange in the very full heart. They bloom on a bushy plant with shiny, dark green leaves, which open out to reveal a red tinge.

✺✺ 35h ♀♀♀ ⌢

Rosa **Pink Babyflor®**

(TANybab) Tantau (1993)

The very full flowers of this miniature rose have a strikingly globular form. On the outside they are carmine-red; inside more old rose. A remarkable rose for areas with plenty of good weather or for sites protected against rain. Suitable for cultivating in pots and continuously flowering when planted in soil with good nutrients that does not fully dry out. The medium green leaves are relatively large.

▣ 15h ♀♀♀ ⌢

Pink Babyflor®

Pink Abundance

Rosa **Pink Bassino®**

(Korbasren) Kordes (1995)

The bush grows equally wide as tall and branches well. The young leaves are initially a coppery red changing via light green to moss green. The foliage is very healthy and remarkably shiny. New trusses develop throughout summer, bearing single, pink flowers with a white heart with yellow stamens.

◉ 25h ♀♀♀ ⌢ ✚ ADR

Rosa **Pink Chimo®**

(INTerchimp) Interplant (1989)

Long thorny stems bear light green, shiny leaves that have good resistance to fungal diseases such as black spot and mildew. Trusses with small buds develop on top of the stems. Once the numerous trusses develop into single flowers the stems bend under the weight and reach the ground. The bright pink flowers with a light eye and yellow pollen bloom prostrate or against support, as newer stems are already growing

Pink Bassino®

upwards and will be nestling against the older ones. In this way a closed dome is formed that covers the entire ground. Pink Chimo® is particularly suitable for public green areas and for natural gardens.

↔ 25h ♀♀♀ ⌢ ✚ TOP

Pink Chimo®

Rosa Pink Cover™ Towne & Country®

(POUlnoz) Poulsen (1991)

The shrub branches profusely and remains low. It bears small, shiny, dark green leaves and single, pale pink flowers of around an inch wide, which bloom in full trusses.

ⓦ 25h 🌻🌻🌻 ☁

Rosa Pink Decumba®

(HANpidec) Hanekamp (1997)

This low ground cover rose completely obscures the ground with a carpet of soft pink, single flowers and healthy olive-green leaves. In the heart of the lightly fragrant flower there is a thick tuft of golden stamens. Four plants per ten square feet will ensure complete ground cover. The variety belongs to the Stecktii® roses, which are propagated using cuttings. Pink Decumba® is also suitable for natural gardens, in particular for covering a slope.

↔ 10h 🌻🌻🌻 ☁☁ ✚

Pink Cover™ Towne & Country®

Rosa Pink Delight®

(LENpi) Lens (1983)

The wonderfully formed and full, pink flowers resemble a large-flowered rose in all but size, as the entire bush barely reaches fifteen inches tall and the flowers are only around an inch wide. No more than three flowers are borne on a single stem, however new ones are formed throughout summer. A splendid rose for a low bed or for in a pot or container. Pink Delight® is prone to mildew.

▣ 15h 🌻🌻🌻 ☁

Pink Decumba®

Rosa Pink Fire®

(INTerpin) Interplant (1989)

The frilly edges of the pink flowers are particularly noticeable. They are also quite round and semi-double: a combination that is often a problem to the durability. The flowers indeed cannot withstand rain well and lose much of their beauty. The

Pink Delight®

large, shiny, dark green leaves are red-tinged when young.
✿✿ 30h 🌷🌷🌷 ○

Rosa Pink Fizz

(Poulyc001)
see *Rosa* Bournonville™ Courtyard®

Rosa Pink Fringe

(INTerpin)
see *Rosa* Pink Fire®

Rosa Pink Haze®

(TANezahpi) Tantau (2001)
The shiny green leaves contrast sharply against the

Pink Fire®

pink flowers of Pink Haze®. These are single, somewhat star-shaped and lightly fragrant. Twenty-five inches wide, the shrub is a little wider than it is tall. Due to its bushy growth, excellent disease-resistance and the lengthy blooms this rose is popular in public green areas, but they are also suitable for flower boxes.
↔ 20h 🌷🌷🌷 ○ ✪

Rosa Pink La Sevillana®

(MEIgeroka) Meilland (1984)
The very dense foliage of Pink La Sevillana® appears pink throughout the summer due to the extremely rich blooms. The semi-double, cup-shaped flowers have a light but unpleasant fragrance. Red hips appear in fall. This highly recommended variety is a sport from the red-flowering La Sevillana® and

Pink Haze®

only differs in terms of color. The shrub looks beautiful in bedding, and without annual pruning grows to a height and width of fifty inches and so is very good for hedging. The leaves are light green, later turning a medium gray-green. The foliage is extremely resistant to mildew but a little susceptible to black spot.
✿✿ 40h 🌷🌷🌷 ○○ ADR

Rosa Pink Meidiland®

(MEIpoque) Meilland (1984)
This is a very remarkable shrub rose. The salmon-pink flowers reveal a light heart and change color a great deal during blooming. They fade considerably, sometimes leaving only a speckled pattern. Pink Meidiland® is one of the strongest shrub roses for parks and natural gardens: grows wide, has dense foliage and is resistant to mildew, though a little susceptible to black spot. It is no surprise then that it has received some important awards. Pink Meidiland® is also suitable as low hedging.
☀ 25h 🌷🌷🌷 ○○ ADR TOP

Pink La Sevillana®

Rosa Pink Nature®

(INTernatro) Interplant (1998)

Apricot-colored buds open to reveal single, cup-shaped flowers of three inches wide, which have a fresh rose perfume. Initially they are apricot-yellow with orange-red edges. The yellow later fades, leaving a creamy white heart with soft pink edges. The pollen on the coral stamens attracts many bees and other insects. The shrub grows upright with a densely foliated base. The healthy-looking leaves are first olive-green, then later glossy, medium gray-green.

@ 30h 🌺🌺🌺 ⌒⌒

Pink Meidiland®

Rosa Pink Panther®

(MEIcapinal) Meilland (1982)

Many of the large-flowered roses are prone to diseases such as mildew and black spot. Pink Panther® is one of the exceptions. The mat, bronze-tinted leaves stay healthy throughout summer and fall, during which the bush blooms constantly. Particularly

Pink Nature®

during warm periods the flowers are clearly bi-colored: pink with a darker, rose-red edge. They have a beautiful form and are borne on long stems making them suitable as a cut rose.

⚘ 30h 🌺🌺🌺 ⌒⌒ ✪ ADR

Rosa Pink Pavement®

(HANbau) Baum (1991)

This is a rugosa hybrid, a descendant of the ramanas rose. The shrub grows upright, but branches well and grows equally wide as tall. It bears many healthy, medium green leaves and numerous semi-double, violet-pink flowers. They have a wonderful fragrance. In the course of summer they begin to form oranged-red hips, but the shrub continues blooming, though more modestly. The shrub is propagated through cuttings and is often used in public green areas, but it is also suitable for natural gardens. Insects visit the flowers and birds eat the hips.

@ 80h 🌺🌺🌺 ⌒⌒⌒ ✪

Pink Panther®

Rosa Pink Pirouette

(HARboul) Harkness (1998)

The low shrub sometimes disappears behind the rich trusses of light pink flowers. The flowers are semi-double, quickly open to a cup-shape that reveals a large tuft of stamens above a soft yellow blotch in the heart. The shiny, dark green leaves are borne by

Pink Pavement®

a rather irregularly spreading bush, which grows equally wide as tall.

🔲 20h ❦❦❦ ◌◌

Rosa **Pink Robin**®

(-) Lens (1992)

This is a pink flowering relative of the more well-known *Rosa* Red Robin®, also from Louis Lens. The shrub reaches between five and seven feet tall and also gets very wide, due to the sideways bending branches. Pink Robin® is of course pink, whereas Red Robin® is carmine-red with a white line. The shrub is covered with flowers that have a wonderful fragrance. The foliage is gray-green.

�",65h ❦ ◌◌◌

Rosa **Pink Robusta**®

(KORpinrob) Kordes (1986)

Though the name implies otherwise, Pink Robusta®

Pink Pirouette

is not very resistant to black spot. This is unusual as it derives from the ramanas rose (*Rosa* rugosa), which does not suffer much from rose diseases. That aside, Pink Robusta® grows vigorously to around five feet tall. The shrub grows upright with well-branching thorny stems. The flowers are semi-double and light pink with a creamy white heart and yellow stamens. They have a light, fresh fragrance.

🌠 50h ❦❦ ◌◌

Pink Robin®

Rosa **Pink Spray**®

(LENray) Lens (1980)

Both this cultivar and its white-flowering sister White Spray® (see White Spray®) retain their fresh green leaves deep into fall. During exceptionally mild winters they may even stay on the plant. In early summer the shrub is covered with pink flowers with a white eye. They are single and slightly fragrant. Cutting off the spent trusses will encour-

Pink Robusta®

age continuous blooming. Without this measure only repeat blooms will be produced. The branches grow to five feet. If they find support they grow as high, otherwise they will bend and effectively cover the ground, reaching only twenty inches tall in this case.
↔ 20h 🌺🌺 ⌒

Rosa Pink Sunsation

(KORpinka)
see *Rosa* Sommermärchen®

Rosa Pink Torch®

(INTertor) Interplant (1987)
This is quite a remarkable rose. The vertically growing branches bear rich trusses of buds. These trusses form long plumes of up to twenty inches. The one-and-a-half-inch flowers have a very pure form. They are single, with round, bright pink petals and a golden heart of pollen. Insects are frequent visitors, al-

Pink Spray®

though the flowers are scarcely fragrant. The healthy leaves are a glossy dark green.
◍ 40–60h 🌺🌺🌺 ⌒ ✜

Rosa Pink Traumland®

(TANipilanmau) Tantau (1996)
A beautiful floribunda rose that blooms in extremely rich trusses. The bright pink, full flowers are cup-shaped and once fully open reveal their heart. The red-tinged stems branch profusely and hang gracefully, producing a wide bush that can be used as a low shrub and cover the ground quite well. The

Pink Torch®

color of the healthy, shiny, light green leaves combine well with the flowers and stems.
�✿ 30h 🌺🌺🌺 ⌒

Rosa Pink™ Hit®

(POUltipe) Poulsen (1996)
This is a beautiful floribunda rose, but then a smaller version. The full flowers have a silvery pink color that contrasts well with the glossy, dark green leaves. Wonderful for a large flower pot or box, but also good for low bedding and the front of a border.
▦ 20h 🌺🌺🌺 ⌒

Pink Traumland®

236

Rosa **Piroschka**®

(TANpika) Tantau (1972)

The fresh-looking pink flowers have an intense rose perfume. They are semi-double and retain their attractive form for a long time, also during rainy periods. The blooms last the whole summer and fall. The healthy, dark green leaves are borne by a well-branching, wide spreading bush.

⚘ 30h ❦❦❦ ☁☁☁

Rosa **Play Rose**®

(MEInoiral) Meilland (1989)

A very healthy ADR-awarded rose with glossy, medi-

Pink™ Hit®

Piroschka®

um green leaves. The bush reaches thirty to forty inches tall and produces rich blooms throughout the summer. The full flowers, which are often so per-

fectly formed that they look artificial, have a light but pleasant and very fresh rose perfume. Play Rose® is suitable for bedding as well as mixed borders.

✿✿35h ❦❦❦ ☁☁ ✚ ADR

Rosa **Playtime**

(KORpeahn)

see Rosa Roselina®

Rosa **Pleine de Grâce**®

(LENgra) Lens (1984)

In June this enormous shrub is covered with white, single flowers of over an inch wide. They develop from cream-colored buds that are so perfectly arranged along the branches, that the wonderfully fragrant flowers bloom in a continuous line along the branches. Insects visit the yellow pollen. After pollination the flowers develop into orange-red hips in the fall: so twice per

Play Rose®

year the plant is a pretty sight. Pleine de Grâce® reaches eighty inches tall and at least as wide; when supported the rose can reach around thirteen feet tall.

◍ 80h ❦ ☁☁☁ ✚

Rosa **Poker**

(MEIpazdia) Meilland (1998)

Do not confuse this creamy white to light yellow rose with the pink rose Poker® (HAVaps) from breeder Ted Verschuren. The rose pictured here is from the Meilland family and is included in the 'Parfums de Provence' series, due to its intense, spicy rose perfume. The flowers are creamy white, sometimes with a slight hint of light yellow, and have a pink tinge in the heart. With its long stems, Poker is suitable a cut rose.

⚘ 30h ❦❦❦ ☁☁☁

Pleine de Grâce®

Poker®

Rosa Poker®

(HAVaps) Verschuren (1984)

Large, full flowers crowd the ends of the sturdy, upright stems. The flower color is an intense, yet light pink. In part because of its wonderful fragrance, this Poker® is very suitable as cut rose. The shrub has vigorous upright growth and bears large, dark green foliage. Flowers appear throughout summer and fall. Poker® is an excellent rose, which cleans well even with rainy weather. Do not confuse this rose with that of the same name from Meilland.

�֍֍ 35h ♀♀♀ ☁☁☁ TOP

Rosa Polarstern®

(TANlarpost) Tantau (1982)

The beautifully formed, full flowers appear throughout the summer and fall on the robust, upright bushes. The flowers are white with lemon tinges. Excellent as cut rose due to the long, straight stems and light but pleasant fragrance. Outside they appear to be resistant to bad weather. They clean well. The bush bears plenty of mat, dark green leaves, and fill a bed well when planted next to one another. Due to its vigorous growth Polarstern® is also suitable for combination with perennials of medium height. In 1985 this variety was 'Rose of the Year' in Great Britain.

֍ 40h ♀♀♀ ☁☁

Poker

Rosa Polka®91

(MEItosier) Meilland (1996)

Although Polka®91 is a climbing rose, you can also plant it against a pillar where it will grow no taller than this support. The flowers appear in trusses and are the currently popular apricot color with a hint of salmon. They have a light, but pleasant fragrance.

Polarstern®

Rosa Polar Star

(TANlarpost)

see *Rosa* Polarstern®

This climber has vigorous but not wild growth, and has healthy, glossy, medium green leaves.
🌿 50–100h 🌹🌹🌹 ☁☁

Rosa Ponderosa

(KORedan)
see *Rosa* Blühwunder®

Rosa Porcelain

(KORflüg)
see *Rosa* Flamingo®

Rosa Portmeirion

(AUSguard) Austin (1999)
Many English roses grow rather tall and wide, and as shrub roses are particularly suitable for the back of a border or to give color to a group of bushes. For smaller gardens and the fronts of borders David

Polka®91

Austin Roses is now breeding lower English roses, such as Portmeirion. This reaches less than forty inches tall and wide, and branches profusely widthways. Throughout the summer trusses appear with full, bright pink flowers. The flowers have a shallow cup-shape, are approximately three inches wide, and have a delicious old rose perfume.
🌹GB 35h 🌹🌹🌹 ☁☁☁☁

Rosa Postillion®

(KORtionza) Kordes (1998)
'Warm yellow with a hint of apricot' is the best way to describe the flower color of this robust shrub rose. The full flowers develop from copper-red buds. They

Portmeirion

have a delicious fragrance and have a loose look, making this rose suitable for a romantic garden style. The shrub is strong and the glossy, dark green leaves are hardly ever affected by diseases. The rose has won silver medals at tests in Kortrijk (Belgium) and Madrid.
☀ 60h 🌹🌹🌹 ☁☁☁ ✚ ADR

Rosa Preference

(MEImagarmic)
see *Rosa* Princesse de Monaco®

Rosa Prestige de Lyon

(MEInimo)
see *Rosa* Regatta®

Rosa Pride of England

(HARencore) Harkness (1998)
With its vertical shoots of around five feet long Pride of England can hardly be missed. Also the full, vel-

Postillion®

vety red flowers with a width of five inches are an impressive sight. They unfold from dark red buds, which initially appear almost black. The very full flowers have a perfect star shape and open up slowly, thereby preserving the splendid form well. The color also remains regardless of the weather. There is hardly any fragrance. Pride of England is a beautiful, healthy-looking, high bush with dense foliage. The leaves begin light green and change to mat dark green with age.

✱ 50h ♀♀♀ ◌ ✚

Rosa Prima

(HARwanted)
see *Rosa* Many Happy Returns

Rosa Primaballerina®

(-) Tantau (1957)
The full flowers are an attractive dark pink with a silvery haze. They have a very pleasant fragrance, and are borne on sturdy stems above the equally decorative, dark green foliage. The healthy bush branches well and grows vigorously.

✱ 30h ♀♀♀ ◌◌◌

Rosa Prince Meillandina®

(MElrutral) Meilland (1988)
Prince Meillandina® is a true miniature of approximately fifteen inches tall and therefore highly suitable

Pride of England

for small gardens and for pots and flower boxes. The deep to bright red flowers are relatively wide (up to two inches). They have no fragrance, but bloom

throughout the summer. The small bushes branch attractively and bear mat dark green leaves.

⊞ 15h ♀♀♀ ◌

Rosa Prince Sunblaze

(MElrutral)
see *Rosa* Prince Meillandina®

Primaballerina®

Rosa Princess Alice

(HARtanna) Harkness (1985)
The trusses with yellow flowers bloom throughout the summer and fall on long stems. They are raised some forty inches above the ground, so you can also cut them off for display in a vase. The full flowers are initially pompon-shaped, particularly due to the

Prince Meillandina®

wavy edge of the petals. They later open out cup-shaped, revealing the red stamens and golden pollen. The glossy, medium green leaves cover an upright bush, which branches well and can reach thirty inches wide.

✻✻ 45h ❦❦❦ ◌◌

Rosa Princess Grace

(MEImagarmic)
see *Rosa* Princesse de Monaco®

Rosa Princess Grace Kelly

(MEImagarmic)
see *Rosa* Princesse de Monaco®

Rosa Princess of Monaco

(MEImagarmic)
see *Rosa* Princesse de Monaco®

Princess Alice

Rosa Princess of Wales

(HARdinkum) Harkness (1997)
The extremely soft creamy, apricot-colored buds develop into pure white, full flowers. On opening they reveal a remarkably small heart with golden pollen. The bush branches vigorously and has compact growth with many glossy, medium green leaves.

✻✻ 30h ❦❦❦ ◌◌

Rosa Princess Preference

(MEImagarmic)
see *Rosa* Princesse de Monaco®

Rosa Princesse de Monaco®

(MEImagarmic) Meilland (1982)
The pure creamy white with a soft pink edge suits the rose named after the film star and princess Grace Kelly well. The flowers appear practically the whole summer and fall. The flowers are very lightly fragrant and borne singly on sturdy stems, making Princesse

Princess of Wales

de Monaco® suitable as cut rose. The thirty-inch tall bush has upright growth.

✻ 30h ❦❦❦ ◌◌

Rosa Princesse Grace de Monaco

(MEImagarmic)
see *Rosa* Princesse de Monaco®

Rosa Prinsesse Alexandra™ Renaissance®

(POUldra) Poulsen (1998)
The Renaissance series from the Danish breeder

Princess de Monaco®

Rosa pteragonis 'Cantabrigiensis'

see *Rosa* 'Cantabrigiensis'

Rosa Puccini®

(-) Lens (1984)
A moschata hybrid (see also *Rosa moschata*) with strikingly upright growth. The branches reach almost thirty inches high and at the top bear very full trusses of pointed buds. They open to reveal single, pink flowers with a lighter heart. New shoots with flowers appear constantly, but you can encourage the

Pristine

Poulsen is intended to combine the good characteristics of continuous-flowering modern roses with those of the pleasantly fragrant old roses, as Austin had done with his English roses. Princess Alexandra with its full, old rose flowers and wonderful fragrance is an example of this. They bloom the whole summer on a shrub with strikingly shiny, dark green leaves. The flowers can withstand bad weather well.
⊛ 45h ❦❦❦ ◌◌◌◌

Rosa Pristine

(JACpico) Warriner (1978)
On opening, the outer petals of the flower retain the pink of the buds for only a short while. As this wonderfully formed, full flower opens up only a slight tinge of pink remains on the ivory-white flower. Due to its form and enormous size Pristine is popular as a cut rose, which has a light and pleasant fragrance. The blooms are never very rich. The deep red to very dark green foliage contrasts well. The bush has vigorous upright growth.
✻ 40h ❦❦❦ ◌◌

blooms by cutting off the spent trusses. When you stop this in August, round, red hips form in the fall, the size of marbles. A marvelous sight, as they are borne on the top of the shoots.
⊛ 30h ❦❦❦ ◌◌

Prinsesse Alexandra™ Renaissance®

Puccini®

Rosa Purple Haze®

(TANrupeza) Tantau (1998)
The purple-red flowers turn to violet with age. They are approximately two-and-a-half inches wide, single and their heart of yellow stamens contrast well with the rest of the flower. The flowers appear throughout the summer and fall in rich trusses above the very shiny, dark green foliage. The low shrub branches profusely and eventually covers the ground effectively. This variety is used a great deal in public green areas, in part due to its good resistance to rose diseases. This ground cover rose is propagated using cuttings and belongs to the Stecktii® series from Tantau.

↔ 25h 🌿🌿🌿 ⌣ ⊕

Rosa Purple Pavement

(Baum)
see *Rosa* Rotes Meer

Rosa Pussta®

(New Daily Mail) Tantau (1972)
This splendid rose can be used to turn a bed completely red. The bushes grow very vigorously, and bear dense foliage particularly at the base. They bloom long and rich with dark red, yet bright, flowers. The flowers are almost four inches wide, stay

Purple Haze®

attractive during the entire bloom and eventually drop off in their entirety: the bush therefore cleans well. Unfortunately Pussta® has hardly any fragrance. The large, wide, oval leaves are initially

a light, yellowish green, changing to mat dark green with age. They remain healthy the entire season

Pussta®

and so the old floribunda Pussta® is among the new, disease resistant assortment of breeder Tantau.

✻✻ 35h 🌿🌿🌿 ⌣ ⊕ ADR

Rosa Pyrenees

(POUlcov)
see *Rosa* White Cover™ Towne & Country®

Rosa Queen Adelaide

(MEIvildo)
see *Rosa* Yves Piaget®

Rosa Queen Elizabeth®

(-) Lammerts (1954)
This is quite rightly one of the most famous roses from the twentieth century. The bush has vigorous upright growth, whereby the flower trusses are held high on long stems. Queen Elizabeth® is therefore excellent for the background of a border. Depending on the conditions the bush can reach a height of fifty to seventy inches. The full, pink flowers appear the whole summer and fall and have a light fragrance. The dark green, leathery leaves have good resistance to rose diseases.

✻✻ 60h 🌿🌿🌿 ⌣⌣ ⊕ TOP

Rosa Queen Margrethe

(POUlskov)
see *Rosa* Dronning Margrethe™ Palace®

Queen Elizabeth®

Rosa **Queen Mother®**

(KORquermu) Kordes (1998)

The single, soft pink flowers are borne on dense trusses. They produce long and rich blooms, but scarcely have any fragrance. The yellow stamens can be easily seen in the heart of the three-inch, saucer-shaped flowers. The small leaves are fresh green, glossy and resistant to disease. The bush is low growing and produces such regular branching that it resembles a ground cover rose.

✿✿ 15h 🌹🌹🌹 ∽ ✪ ADR

Rosa **Queen Nefertiti®**

(AUSap) Austin (1988)

This English rose is slowly going out of the picture. The buds are deep red but surprisingly open to reveal cream-colored flowers of three inches wide with a soft apricot-yellow heart. They are very full and have a beautiful form, like a Hybrid Tea. The edges are pink-tinged. The flowers have a light, but fresh and fruity fragrance. Older flowers may smell unpleasant. The shrub has good regular branching

Queen Mother®

growth, producing a full shrub with many light green leaves, which turn dark green with age. All good qualifications, so why has breeder Austin taken this rose, named after an Egyptian Pharaoh, from his catalogue. The flower is actually only suitable for warm and dry climates. In wetter climates the edges of the flowers get a dirty color and the flowers clean badly.

🌹GB 35h 🌹🌹🌹 ∽∽

Rosa **Queen of Hearts**

(Lens)

see *Rosa* Dame de Coeur

Rosa **Queen of Roses**

(KORbico)

see *Rosa* Königin der Rosen®

Rosa **Queen of the Violettes**

(Millet-Malet)

see *Rosa* Reine des Violettes

Queen Nefertiti®

Rosa **Queen's™ Palace®**

(POUlelap) Poulsen (1997)

A miniature rose with the softest pale pink imaginable. The full flowers contrast well with the shiny, dark green leaves of the low bushes. Queen's™ Palace® is suitable for smaller gardens and for large pots and containers.

▣ 20h 🌹🌹🌹 ∽

Rosa Rainbow Nation

(DELstricol)
see *Rosa* Camille Pisarro®

Rosa Rainy Day®

(MACraida) McGredy (1982)
A splendid bedding rose due to its regular, upright growth and the attractive contrast between the dark green, mature leaves and the bright pink flowers. They are full, bloom cup-shaped up to four inches wide and clean very well. Unfortunately this rose is susceptible to black spot. It has a light fragrance,

Queen's™ Palace®

though fresh and fruity. Bees visit the flower as soon as it reveals its heart.
⚹ 30h 🌹🌹🌹 ⌣⌣ TOP

Rosa Raubritter®

(-) Kordes (1936)
The globular form of the small, pink flowers are quite eye-catching. Many petals overlap one another. It is primarily because of this unusual form that this old rose is still sold, as it has not much else to offer: it is once-blooming, has an uninteresting fragrance, stringy branches and leathery, medium green leaves that are susceptible to mildew. Its loose growth habit

makes it suitable for combining with perennials or as rambler.
◍ -꒰ 40–100h 🌹 ⌣⌣

Rainy Day®

Rosa Rebecca®

(TANrekta) Tantau (1970)
The striking bi-colored flowers of Rebecca® are full and have a wonderful shape. The outside of the petals are warm yellow, the inside a warm red. In 1972 the variety received the prestigious ADR award, but in recent tests in rosariums it has not been counted among the most disease-resistant large-flowered roses. In part due to its very slight fragrance and its currently unfashionable color, Rebecca® will probably disappear from the assortment. The reasonably

Raubritter®

healthy, large, medium green leaves cover a vigorously upright bush.

✿ 30h 🌱🌱🌱 � ADR

Rosa Rebell®

(KORvegata) Kordes (1996)
The full, medium-sized flowers of Rebell® are bright crimson. They are borne singly or several on one branch. Due to the upright growth habit of the bush the flowers are suitable as cut rose. Unfortunately they are only slightly fragrant. The shiny leaves are initially olive-green and later turn a dark blue-green. The bush reaches twenty-five to thirty inches tall. In 1974 Kordes introduced a rose with the same trade

Rebecca®

name, and the patent name FEYbell. This rose is no longer available but it may still be found in (rose) gardens.

✿ 30h 🌱🌱🌱 ⌑

Rebell®

Rosa Red Ballerina

(HARhero)
see *Rosa* City Livery®

Rosa Red Blanket®

(INTercel) Interplant (1981)
The single to semi-double flowers have a rare rose-red color that turns to white in the heart. In the young flowers the golden pollen provides an attractive contrast. They have no fragrance and reach almost two inches wide. The shrub blooms throughout the summer and deep into fall, and grows to forty inches tall. It is used primarily in public green areas, but does not look out of place in a large natural garden. The leaves are initially gray-green, later turning glossy, dark green.

🌐 50h 🌱🌱🌱 ⌑ ✚

Rosa Red Coat

(-) Austin (1973)
This modern shrub rose produces rich blooms of carmine-pink, single flowers throughout the summer and fall. They have a light musk fragrance.

🌐 60h 🌱🌱🌱 ⌑⌑

Red Blanket®

Rosa Red Dagmar Hastrup

(SPEruge)
see *Rosa* Red Dagmar®

Red Coat

Rosa Red Dagmar®

(SPEruge) Spek-Geers (1997)

Red Dagmar® is a rugosa hybrid that resembles *Rosa* Dagmar Hastrup, but remains much lower and the flower color is far deeper. This form of the ramanas rose, too, is used frequently in public green areas. The single, carmine-red flowers have a pleasant, mildly sweet rose perfume, which attracts bees. The flowers produce richer blooms in early summer, after which it continues blooming but moderately above the rugose leaves.

☼ 20h 🌳🌳🌳 ☁☁☁☁

Red Dagmar®

Rosa Red Decumba®

(KORmarec) Kordes (1998)

Red Decumba® is a healthy growing ground cover rose with glossy, bronze-tinged leaves and full truss-

es with bright, single flowers, containing golden pollen. The shrub, which belongs to the Stecktii® series and is propagated by cuttings, is suitable for public green areas as well as private gardens. It reaches thirty inches wide.

↔ 15h 🌳🌳🌳 ☁☁☁ ✚

Red Decumba®

Rosa Red Dorothy Perkins

(Walsh)
see *Rosa* Excelsa

Rosa Red Dot®

(INTermunder) Interplant (1989)

The white eyes seem to be staring at you from the heart of the bright red flowers. The conspicuous golden pollen inside is as attractive as the flower itself. They are popular with bees and other in-

Red Dot®

247

sects. New flower trusses appear throughout summer on this compact shrub with shiny, olive-green leaves.

ⓦ 40h 🌺🌺🌺 ☁

Rosa **Red Flower Rain**

(TANklesant)
see *Rosa* Santana®

Rosa **Red Friendship**

(HAVership) Verschuren (1986)
The flowers are only just over an inch wide but the shrub is completely covered by them. They are cherry-red, semi-double, have no fragrance and appear in extremely rich trusses on the ends of the long shoots. These bend under the weight, forming excellent ground cover, all the more because the branches are well covered in healthy-looking leaves. A leaf comprises of seven remarkably long leaflets. They are glossy, medium green.

ⓦ 35h 🌺🌺🌺 ☁

Red Friendship

Rosa **Red Haze**®

(TANzahde) Tantau (1999)
If you wish to cover a piece of ground with a bright red carpet, look no further than Red Haze®. The shiny, dark green leaves of this wide-spreading shrub is sometimes completely engulfed by the single, red flowers. The golden pollen in the heart provides contrast. Flowering continues throughout summer and fall. The rich blooms and good disease resistance

Red Haze®

make Red Haze® a popular choice for public green areas. They are supplied as a cutting.

↔ 20h 🌺🌺🌺 ☁ ✚

Rosa **Red Meidiland**®

(MEIneble) Meilland (1989)
These shrubs are ideal for an informal setting, due to their wide, overhanging growth. The leaves stay healthy for long, but are somewhat susceptible to black spot. The single, red flowers have a white eye that contains yellow stamens. They are slightly fragrant. Insects pollinate the flowers, which change into red hips. Despite this the shrubs bloom the whole summer.

ⓦ 25h 🌺🌺🌺 ☁

Red Meidiland®

Rosa **Red Meilove**®

(MEIrokad) Meilland (1999)
The semi-double flowers of this red-flowering patio rose of around twenty inches tall appear in trusses.

They are fragrantless and do not attract any insects. White streaks can sometimes be seen in the heart. The shrub grows widthways, but does not cover the ground.
🔲 20h 🌹🌹🌹 ☁

Red Meilove®

Rosa Red Nostalgie®

(TANumleh) Tantau (1996)

Round buds open to reveal very full, remarkably large, dark red flowers. They bloom wide open, yet despite this can withstand rain well. Due to the strong stems they are popular as cut rose, even though they are practically fragrantless. The shrub bears large, shiny, dark green leaves.
✳ 30h 🌹🌹🌹 ☁

Red Nostalgie®

Rosa Red Peace

(Lens)

see *Rosa* Dame de Coeur

Rosa Red Rugostar®

(MAGseed) Meilland (1995)

A typical descendant of the ramanas rose (Rosa rugosa) with vertical stems that grow to around thirty inches high and some twenty inches wide. The single flowers are cherry-red with a light, open heart and yellow stamens. They are slightly fragrant, but bloom very long for a rugosa hybrid. Suitable for hedging.
🌙 30h 🌹🌹🌹/🌹🌹 ☁ ✚

Rosa Red Sunblaze

(MEIrutral)

see *Rosa* Prince Meillandina®

Rosa Red Velvet®

(NOAre)

see *Rosa* Alcantara®

Rosa Red™ Paillette®

(POUlsint) Poulsen (1998)

Although it is usually the long-stemmed roses that are cultivated as cut roses, the Danish breeder Poulsen came out fairly recently with the Pailette series which included miniature roses that were bred as cut roses. They have rich trusses of full flowers on each stem. This rose is not suitable for outdoors.
🔲 20h 🌹🌹🌹 ☁

Red™ Paillette®

Rosa Redouté

(AUSpale) Austin (1992)

This is a sport of *Rosa* Mary Rose, which is also included in this encyclopedia. A 'sport' is a spontaneous deviation. In the case of Redouté it is only the color that differs; this is a softer shade of pink. The very full flowers develop in trusses on top of the stems. They open in a ball, eventually having a more loose form, reach over three inches wide and clean extremely well when spent. They have a strong, sweet yet fresh rose perfume. The shrub branches well and forms many mat, medium leaves, which remain healthy.

🌹GB 45h ❀❀❀ ☁☁☁ ✛

Redouté

Rosa Redwood

(POUltry)
see *Rosa* Kronborg™ Castle®

Regatta®

Rosa Regatta®

(MEInimo) Meilland (1994)
In the salmon-pink, full flowers of Regatta the yellow clearly permeates through. They have a wonderful fragrance, which won Regatta the Fragrance Prize at Geneva in 1989. The bushes have vigorous upright growth with mat, dark green leaves and few thorns. For a large-flowered rose it is relatively resistant to diseases.

✳ 30h ❀❀❀ ☁☁☁

Rosa Reikor

(KORrei)
see *Rosa* Träumerei®

Rosa Reine des Neiges

(Lambert)
see *Rosa* Frau Karl Druschki

Rosa Reine des Roses

(KORbico)
see *Rosa* Königin der Rosen®

Rosa Reine des Violettes

(-) Millet-Malet (1860)
This is a remontant rose with full carmine-red flowers, that later turn violet. They have several blooms per season and have a pleasant sweet fragrance. The shrub has practically thorn-free stems and gray-green leaves. The stems initially grow upright then bend. The entire

Reine des Violettes

bush grows around eighty inches tall and wide.
◉ 80h ♀♀ ◌◌◌◌

Reine Victoria

Rosa **Reine Victoria**

(-)Schwarz (1872)
An old Bourbon rose with cup-shaped, full, pink flowers. They have a wonderful fragrance. The main flush of blooms is in early summer, with a more modest second flush in late summer. The shrub has vigorous upright growth, but grows less tall than many other old roses. The gray-green foliage is susceptible to black spot.
◉ 40h ♀♀ ◌◌◌◌

Rosa **Relax Meidiland®**

(MEIdarwet) Meilland (1993)
Particularly the orange stamens in the salmon-pink

Relax Meidiland®

(later light pink) flowers give this rose a unique look. The semi-double flowers have a light apple fragrance. They are visited by insects and develop red hips in late summer. The shrub grows vigorously widthways up to hip height and can cover the ground. The leaves are medium green, bronze and very glossy when young. It has an average susceptibility to black spot.
◉ 30h ♀♀♀ ◌◌ TOP

Rosa **Relax Meillandecor**

(MEIdarwet)
see *Rosa* Relax Meidiland®

Rosa **Release**

(-) McGredy (1984)
A fine rose for relatively dry climates, as the flowers clean badly with rain. For the rest, a wonderful rose. The amber-colored, full flowers have an attractive shape. They eventually open out cup-shaped and then turn a light creamy yellow. The gray-green stems bear remarkably few thorns. They grow upright, but with their excellent branching they can fill a bed well widthways with very large leaves, which can reach almost five inches long and three inches wide. The young leaves are rose-red, later via olive turning glossy dark green.
✿✿ 30h ♀♀♀ ◌

Release

Rosa **Remembrance**

(HARxampton) Harkness (1992)
The full flowers are bright red. They are three inches wide and appear throughout the summer in trusses of five to seven on a bushy, dense plant with glossy, dark green leaves. Place this rose in a bed or

Remembrance

in a row as a low hedge. Flowers also appear on the sides.

✲✲ 30h ✿✿✿ ☁

Rosa Rendez-vous®

(MEIpobil) Meilland (1987)

The cherry-red, full flowers of this rose from the Parfums de Provence® series of breeder Meilland have a wonderfully fruity fragrance. Rendez-vous® won the Belfast Fragrance Prize in 1990. The upright bush reaches around thirty-five inches tall and bears bright green leaves. It is suitable as cut rose. Do not confuse this rose with the red-flowering shrub rose Rendez-vous (LUCdod).

✲ 35h ✿✿✿ ☁☁☁☁

Rendez-vous®

Rosa Repandia

(KORsami) Kordes (1982)

This rose is suitable for ground cover, though it does take some years before the carpet of glossy, dark green leaves completely closes up. The bending stems grow to ten feet in all directions. In early summer trusses of single, soft pink, lightly fragrant flowers appear. The heart is ivory-white with yellow stamens. This very healthy rose reaches twenty inches tall.

↔ 20h ✿ ☁☁ ✚ ADR

Repandia

Rosa Riberhus™ Floribunda Poulsen®

(POUlriber) Poulsen (1998)

The blooms of this floribunda rose are sometimes so rich that the bush is almost completely covered with flowers. The full flowers are almost four inches wide and a little too bright and orange to be called salmon-pink. They have a fresh and fruity fragrance. The bush is attractive and compact. The olive-green

Riberhus™ Floribunda Poulsen®

leaves are resistant to rose diseases. This excellent rose has won numerous prizes.
✿✿ 30h 🌿🌿🌿 ⌒⌒ ✛

Rosa Rita Barbera

(POUlen002)
see *Rosa* Solo Mio™ Renaissance®

Rosa Roberta

(AUSblush)
see *Rosa* Heritage®

Rosa Robusta

(KORgosa) Kordes (1979)
Plant a row of these descendants of the ramanas rose and you will have an impenetrable hedge. The shrubs grow densely upwards, with very thorny stems. They bear healthy, large, glossy, dark green leaves, forming a well-closed hedge. The flowers first appear in May with a few repeat blooms during the rest of the season. The large, single, crimson flowers can withstand bad weather well, but are only slightly fragrant. There are two other roses with the name Robusta: a pink flowering, large-flowered climber and a very full, red old Bourbon rose.
⊕ 80h 🌿🌿 ⌒ ✛ ADR

Robusta

Rosa Rock 'n' Roll

(MACfirwal) McGredy (1988)
The very rich blooms (in multiflorous trusses) make this an attractive rose for public green areas and for

Rock 'n' Roll

those who dare to have this color in their garden. The young flowers have a very striking, fluorescent orange color. The older flowers fade a great deal at the edges and from the creamy white eye. This can be clearly seen, as the semi-double flowers open cup to saucer-shaped to expose their golden pollen. The shrub has vigorous, upright growth, branches profusely and bears many olive-green (later dark green) leaves.
⊕ 30h 🌿🌿🌿 ⌒

Rosa Rody®

(TANydor) Tantau (1994)
You will seldom see a rose with so many leaves and flowers. The shrub bears full trusses of semi-double, bright raspberry-red flowers, which are two inches wide. They have hardly any fragrance. The stems bend

Rody®

under the weight and rest on the lower branches. This forms a dense bush of leaves and flowers, which in turn is covered by another layer of bending stems. The ground is completely hidden from view. Rody® is often used for public green areas due to its excellent ground cover habit and its excellent resistance to disease. Rody® is also very suitable for private gardens.
↔ 30h �]🌷🌷 ⌖ ✚

Rosa Rokoko®

(TANokor) Tantau (1987)
The very large, full flowers have a most unusual creamy white color with a pink glow. They open out wide, have the fragrance of wild roses and clearly display their heart of golden pollen. The petals are attractively arched. Such flowers are not expected on a shrub rose. The shrub reaches five feet tall. It has profuse branching, also widthways, and so needs plenty of room. The leaves are large and a glossy medium green.
🌑 50h 🌷🌷🌷 ⌖⌖⌖

Rosa Romance

(TANezamor)
see *Rosa* Romanze®

Rokoko®

Rosa Romantic Days

(MEIparnin)
see *Rosa* Honoré de Balzac

Rosa Romantic Meillandina®

(MEIdanclar) Meilland (1991)
The outer petals of this miniature rose with deep pink, full flowers fade with age. There is no appreciable fragrance. The compact bush bears glossy, dark green leaves. Very suitable for pots and flower boxes.
🌼 15h 🌷🌷🌷 ⌖

Rosa Romantic Occasion

see *Rosa* Cesar

Romantic Meillandina®

Rosa Romantic Serenade

see *Rosa* Abbaye de Cluny

Rosa Romantique Meillandina

(MEIdanclar)
see *Rosa* Romantic Meillandina®

Rosa Romanze®

(TANezamor) Tantau (1984)
Romanze® is first and foremost a vigorous upright and branching shrub, with many thorns. The bush can therefore form an impenetrable hedge. It produces rich and long-lasting blooms of semi-double, large, pink flowers that are lightly fragrant. The shiny, dark green leaves have good resistance to fungal diseases: the rose is known for its disease resistance.
🌑 /↔ 50h 🌷🌷🌷 ⌖⌖ ✚ ADR

Romanze®

Rosali® 83

out the summer and fall. The flowers are very large and full compared to the size of the bush. Once spent the petals fall off, keeping the fragrantless flowers clean. Damage caused by disease is quickly grown over; therefore a robust rose.

✺✺ 25h ♀♀♀ ⌒

Rosa Romeo Meilove

(MEIvapium) Meilland (1998)
This patio rose that grows vigorously widthways bears light pink flowers. They are semi-double and fragrantless. Six bushes per ten square feet will completely cover the ground.

▣/↔ 20h ♀♀♀ ⌒

Rosa Rosalina™

(KORpeahn)
see *Rosa* Roselina®

Rosa Rosalinde

(-) Krause (1944)
The rich trusses of full flowers are simply too much for this rose. The vertical stems bend under the weight of the full, pink flowers. The wide, round buds open to reveal attractive, cup-shaped flowers that bloom throughout the summer and fall. The slight fragrance is unpleasant. The medium green leaves are relatively small, making the bush rather sparse in foliage, particularly at the base.

✺✺ 40h ♀♀♀ ⌒

Romeo Meilove

Rosalinde

Rosa Rosali® 83

(TANilasor) Tantau (1983)
This low-growing floribunda rose is highly suitable for bedding and low hedging. The rich trusses of full pink flowers appear on the compact bush through-

Rosa Rosalita®

(-) Lens (1997)

For a moschata hybrid (see also *Rosa moschata*) Rosalita® has relatively large flowers, reaching over two inches wide. The buds are soft yellow, which can still be seen in the heart of the open flowers. The flowers eventually change to pure white, with an attractive tuft of yellow stamens and pollen. They have a light musk fragrance. The leaves with large leaflets are a browny green. The upright - then later sideways bending - bush reaches fifty to sixty inches tall.

50h

Rosalita®

Rosa Rosario®

(TANoras) Tantau (1993)

The semi-double, soft pink flowers of around three inches wide appear in full trusses on the shrub. The stems bend under the weight. The flowers have a light but pleasant rose perfume. Unfortunately, they clean badly after rain. The shrub is often planted in public green areas due to its good disease resistance and dense foliage. The leaves are glossy and attractive, turning dark green with age.

40h

Rosario®

Rosa Rosarium Glücksburg

(AUSren)

see *Rosa* Charles Rennie Mackintosh

Rosa Rosarium Uetersen®

(KORtersen) Kordes (1977)

This climbing rose can also be planted as a solitary: it then eventually forms a wide dome. The shrub bears dense glossy, medium green leaves. At the height of its blooms it is covered with full flowers of around three inches wide. The flowers are slightly fragrant, but have an attractive deep pink color, which changes to silver with age. After the main flush a second modest flush of blooms appears in late summer or fall. Hips often form in fall.

/ 60–120h

Rosarium Uetersen®

Rosa Rose Cascade®

(DELcouro) Delbard (1995)

A good rose to disguise a difference in height, for example by planting above a terrace wall or in a stone container. The bending stems bear fresh and slender green leaves. Particularly in early summer Rose Cas-

Rose Cascade®

Rosa Rose Gaujard®

(GAUmo) Gaujard (1957)

The bushes of Rose Gaujard® do not really have that much to offer. They have rather irregular growth with olive-green leaves that later turn a glossy, medium green. However, throughout summer and fall the red-tinged stems bear loose trusses of full flowers with a striking color: inside they are bright fluorescent pink, and outside a pale pink, giving a bi-colored look. They have a light, fresh and fruity fragrance with a hint of rose perfume.

✳ 35h 🌷🌷🌷 ☁☁

cade® is covered with trusses of single, pink flowers with a white eye and yellow pollen.

‹› 30h 🌷🌷🌷 ☁

Rosa Rose des Cisterciens®

(DELarle) Delbard (1998)

The ninth centennial celebration of Citeaux Abbey was the reason behind naming this rose after this order of monks, whilst this rose actually belongs to the series that breeder Delbard named after impressionist painters. The very full flowers look frivolous. The petals are scalloped and vary a great deal in color. Individual flowers on the same bush can have very diverse colors such as cream, bright pink and deeper old rose, often with yellow on the base of every petal. Rose des Cisterciens® is also available as a tree rose.

✳✳ 40h 🌷🌷🌷 ☁

Rose des Cisterciens®

Rose Gaujard®

Rosa Rose Iga

(MEIbalbika)

see *Rosa* Iga®'83 München

Rosa Rosehill

(POUlrohill)

see *Rosa* Egeskov™ Castle®

Rosa Roselina®

(KORsaku) Kordes (1992)

In a sunny site Roselina® grows no taller than forty inches; in the shade this rose can reach five feet tall. What is remarkable for a descendant of the ramanas rose is the lengthy blooms. The flowers have a mild, old rose perfume. A small part of the heart is white. The flowers are slightly fragrant, and although the stamens appear quite enticing they do not have many insect visitors. The shrub has a compact growth habit

Roselina®

and is well covered with grass-green leaves, which remain healthy.

☼ 40h–60h ❀❀❀ ☁ ✚

Rosa Rosemary Harkness

(HARrowbond) Harkness (1985)

The popular climbing rose Rosa Compassion was the parent plant of this large-flowered rose, from which it has inherited the delicious fragrance and subtle flower colors. The flowers initially appear primarily orange, later changing via apricot to a mild salmon-pink. The outer petals of the full flowers are more orange with yellow. The blooms appear in waves. The bushy rose bears many glossy, medium green leaves. It grows up to forty inches tall.

✲✲ 45h ❀❀ ☁☁☁

Rosemary Harkness

Rosa Rosenborg™ Castle®

(POUlasor) Poulsen (2000)

Extremely full trusses of pink buds develop into full, cup-shaped flowers with a very soft pink color. There is no appreciable fragrance. The flowers bloom on a low bush, which the Danish breeder included in his Castle series and is regarded by some as a low shrub rose.

✲✲ 25h ❀❀❀ ☁

Rosenborg™ Castle®

Rosa Rosenburg Riederburg

(POUldron)

see *Rosa* Schackenborg™ Castle®

Rosenprofessor Sieber®

Rosa Rosenprofessor Sieber®

(KORparesni) Kordes (1997)

This is a variety of the new generation of floribunda roses: the fresh green (later dark green) leaves remain quite healthy. Throughout the summer above the foliage bloom full flowers, which are soft pink and later turn even milder. The fragrance is not too intense but is fresh and apple-like. The bush reaches twenty-five to forty inches tall. A fine rose for bedding as well as in flower borders in combination with perennials.

�֍֍ 30h ♀♀♀ ◌◌ ✚ ADR

Rosa Rosenresli®

(KORresli) Kordes (1986)

The flowers of Rosenresli® have a striking, intense fragrance, with the wonderful traditional perfume of tea roses. They are full and deep red, but with subtle shades of carmine, salmon and apricot. They are borne singly or in small trusses. They have vigorous upright growth and hang wide, thereby forming a large shrub. Rosenresli® can also be used as a low climber. The dark green, shiny leaves have good resistance to fungal disease. Highly recommended.

֍ / ֎ 50–85h ♀♀♀ ◌◌◌◌ ✚ ADR

Rosenresli®

Rosa Rosy Carpet®

(INTercarp) Interplant (1984)

The extremely rich blooms and wide-spreading growth make this shrub very suitable for public green areas. The base is full with glossy, medium green leaves. From here the shrub sends out thorny shoots, which on the top bear trusses with thin

Rosy Carpet®

buds. Despite the length and the weight of the trusses, they remain upright. The single, carmine-pink flowers are slightly fragrant. They are just over two inches wide and have a white eye with yellow pollen in the heart.

֍ 100h ♀♀♀ ◌ TOP

Rosa Rosy Cushion®

(INTerall) Interplant (1981)

Rosy Cushion® blooms throughout summer and fall with single flowers that appear pale pink due to their practically white heart, apart from the small tuft of golden pollen. The flowers are slightly fragrant, and grow to two inches wide. The shrub has vigorous growth and bears glossy, dark green leaves. Although the variety has received awards and is intended for public green areas, it is susceptible to mildew.

֍ 150h ♀♀♀ ◌

Rosy Cushion®

259

Rosa Rotary International

(-) Leenders (unknown)

A rose with such a flower color should do well. The soft pink seems to be undecided between orange and salmon. The petals have a satin sheen. However, this large-flowered rose produces sparse blooms, cannot withstand rain and cleans badly. The rose is decreasing in popularity.

⚹ 30h ♀♀ ☁☁

Rotary International

Rosa Rote Max Graf®

(KORmax) Kordes (1980)

This is one of the numerous varieties that arose from *Rosa* x *kordessi*, a cross between *Rosa wichuriana* and *Rosa rugosa*, created by breeder Wilhelm Kordes. The flowers of Rote Max Graf® are pure red with a little white in the open heart. They are single, lightly fragrant and bloom only in early summer on wood formed the previous year. Any pruning should therefore be carried out straight after the blooms are finished. The shrub has vigorous growth with over-hanging branches; it can be used for ground cover. The foliage stays on the shrub for a long time and seems resistant to mildew but a little susceptible to black spot.

☀ / ↔ 30h ♀ ☁☁ ✛

Rote Max Graf®

Rosa Rotes Meer

(-) Baum (1986)

This is one of the healthiest and strongest roses. No wonder that it is popular in public green areas, in part due to its ease of maintenance. Its growth is the same as with an average rugosa hybrid: dense upright stems. Growth widthways is provided by suckers and branching at the top of stems during blooming. As of June, the stems bear large, semi-double, purple-red flowers. They have a wonderful sweet fragrance and attract many insects. Moderate blooms continue throughout summer, during which large orange-red hips begin to form, which provide decoration in fall together with the fall colors of the rough leaves. Rotes Meer is also suitable as tree rose.

☀ 40h ♀♀♀ ☁☁☁☁ ✛ ADR

Rotes Meer

Rosa Rotilia®

(KORvillade) Kordes (2000)

One of the latest low floribunda roses, specifically intended for bedding. The bush grows no more than twenty-five inches tall and bears semi-double, bright carmine-red flowers throughout the summer into the fall. They have a weak rose perfume. The olive-green young leaves, with a beetroot-red edge, eventually change to mat dark green.

⚹⚹ 25h ♀♀♀ ☁☁

Rotilia®

Rosa Rouge Meilland®

(MEImalyna) Meilland (1984)
The upright bush reaches over forty inches tall and is covered with large, glossy, dark green leaves. The large, full, velvety red flowers appear throughout summer and fall, but not in large numbers. Never more than three flowers are borne on the stems. They have a very light, fresh rose perfume. Despite this Rouge Meilland® is a beautiful cut rose, which stays attractive for long.
✻ 45h 🌹🌹🌹 ☁

Rouge Meilland®

Rosa Rouge Meillandecor

(MEIneble)
see *Rosa* Red Meidiland®

Rosa Roy Black™

(POUlari)
see *Rosa* Karen Blixen™ Hybrid Tea Poulsen®

Rosa Roy Castle Rose

(POUlduf)
see *Rosa* Courage™ Paramount®

Rosa Royal Bassino®

(KORfungo) Kordes (1991)
The shrub is wider than it is tall and so is also described as a ground cover rose. And if you plant a few bushes alongside one another, forty inches apart, they will indeed hide the ground from view with large, wonderfully glossy, dark green leaves and bright red, semi-double flowers. The flowers fade to rose-red with age. The petals fall off the spent flowers. This shrub therefore cleans well.
◔ /↔ 25h 🌹🌹🌹 ☁☁

Royal Bassino®

Rosa Royal Bonica®

(MEImodac) Meilland (1994)
Royal Bonica® originated as a sport of the popular shrub rose Bonica®. The flowers of the sport appear larger, retain their color better and are fuller than those of Bonica®. They are slightly fragrant, but can withstand bad weather well and appear throughout the summer and fall on the upright bushes. The mat, medium green leaves are

Royal Bonica®

borne on a vigorous shrub that can cover large areas, but can also be used in hedging.
⊕ 30h 🌹🌹🌹 ☁

Rosa Royal Dane

(POUltroi)
see *Rosa* Troika™ Hybrid Tea Poulsen®

Rosa Royal Occasion

(Tantau)
see *Rosa* Montana®

Rosa Royal Philharmonic

(HARdeed) Harkness (1997)
The full flowers open to a splendid white star form above the dark green foliage. They are not pure white, but have a pink haze, particularly in the heart. They are pleasantly fragrant, which in part contributes to their popularity as a cut rose. Royal Philharmonic is one of the stronger large-flowered roses. The leaves are quite resistant to fungal diseases.

Royal Philharmonic

This and its long-lasting blooms make this rose one of the most popular Hybrid Teas.
✴ 35h 🌹🌹🌹 ☁☁☁

Rosa Royal William

(KORzaun)
see *Rosa* Duftzauber 84®

Rosa rubiginosa

(-) botanical rose (-)
The eglantine is not so much famous for its flowers but its leaves that smell of apples. The wild rose grows throughout Europe and neighboring areas in Asia and Africa. They form a man-sized shrub, which also grows vigorously widthways and blooms in early summer with pink flowers of around one-and-a-half inches wide. These flowers, too, have an apple fragrance. In fall the shrub is decorated with orange-red hips, which are eaten in winter by birds.
⊛ 80–120h 🌹 ☁☁☁ ✚

Rosa rubiginosa

Rosa rubra

see *Rosa gallica*

Rosa rubrifolia

see *Rosa glauca*

Rosa rubus

(-) botanical rose (-)
This wild rose from West China was discovered in 1888 and was given the name blackberry rose because

Rosa rubus

it was thought that the leaves resembled that of the blackberry. The leaves are hairy. In summer single, white flowers appear with a little creamy yellow in the heart. They have a delightful musk fragrance. The shrub can grow over ten feet tall and wide, but in our gardens usually stays lower. The rose can be seen in botanical collections, but is not widely sold.

⊛ 80h ♀ ☞☞☞ ✚

Rosa Rugelda®

(KORruge) Kordes (1989)

The majority of the descendants of the ramanas rose *(Rosa rugosa)* bloom either red or pink. Rugelda® has full, practically fragrantless lemon-yellow flowers, which develop from thick, red buds. The flower petals are sometimes red on the edges. The blooms occur in bursts. The shrub grows upright up to eighty inches tall and over forty inches wide. It is therefore very suitable as hedging. For the best blooms, prune no more than a third of the length of the stem in the

Rugelda®

spring. The glossy, dark green leaves are very disease resistant.

⊛ 70h ♀♀ ☞ ✚ ADR

Rosa Rugelda® Pavement®

(KORgeru) Kordes (1998)

Rugelda® Pavement® is in every respect, but one, the same as Rosa Rugelda®: the Pavement version is propagated from a cutting and so belongs to the Stecktii® roses. They are particularly intended for use in public green areas.

⊛ 70h ♀♀ ☞ ✚

Rugelda® Pavement®

Rosa rugosa

(-) botanical rose (-)

The ramanas rose grows so well in our regions that they seem indigenous here. However, its origins are in Eastern Asia, Japan for example. That's why it is sometimes called the Japanese rose. It does not have any special soil requirements. Even in fairly poor sandy soils the very prickly, vertical stems branch

Rosa rugosa

out profusely widthways, with underground suckers. The leaves are quite rough and wrinkled. The single, carmine-red to pink flowers appear in early summer on the tops of the shoots. They are relatively large and have a good fragrance. Although the ramanas rose blooms throughout the summer, the main bloom is clearly June-July; the subsequent ones are really just a bonus. This rose has other extras to offer. It develops large, orange-red hips that are very popular with birds. Greenfinches enjoy the seeds. What's more, the leaves turn a marvelous yellow to orange fall color. The ramanas rose is the ancestor of numerous crosses that have been indicated in this encyclopedia as rugosa hybrids. Some develop better than the original, others remain lower than average, whilst others may produce better blooms. The name Carpet rose is often seen in the name of the cultivated form.

⊛/◍ 50h ❀❀❀ ❀❀❀❀ ✚

Rosa rugosa Foxi®

(UHLwa) Uhl (1989)

Although the wide, round hips appear early in the year, this cultivated strain of the ramanas rose blooms throughout the summer. The large, semi-double pink flowers are pleasantly fragrant. They display yellow pollen in the open heart. The shrubs have compact growth and four plants can very effectively cover ten square feet of ground. They are therefore very popular in public green areas, particularly because of their excellent disease-resistance.

◍ 30h ❀❀❀ ❀❀❀❀ ✚ ADR

Rosa rugosa Foxi®

Rosa rugosa Pierette®

(UHLater) Uhl (1988)

For a descendant of the ramanas rose the shrub grows with remarkably horizontal stems. They initially grow upwards but then predominantly sidewards. In summer and early fall large, semi-double, old rose-colored flowers appear amid the large, light green foliage. They have a pleasant fragrance and change into large orange-red hips. Young shoots continually produce new blooms. An excellent and extremely disease-resistant variety for public green areas and for natural gardens.

◍ 40h ❀❀❀ ❀❀❀ ✚ ADR

Rosa rugosa Pierette®

Rosa rugosa scabrosa

see *Rosa* Scabrosa

Rosa rugosa Schnee-Eule®

(UHLensch) Uhl (1989)

Due to the wide growth of this rugosa hybrid a bed can be completely hidden from view, though this is not a typical ground cover rose. The semi-double,

Rosa rugosa Schnee-Eule®

snowy white flowers appear throughout the summer on a well-branching shrub. They smell delightful. After blooming the flower petals fall before turning brown, cleaning the shrub well. Numerous large orange-red hips form already during summer.

🌑 40h 🌷🌷🌷 ∽∽∽ ✚

Rosa rugosa superba

see *Rosa* Scabrosa

Rosa Rush®

(LENmobri) Lens (1983)

Trusses with cherry-red buds open to reveal ivory-white flowers with a pink edge, resembling apple blossom. They are two-and-a-half inches wide, single, slightly fragrant and are held high above the foliage. The leaves are initially light green with red leaf stalks, later turning glossy, dark green. The profusely branching shrub bears many leaves. The rose is a descendant from, amongst others, the large-flowered rose. It is extremely popular and has a long list of awards to its name. This is in part due to its lengthy, uninterrupted blooms from June to the start of winter. The shrub is particularly suitable for larger, natural gardens and for public green areas. With hard pruning, Rush® can be planted in beds.

🌑 60h 🌷🌷🌷 ∽

Rushing Stream

belong to this group. Rushing Stream is such a rose. It is a ground cover rose with small, white, single flowers (sometimes with a tiny flush of apricot). Large numbers of flowers appear in trusses throughout summer and fall. The shrub bears light green leaves. In fall bright red hips develop.

↔ 20h 🌷🌷🌷 ∽∽

Rosa Sahara®

(TANarasah) Tantau (1996)

The full flowers have the form of a large-flowered rose (Hybrid Tea), but they appear throughout summer on a shrub rose that grows to over forty inches. The medium green leaves are red tinged, contrasting well with the golden to bronze-orange flowers.

🌑 45h 🌷🌷🌷 ∽

Rush®

Rosa Rushing Stream

(AUStream) Austin (1996)

David Austin, the renowned 'father' of the English rose, has also developed a few varieties that do not

Sahara®

Rosa Saint-Vincent®

(DELtrap) Delbard (1993)

Robust upright stems bear rich trusses of buds on their ends. The flower stems are long and weak, making the semi-double, crimson flowers hang to the side. They bloom throughout summer and fall like bouquets above the low shrub. The young shoots are mahogany-colored, later turning glossy, dark green. Despite the rather flimsy flower stems a highly recommended rose.

✿✿ 30h ♥♥♥ ☁

Saint-Vincent®

Rosa Salita®

(KORmorlet) Kordes (1987)

The slow climbing Salita® reaches almost seven feet tall. The striking, red-orange flowers are too heavy for the weak stems and hang. However, this way they can be seen better. They are medium-sized, full, practically fragrantless and appear continuously on the climber, which is seldom without flowers. The leaves are reddish and change to mat olive-green.

🌿 70h ♥♥/♥♥♥ ☁

Salita®

Rosa Samaritan

(HARverag) Harkness (1991)

Above the bushy plant, some thirty inches tall and over twenty inches wide, bloom the full flowers with sometimes up to ninety petals. They are multi-colored: orange, amber, peach to salmon. The colors blend into one another creating a soft look. Blooms start early and continue throughout summer. Samaritan has a light, pleasant fragrance.

✿ 30h ♥♥♥ ☁☁

Samaritan

Rosa Samba®

(KORcapas) Kordes (1964)

The young flowers of Samba® are predominantly golden, but red slowly begins to develop from the

Samba®

266

edges inwards, producing a bi-colored flower. They are full and slightly fragrant and are borne in trusses on the low bush, which branches well and bears glossy, blue-green leaves.
✿✿ 20h �--- ☁

Rosa Sander's White Rambler

(-) Sander&Sons (1912)

The blooms of this rambler reach their peak early July. The rose is then covered with semi-double, white flowers that have a light fruity fragrance. After a few weeks of pleasure the blooms are over. The thin, long branches can reach thirteen feet with a little help. Without support they have a creeping habit. It bears attractively formed leaves, usually with seven leaflets. They are glossy, fresh, light green and remain healthy.
🌿 120h 🌸 ☁☁ ✚

Sander's White Rambler

Rosa Sander's White

see Rosa Sander's White Rambler

Rosa Sandton Smile

(KORmetter)

see *Rosa* Trier 2000®

Rosa Santana®

(TANklesant) Tantau (1985)

Santana® is a crimson flowering climbing rose with full flowers. They are only slightly fragrant. There are many other red climbers, so what's so special

Santana®

about this one? This climber stands out due to its weather-hardiness. The flowers stay attractive even after long spells of rain. What's more, it has good branching growth, so that also the base - through training - is full with foliage (and flowers). The shiny leaves are leathery, medium green and remain healthy.
🌿 120h 🌸🌸🌸 ☁ ✚

Rosa Satellite®

(DELsatel) Delbard (1982)

The full orange-red flowers have a wide, loose form, but seem to last well as cut rose. They have a light, spicy fragrance. The moderately-growing bush bears glossy, medium green leaves.
✿ 35h 🌸🌸🌸 ☁

Satellite®

Rosa Satina®

(TANinaso) Tantau (1992)

Above a wide-growing shrub with very shiny light green leaves develop numerous semi-double flowers with a soft pink color throughout the summer and fall. The heart is yellow and the stamens are clearly visible. The flowers are very weather-hardy and clean well. They are fragrantless. An excellent rose for public green areas and for beds in natural gardens, and even in flower boxes. The shrub grows around twenty inches tall and wide. It is propagated from cuttings.

⚈ /↔ 20h ♀♀♀ ⌇ ✛

Satina®

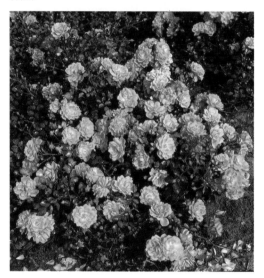

Rosa Savoy Hotel

(HARvintage) Harkness (1989)

This is one of the strongest and most popular large-flowered roses at the moment. They were introduced way back in 1989. Despite this at recent ADR tests of large-flowered roses (1995-1998) it was one of the healthiest roses. The full flowers are a bright, light pink color and are lightly fragrant. The squat buds open to reveal tapered flowers. With sufficient feed and warmth they bloom the whole summer, especially when old flowers are removed. Without pruning green hips will develop.

⚘ 35h ♀♀♀ ⌇⌇ ✛

Savoy Hotel

Rosa Saxo

(HARqueterwife)

see *Rosa* Paul Shirville

Rosa Scabrosa

(-) Harkness (1950)

The single flowers of Scabrosa do not all appear in spring and early summer. They also continue blooming through the rest of the season - though in smaller numbers. They are over four inches wide, magenta red and have a sweet fragrance of carnations: a beacon for insects. Large hips already begin to form in summer, which in late summer turn orange, then bright red and are eaten by birds. The shrub reaches over five feet tall and also has vigorous sideways growth. An excellent choice if you want a rough hedge or wish to encourage wildlife in the garden.

⚈ 70h ♀♀♀ ⌇⌇⌇⌇

Scabrosa

Rosa Scarlet Meidiland®

(MEIkrotal) Meilland (1987)

The shrub grows with vigorous shoots that bend under their own weight, resulting in a ground cover habit. The glossy, dark green leaves are a little susceptible to black spot, but remain free of mildew. The semi-double cherry-red flowers appear throughout summer and fall in multiflorous trusses. They are slightly fragrant and only open fully with warm weather.

☁ 25h 🌷🌷🌷 ☁

Scarlet Meidiland®

Rosa Scarlet Meillandecor

(MEIkrotal)
see *Rosa* Scarlet Meidiland®

Rosa Scarlet™ Hit®

(POUlmo) Poulsen (1996)

The crimson, full flowers of this miniature rose open cup-shaped. They bloom throughout summer in trusses on a low bush with glossy, medium green leaves.

▦ 15h 🌷🌷🌷 ☁

Scarlet™ Hit®

Rosa Scarlet Pavement®

(HANuhl) Uhl (1991)

Scarlet Pavement® is one of the rugosa hybrids derived from the ramanas rose. The ribs in the dark green leaves lie somewhat lower, giving a wrinkled look. The semi-double flowers are carmine-red and have a wonderful fragrance. They change in the summer into deep red hips, whilst the shrub continues blooming well. It is used primarily in public green areas due to its relatively low, bushy growth.

☁ 30h 🌷🌷🌷 ☁☁☁ ✚

Scarlet Pavement®

Rosa Scented Dawn

(MEItosier)
see *Rosa* Polka®91

Scepter'd Isle

Rosa Scepter'd Isle

(AUSland) Austin (1996

The vigorously upright growing bush develops trusses with soft pink flowers. The flowers are full, have a deep cup-shape and eventually open out to reveal the golden pollen. They have a pleasant fragrance of myrrh and old roses. The mat, gray-green leaves are large and borne on a relatively low shrub.
GB 35h 🌹🌹🌹 ☁☁☁

Rosa Schackenborg™ Castle®

(POUldron) Poulsen (1998)

Very full flowers with a salmon-pink to orange-pink color bloom in trusses above the shiny, dark green foliage. A splendid rose for small gardens. Suitable also for large pots or flower boxes. This floribunda rose is sometimes regarded as a low shrub rose.
✻✻ 25h 🌹🌹🌹 ☁

Schackenborg™ Castle®

Scharlachglut

Rosa Scharlachglut

(-) Kordes (1952)

This is still a very popular shrub rose, even though they often grow to around seven feet tall and wide. In June-July the shrub produces rich blooms of large, single, scarlet flowers. They are scentless but attract insects to their pollen. Large, orange-red hips are produced in fall. The branches a red-tinged, with gray-green leaves.
80h 🌹 ☁ ✛

Rosa Schleswig 87®

(KORtara) Kordes (1987)

Certain roses with outstanding characteristics seem for some unknown reason not to be very popular. Schleswig 87®, for example, deserves more appreciation, if only for its good disease-resistance. The bush grows upright yet branches well. It produces long-lasting rich trusses of semi-double flowers that can withstand bad weather. The flowers clean well. The flower color is intense pink, with a silvery salmon-pink, which is particularly eye-catching from a distance.
✻✻ 30h 🌹🌹🌹 ☁ ✛

Schleswig 87®

Rosa Schloss Balthasar®

(KORpalmor) Kordes (1997)

The large, salmon-pink, semi-double flowers of this floribunda rose have a light, fresh apple fragrance, and develop in mid-summer into long hips. And considering a rose blooms to produce seeds, now that this task seems complete, fewer flowers are produced. You can trick the rose by cutting off the spent flowers so that no fruit is produced. Later you can leave the hips for fall decoration and as food for the garden birds.

Schloss Balthasar®

In 2001 Schloss Balthasar® was awarded the highest distinction (Golden Rose) at the international rose show in The Hague, in the Netherlands.

�֍�֍ 25h ♀♀ ⌲ ✚

Rosa Schloss Herrenchiemsee

(POUlmax)
see *Rosa* Fredensborg™ Castle®

Rosa Schloss Linderhof

(POUltry)
see *Rosa* Kronborg™ Castle®

Rosa Schloss Mannheim®

(KORschloss) Kordes (1975)
A richly blooming floribunda rose of over twenty inches tall, which branches well and grows equally wide and tall. In summer full trusses of red-orange, semi-double flowers appear. They are saucer-shaped. As the petals become shorter nearer to the heart, the

full flowers appear globular. They have a light fragrance. The long-lasting, rich blooms, the healthy foliage and the flowers that clean well have earned the rose the ADR award.

�֍✖ 25h ♀♀♀ ⌲⌲ ✚ ADR

Rosa Schloss Neuschwanstein

(POUlreb)
see *Rosa* Marselisborg™ Castle®

Rosa Schloss Neuschwanstein™

(POUlreb)
see *Rosa* Marselisborg™ Castle®

Rosa Schnee-Eule®

(UHLensch)
see *Rosa* rugosa Schnee-Eule®

Rosa Schneeflocke®

(NOAschnee) Noack (1991)
The good characteristics of this ground cover rose are universally praised: semi-double, pure white flowers in trusses of up to twenty-five scentless flowers; each flower grows to over two inches wide; the blooms begin already in May and continue into fall. The glossy, gray-green leaves are very resistant to fungal diseases and so remain on the shrub into fall. By the second year Schneeflocke® will cover ninety per cent of the ground.

↔ 25h ♀♀♀ ⌲ ✚ ADR TOP

Schloss Mannheim®

Schneeflocke®

Rosa Schneekönigin

(Lambert)
see *Rosa* Frau Karl Druschki

Rosa Schneekönigin®

(TANigino) Tantau (1992)
The semi-double, white flowers with a yellow heart bloom in large numbers on the wide-hanging branches. A ground cover form eventually results, covered with lightly fragrant flowers. The rose is used primarily in public green areas, partly because of its excellent resistance to black spot and mildew. Schneekönigin® is also highly recommended for private gardens as it can be combined well with perennials in a garden with a natural feel.
↔ 30h 🌹🌹🌹 ⌾⌾ ✚ ADR

Schneekönigin®

Rosa Schneesturm®

(TANmurse) Tantau (1990)
With two plants per ten square feet in two years' time seventy per cent of the ground will be covered by this wide-spreading, vigorous shrub. Throughout summer and fall they produce rich trusses of creamy white flowers that sometimes change to pink. The semi-double flowers are slightly fragrant. Schneesturm® is primarily used in public green areas, but is also suitable for gardens and even pots and tubs. Although the variety is an ADR recipient and so has been tested for rose diseases, extensive tests in Dresden have shown it to be a little susceptible to black spot and even very susceptible to mildew.
↔ 30h 🌹🌹🌹 ⌾ ADR

Schneesturm®

Rosa Schneewalzer®

(TANrezlaw) Tantau (1987)
The flowers of climbing rose often have a less refined form than those of bush roses. Schneewalzer® is an exception to this. The strikingly large, full flowers have a wonderful classic form. They are pure white, with a little creamy white in the heart and have a light, sweet fragrance. They bloom throughout summer on a vigorously branching climbing rose with large, dark green leaves. It has good resistance to rose diseases.
⚲ 80–120h 🌹🌹🌹 ⌾⌾ ✚

Schneewalzer®

Rosa Schneewittchen®

(KORbin) Kordes (1958)

This is one of the legendary roses: a refined form, snow-white, light and fresh fragrance, weather-hardy, cleans well, produces rich blooms, loose growth habit and so highly suitable for romantic gardens (especially in combination with perennials), and also quite healthy. It can, however, sometimes be affected by mildew. The long stems bear few thorns and have slender, medium green, mat leaves. In 1983 Schneewittchen was proclaimed the best rose in the world. This rose can be bred as a solitary as well as a floribunda, but also – by pruning less – as a shrub rose.

✿✿/◍ 30–50h ❦❦❦ ✿✿ ✪ ADR TOP

Schneewittchen®

Rosa Schöne Berlinerin®

(TANireb) Tantau (1986)

Outside Germany this large-flowered rose is primarily sold in southern European countries, where they grow and bloom wonderfully. The soft salmon-pink flowers look like candy. They usually bloom singly above the glossy, medium green leaves. Although the flowers are lightly fragrant they are suitable as cut roses.

✿ 30h ❦❦❦ ✿✿

Schöne Berlinerin®

Rosa Schubert

(LENmor) Lens (1984)

This is a fine, low-growing moschata hybrid (see also *Rosa moschata*). On the top of the shoots bloom rich trusses of cup-shaped, single flowers. The edge is carmine red and the heart is white. The yellow pollen quickly turns brown, whilst the flowers remain for long on the shrub. The shrub grows upright and bears long, dark green, rough-looking leaflets.

◍ 30h ❦❦❦ ✿✿

Schubert

Rosa Schwarze Madonna®

(KORschwama) Kordes (1992)

Schwarze Madonna® is a perfectly formed, full, large-flowered rose. The velvety, deep red color contrasts wonderfully with the shiny grass-green leaves. The young leaves are wine-red. A good cut rose, which unfortunately is only slightly fragrant. The bush grows upright and branches well.

✿ 30h ❦❦❦ ✿

Schwarze Madonna®

Rosa Schwarzwaldfeuer

(POUlharmu)
see Rosa Charming Cover™ Towne & Country®

Rosa Seagull

(-) Pritchard (1907)
Seagull is one of the most popular white ramblers due to its rich blooms, even though they do not last long. In July this rambler is covered for two to three weeks with white flowers, which are pleasantly fragrant. The single to semi-double flowers display a tuft of golden stamens in the heart. Hips later form but they have little decorative value. The leaves consist of seven to nine large, glossy, gray-green leaflets. The stipule on the base clearly shows its relationship with *Rosa multiflora* (see *Rosa multiflora*). Seagull forms long shoots with backward-pointing hooked thorns, which help the branches to reach great heights.
ᕲ 210h ♀ ◌◌◌ ✛

Seagull

Rosa Sebastien KNEIPP®

(KORpastato) Kordes (1997)
The loose growth habit of the bush goes wonderfully with the soft color of the very full, quartered flowers. They have a delicious, sweet fragrance and are borne on small open trusses. Sebastien KNEIPP® is very suitable in romantic gardens, as well as in combination with perennials. This attractive large-flowered rose is cream with soft pink, which contrasts wonderfully with the dark green, glossy leaves.
✳ 30h ♀♀♀ ◌◌◌

Sebastian KNEIPP®

Rosa Selfridges

(KORpriwa)
see Rosa Berolina®

Rosa Senator Burda®

(MEIvestal) Meilland (1988)
The wide, full, bright red flowers of Senator Burda® have an intense, apple rose perfume. This variety won the Fragrance Prize in The Hague, the Netherlands, in 1985. The flowers appear singly on sturdy stems, making it ideal as a cut rose. The plant has vigorous, bushy growth, reaching forty inches.
✳ 45h ♀♀♀ ◌◌◌

Senator Burda®

Rosa Senteur des Iles

(COCdana)
see Rosa Fulton Mackay

Rosa Senteur Royale

(TANschaubud)

see *Rosa* Duftrausch®

Rosa Sentinel

(LENblank)

see *Rosa* White Dream®

Rosa Serpent Vert

(Lens)

see *Rosa* Green Snake®

Rosa Sharifa

(AUSreef)

see *Rosa* Sharifa Asma

Rosa Sharifa Asma

(AUSreef) Austin (1989)

The very full and often quartered flowers have a sweet rose perfume. They are sometimes borne singly but more often in trusses at the end of thin stems that tend to bend. The flower stems sometimes break under the weight of the deep cup-shaped flowers. The outer petals are pale pink, the inner ones becoming a more intense pink, with a little yellow on the base. Sometimes with bright sunshine after rain the flowers do not open well, and the flower buds eventually rot. You can save them by picking them open (see 'balling' in the chapter Rose Care). The open flowers have an intense, fresh, sweet fragrance. The shrubs have vigorous growth, initially upright, but under the weight of the flowers they acquire a spreading habit. The mature leaves are dull medium green.

🌿GB 50h 🌷🌷🌷 ✿✿✿✿

Rosa Sharifa Asthma

(AUSreef)

see *Rosa* Sharifa Asma

Rosa Sharon's Love®

(-) Lens (1998)

In the large, single flowers of this continuous-flowering shrub rose the pink stamens are particularly eye-catching. The four-inch-wide flower has five wavy petals with a very soft pink color. The leaves are glossy, dark green and are borne on an upright shrub.

@ 50h 🌷🌷🌷 ✿

Sharon's Love®

Sharifa Asma

Shocking Blue®

Rosa Shocking Blue®

(KORblue) Kordes (1975)

Lilac, magenta and mauve are the colors mentioned when describing Shocking Blue®; the color is in any case remarkable. They are semi-double and unfold spiral-like. They have an intense fragrance and are suitable as cut rose. Cut off old flowers to encourage further blooms. It has bushy growth, reaching around forty inches tall and has large, dark green, shiny leaves.
✳ 30h 🌹🌹 ☁☁☁

Rosa Shogun®

(TANugosh) Tantau (1999)

Breeder Tantau specializes in creating strong rose varieties, which seem resistant to fungal diseases. This is one of the new climbing roses. The attractively formed, full flowers can withstand bad weather. This vigorous climber is not adversely affected by any disease damage. The carmine-pink flower color may take some getting used to.
🏵 120–160h 🌹🌹🌹 ☁☁ ✪

Shogun®

Rosa Showbiz

(TANweieke)
see *Rosa* Ingrid Weibull®

Rosa Sibelius®

(-) Lens (1984)
Sibelius® is a moschata hybrid (see also *Rosa moschata*) with flowers that very much resemble

those of the rambler *Rosa* Veilchenblau. They are lavender-colored with dabs of white, and are semi-double. However, in this case they are in full trusses on a shrub of no more than forty inches tall, which has a spreading growth habit. The leaves are somewhat ribbed and dark green.
🌐 35h 🌹🌹🌹 ☁☁

Sibelius®

Rosa Silver Anniversary

(POUlari)
see *Rosa* Karen Blixen™ Hybrid Tea Poulsen®

Rosa Silver Jubilee

(-) Cocker (1978)
The Scottish breeder Cocker introduced this large-flowered rose some time ago now.

Silver Jubilee

It is, however, still very popular. In its time the rose won a whole catalogue of important prizes and distinctions. The full flowers, which can reach some five inches wide, have a wonderful form. They display various pink hues, and are lightly fragrant and suitable as cut rose. The plant has bushy growth, branches well and has many glossy, dark green leaves.
✲ 45h ✿✿✿ ☁☁

Rosa Silver Queen

(INTerway)
see *Rosa* Milky Way®

Rosa Silver River®

(-) Lens (1989)
Stems grow diagonally upwards from the heart of this shrub. It bears relatively large leaves with a maximum of seven dark green, glossy leaflets on red leaf stalks. At the end of the stems are rich trusses of ivory-white flowers a little under two inches wide. They are single, and in addition to a pink sheen they have golden pollen that is feasted upon by many insects. Silver River® has a very light, fresh fragrance. The stems are around thirty inches long, but the shrub reaches no taller than twenty inches as the stems bend and cover the ground.
↔ 20h ✿✿✿ ☁☁ TOP

Silver River®

Rosa Sissi

(TANnacht)
see *Rosa* Mainzer Fastnacht

Rosa Smarty®

(INTersmart) Interplant (1977)
Very thorny stems grow upwards but eventually bend under the weight of the very full flower trusses. As these stems branch, a shrub of over forty inches tall and wide is produced. The single flowers of over two inches wide are initially soft pink, later fading to almost white. The heart reveals an attractive tuft of golden pollen. The flowers have a pleasant, light, fruity fragrance. The dark, gray-green leaves are somewhat susceptible to black spot.
⊛ 45–60h ✿✿✿ ☁☁

Smarty®

Rosa Snow Ballet®

(Claysnow) Clayworth/Harkness (1977)
Harkness introduced this rose that was bred in New Zealand. It is suitable as a weeping tree rose, but also particularly as a low shrub rose in low beds or along the front edge of a border. The blooming stems bend a great deal and end up on the ground. The slightly fragrant white flowers, which can reach four inches wide, are sensitive to rain.

Snow Ballet®

They are full and appear throughout the summer in trusses with red stems.

⚇ 15h 🌹🌹🌹 ☁

Rosa Snow Cover™ Towne & Country®

(POUlmulti) Poulsen (1996)
Trusses with red-tinged stems bear the full white flowers. They are only about an inch wide, but appear in large numbers on the low shrub, which grows wider than its full height. The leaves are also small and a glossy dark green.

⚇ 15h 🌹🌹🌹 ☁

Snow Cover™ Towne & Country®

Rosa Snow Goose

(AUSpom) Austin (1996)
The flowers are very full with elongated white petals, looking like full giant daisies. They have a musk fragrance and bloom on a low climbing rose, which

Snow Goose

grows no more than ten feet tall, but usually remains lower. The same rose is sometimes sold under the name *Rosa* Snow Goose Climbing.

⚘ 100h 🌹🌹 ☁☁

Rosa Snow on the Heather

(KORconta)
see *Rosa* Heideschnee®

Rosa Snow Owl

(UHLensch)
see *Rosa* rugosa Schnee-Eule®

Rosa Snow Queen

(Lambert)
see *Rosa* Frau Karl Druschki

Rosa Snow Waltz

(TANrezlaw)
see *Rosa* Schneewalzer®

Rosa Snowcap

(HARfleet) Harkness (1999)
The numerous pompon-shaped flowers emerge from red-tinged buds. They are borne on a low bush that is equally wide as it is tall. The flowers are very full and creamy white with a butter-yellow heart.

▣ 20h 🌹🌹🌹 ☁

Snowcap

Rosa Snow™ Hit®

(POUlsnows) Poulsen (2000)

Snow™ Hit® is a miniature rose with full, white flowers of two inches width. They are lightly fragrant and bloom above shiny, dark green leaves. Suitable for low hedges, beds in small gardens and for pot culture.

🔲 15h 🌺🌺🌺 ☁☁

Snow™ Hit®

Rosa Snowwhite

(HARfleet)
see *Rosa* Snowcap

Rosa Snowy Summit

(DELblan)
see *Rosa* Clos Fleuri® Blanc

Rosa Sofiero™ Castle®

(POUlsak) Poulsen (2000)

Sofiero™ Castle®

This is one of the latest varieties from the Castle series, in which the Danish breeder Poulsen includes floribunda roses that remain relatively low and so are regarded by some as low shrub roses. Above the bushy, branching plant appear the full, salmon-pink, sometimes orange, flowers. They have no fragrance.

✹✹ 25h 🌺🌺🌺 ☁

Rosa Sogno Rosa

(TANipilanmau)
see *Rosa* Pink Traumland®

Rosa Solliden

(POUlmax)
see *Rosa* Fredensborg™ Castle®

Rosa Solo Mio™ Renaissance®

(POUlen002) Poulsen (2000)

A beautiful rose for the romantic garden. The full flowers have the form of old roses and a soft yellow color. They are lightly fragrant and seem particularly suitable for areas with warm and dry climates.

◉ 45h 🌺🌺🌺 ☁☁

Solo Mio™ Renaissance®

Rosa Sommerabend®

(KORmarec) Kordes (1995)

The first flush of blooms of Sommerabend® is extremely rich. This ground cover rose with its glossy, medium green and very healthy leaves is covered with a carpet of single, bright red flowers. Later in the

Sommerabend®

Sommermärchen®

season regular repeat blooms appear, leaving the shrub seldom without flowers. The stems creep approximately forty inches from the heart of the shrub in all directions and provide effective ground cover.
↔ 15h ❀❀ ✿ ✚ ADR

Rosa Sommerduft®

(TANfundermos) Tantau (1986)

The wonderfully formed flowers of this large-flowered rose have a deep red color. They are full and have a pleasant, spicy fragrance. They are borne on sturdy stems. The large leaves are also quite robust. When young they are burgundy, later glossy dark green. The foliage is quite healthy.
✳ 30h ❀❀❀ ✿✿✿

Sommerduft®

Rosa Sommermärchen®

(KORpinka) Kordes (1992)

The shrub reaches around twenty inches tall and forty inches wide. The stems branch profusely,

completely obscuring the ground from view. During the first flush of blooms in early summer the strikingly glossy, dark green leaves can only be seen here and there: they are largely covered by the full trusses of cherry-red buds and semi-double, deep pink flowers. The flowers clean well. Although Sommermärchen® is known to be resistant to rose diseases, it is a little susceptible to black spot.
✿ /↔ 20h ❀❀ ✿ TOP

Rosa Sommerwind®

(KORlanum) Kordes (1985)

The ends of the petals of Sommerwind® have ruffled lobes. The semi-double, light pink flowers of some three inches wide are grouped in loose trusses. The rich blooms are borne on a shrub of around thirty inches tall. With its wide-spreading growth and profuse branching it can be regarded as a ground cover rose. The rose has fresh, glossy leaves that are fairly resistant to mildew, but is often affected by black spot, though growth continues unaffected. The variety was produced from Rosa The Fairy, pol-

Sommerwind®

linated by the pollen of an unknown seedling. Sommerwind® produces more continuous blooms (into fall), which has won it many awards and distinctions.
⊛ /↔ 30h 🌹🌹🌹 ✿ ✚ ADR TOP

Rosa **Sonia Meilove®**

(MEIprille) Meiland (1998)

Sonia Meilove® is a compact patio rose of around twenty inches tall. The bright pink flowers are very full and scentless. The bushes are supplied in pots.
▣ 20h 🌹🌹🌹 ✿

Sonia Meilove®

Rosa **Sonnenschirm®**

(TANmirsch) Tantau (1993)

Sonnenschirm®

This ground cover rose is propagated using cuttings, and is used primarily for public green areas. It is also ideal for gardens, with its rich and long-lasting blooms of cup-shaped, full flowers, which eventually reveal their heart. The lemon-yellow flower color goes well with the shiny, medium green leaves. In the summer the full trusses have a pleasant, fresh fragrance. No wonder that this has become one of the most popular ground cover roses.
↔ 25h 🌹🌹🌹 ✿✿

Rosa **Sophia Renaissance**

(POUlen002)

see *Rosa* Solo Mio™ Renaissance®

Rosa **Sophy's Rose**

(AUSlot) Austin (1997)

The light pink, full flowers of Sophy's Rose bloom wide open rosette-shaped. They have a light tea rose fragrance and are borne on a profusely branching shrub with elongated leaves.
🌹GB 35h 🌹🌹🌹 ✿✿

Sophy's Rose

Rosa **Sorbet®**

(MEIpeluj) Meilland (1993)

The large, light salmon-pink flowers of this moderately growing climbing rose hang loosely to the side. Creamy yellow tints permeate through the flower.

Sorbet®

The wide upright plant has olive-green leaves. Sorbet® is not widely available.

🌱 60–80h 🌷🌷🌷 ☁☁

Rosa Søren Kanne™ Floribunda Poulsen®

(POUlege) Poulsen (1996)

The semi-double flowers are red-orange with subtle shades of pink. They grow to almost four inches wide and bloom in trusses on a bushy branching plant.

✲✲ 45h 🌷🌷🌷 ☁

Søren Kanne™ Floribunda Poulsen®

Rosa Sourire Rose®

(-) Lens (1996)

Sourire Rose® is a moschata hybrid (see also *Rosa moschata*) with an abundance of medium green leaves. The shrub branches well and grows upright with shoots that end in flower trusses. The semi-double flowers are two-and-a-half inches wide. They

Sourire Rose®

are initially soft pink – in perfect harmony with the golden pollen in the heart – and they have a fresh rose perfume. Older flowers fade to ivory-white.

◉ 60h 🌷🌷🌷 ☁☁

Rosa Southampton

(-) Harkness (1972)

The fact that this old floribunda is still being sold shows its class. It blooms throughout summer in trusses of semi-double flowers. The flowers look initially orange, but on closer inspection can be seen to be multi-colored, between ochre-yellow and salmon-pink. They have a pleasant fragrance and grow on an upright bush with strikingly glossy, dark green leaves.

✲✲ 45h 🌷🌷🌷 ☁☁☁

Southampton

Rosa Souvenir de Louis Amade®

(DELalac) Delbard (1998)

The full pink flowers form an open cup-shape, revealing a full tuft of golden pollen. New flower trusses appear throughout summer, particularly in regions with warm summers. There the flowers also

Souvenir de Louis Amade®

Souvenir de Rose-Marie®

have a more intense fragrance: a fresh aniseed perfume. Souvenir de Louis Amade® is also available as a tree rose.
�֍֍ 30h ❀❀❀ ☁☁

Rosa **Souvenir de Marcel Proust®**

(DELpapy) Delbard (1993)
This modern large-flowered rose has characteristics of old roses. The thin stems bend under the weight of the flowers. These flowers have a classic form: globular to cup-shaped with very many yellow petals overlapping one another. However, this does make the flower sensitive to bad weather. It is therefore best to only choose this variety if you live in a region with relatively warm, dry summers. The fresh yet sweet fragrance is also at its most intense under these weather conditions. After each flush of blooms the rose needs time to regain its strength.
✯ 35h ❀❀ ☁☁☁

Souvenir de Marcel Proust®

Rosa **Souvenier de Rose-Marie®**

(LENtrita) Lens (1998)
A moschata hybrid (see also *Rosa moschata*) with creamy white flowers. The apricot-colored buds open

up to reveal initially yellow with salmon-pink flowers. With a width of two inches, the single flowers are large for this type of rose. Souvenir de Rose-Marie® is suitable as a cut rose. The medium-sized shrub produces long-lasting blooms.
☺ 45h ❀❀❀ ☁☁

Rosa **Sparkler**

(POUlcov)
see *Rosa* White Cover™ Towne & Country®

Rosa **Sparkling Pink**

(POUleas)
see *Rosa* Easy Cover™ Towne & Country®

Rosa **Sparkling White**

(POUlcov)
see *Rosa* White Cover™ Towne & Country®

Rosa **Sparkling Yellow**

(POUlgode)
see *Rosa* Golden Cover™ Towne & Country®

Rosa **Speelwark®**

(KORwarpeel) Kordes (1999)
The large, full flowers give a bi-colored impression, with a peach to yellow heart with smudges of rose-red, which become more intense with age. They have an intense, fresh apple fragrance with a hint of vanilla. The strikingly shiny leaves are initially wine-red, changing later to dark green.

St. Cecilia

Speelwark® has an upright growth habit.
✳ 30h 🌹🌹🌹 ☁☁

ceptible to rust.
🌹GB 45h 🌹🌹🌹 ☁☁☁☁

Rosa Spellbound

(POUlrim)
see *Rosa* Flora Danica™ Paramount®

Rosa Spirit of Youth

(MElvestal)
see *Rosa* Senator Burda®

Rosa Spring Fragrance

(Kordes)
see *Rosa* Frühlingsduft

Rosa Spring Gold

(Kordes)
see *Rosa* Frühlingsgold

Rosa St. Cecilia

(AUSmit) Austin (1987)
The flowers of St. Cecila are initially globular-shaped. They later form into deep cups, in which the petals tightly overlap one another. They are a very soft, light pink color (later almost white) with a hint apricot. The flowers appear in small trusses or singly and bend at the end of their stalks. They have a striking fragrance, a penetrating sweet aroma of peardrops. The shrub shows irregular, upright growth with thin, thorny stems that bear gray-green leaves. The leaves are sus-

Rosa St. John

(HARbilbo) Harkness (1995)
The bush grows almost equally wide as tall and forms a dome shape. This makes it very suitable for

St. John

combinations with perennials in a border. Creamy white flowers bloom throughout summer above the glossy, medium green leaves. The two-inch flowers appear in large numbers, are semi-double to full and slightly fragrant.
✳✳ 45h 🌹🌹🌹 ☁

Rosa St. Swithun™

(AUSwith) Austin (1993)
The cup-shaped soft pink flowers of St. Swithun™ have a rosette form. They are very full, with curled petals in the heart. The edges of the wonderfully fragrant flowers eventually fade to white. The

St. Swithun™

flowers appear the whole summer on a bushy branching shrub. It can also be used as a low climber, then going under the name of Rosa St. Swithun Climbing. Depending on the available support and the way they are tied they reach four to seven feet tall.
🌹GB/🌿 50–100h 🌹🌹🌹 ◌◌◌◌

Rosa St. Vincent

(DELtrap)
see *Rosa* Saint-Vincent®

Rosa Stadt Eltville®

(TANelliv) Tantau (1990)
The full, bright red flowers are borne in dense trusses throughout the summer. The bush has vigorous branching growth and a wide-spreading habit, covering a bed well with glossy, medium green leaves. The leaves are initially deep red, going well with the flowers. The flowers have practically no fragrance.
✹✹ 30h 🌹🌹🌹 ◌

Stadt Eltville®

Rosa Stardust®

(INTerdust) Interplant (1993)
The red-tinged stems grow mainly widthways, creating a low, densely branched bush of around fifteen inches height. There is an abundance of glossy, dark green leaves and trusses of fragrantless, semi-double, yellow flowers of two inches wide. They fade with age. You can use this variety in many ways: for ground cover, as patio rose and even as pot rose, but then in a large pot or tub.
↔/PA 15h 🌹🌹🌹 ◌

Rosa Starlight™ Parade®

(POUlstar) Poulsen (1996)
The roses from the Parade series of the Danish breeder Poulsen can be used both inside and outside.

Stardust®

Inside they require a cool, light location to get the most out of these miniature roses. Outside they grow best in a pot, flower box or tub. The flowers are full and white; the foliage is a mat medium green.
▣ 15h 🌹🌹🌹 ◌

Starlight™ Parade®

Rosa **Stella Dorata**

(TANtern)
see *Rosa* Goldstern®

Rosa **Stella Polara**

(TANlarpost)
see *Rosa* Polarstern®

Rosa **Stretch Johnson**

(MACfirwal)
see *Rosa* Rock 'n' Roll

Rosa **Sue Hipkin**

(HARzazz) Harkness (1997)
The very full flowers of this large-flowered rose are cup-shaped. Pure orange is revealed in the heart. Towards the edges they fade via apricot to yellow and then light pink. The flowers bloom singly or in small numbers on sturdy stems. They have a wonderful fragrance.
✳ 45h ♀♀♀ ◌◌

Rosa **Suffolk**

(KORmixel)
see *Rosa* Bassino®

Sue Hipkin

Rosa **Suffolk**

(POUlgode)
see *Rosa* Golden Cover™ Towne & Country®

Rosa **Sugar Baby**®

(TANabagus) Tantau (1997)
The full, pink flowers are cup-shaped, giving a glimpse of their pollen. Though not large, the flowers have an attractive shape and their color is attention grabbing even from a distance. The rose can be difficult to combine with other flowers, and is best planted in a bed. The low bushes have dense light to olive-green foliage.
▣ 20h ♀♀♀ ◌

Rosa **Summer Dance**®

(INTerdan) Interplant (1993)
Large trusses of rose-red flowers bend under their

Sugar Baby®

own weight. The single, three-inch-wide flowers have an ivory-white eye. There the young flowers bear golden pollen, which later turns black. By that time the flowers will have lost their charm. The shrub grows upright and then wide spreading. It bears large, glossy, dark green leaves.
◉ 55h ♀♀♀ ◌

Summer Dance®

Rosa Summer Fragrance

(TANfundermos)
see *Rosa* Sommerduft®

Rosa Summer Gold

(POUlreb)
see *Rosa* Marselisborg™ Castle®

Rosa Summer Lady®

(TANydal) Tantau (1991)
Tapered buds open to reveal beautifully formed, full, light pink flowers. Though they are only slightly fragrant, they are suitable as cut rose as they keep for long on attractive, straight stems. The upright bush blooms continuously.
✽ 35h ♣♣♣ ⌒

Rosa Summer Wine

(KORizont) Kordes (1985)
An exceptional color for a climbing rose: coral-pink buds open to reveal salmon-pink flowers. The

Summer Lady®

flowers are semi-double and saucer-shaped with an open heart, clearly revealing the deep red base of the stamens. The flowers appear throughout summer, but in waves. They have a wonderful, fruity fragrance. The climber reaches heights of seven to ten feet, and so is very suitable for rose arches and pillars, as well as against walls. The color can be combined well with almost any wall color. The glossy leaves are a very dark green.
↗ 80–120h ♣♣♣ ⌒⌒⌒

Summer Wine

Rosa Summer™ Palace®

(POUlcape) Poulsen (1998)
Summer™ Palace® is a typical miniature rose with full, white flowers. They have a light fragrance and grow to around three inches wide. The leaves are a glossy, dark green. This rose is suitable for tubs, flower boxes and large pots. With sufficient feed and water the rose will bloom the whole summer.
▣ 20h ♣♣♣ ⌒⌒

Rosa Sun Cover™ Towne & Country®

(POUlurt) Poulsen (1996)
The low shrub with fine, shiny, dark green leaves bears trusses of semi-double to full flowers in a soft

Summer™ Palace®

yellow color. The flowers are two inches wide and are loosely cup-shaped. They have a light fragrance of wild roses.
◍ 15h ♣♣♣ ⌒⌒

Sun Cover™ Towne & Country®

Rosa Sunset Boulevard

(HARbabble) Harkness (1997)

This rose was awarded immediately after its introduction; not only because of the beautifully formed buds, the splendid full flowers, the subtle colors (from mild orange to salmon-pink) and the long-lasting blooms, but also because they are resistant to fungal diseases. The compact shrub has vigorous branching growth.

✻✻ 35h 🌹🌹🌹 ☁☁ ✛

Rosa Sunset Celebration™

(FRYxotic)
see *Rosa* Warm Wishes

Rosa Sunblest

(Tantau)
see *Rosa* Landora®

Rosa Sun™ Hit®

(Poulsun) Poulsen (1996)

The over two-inch-wide, cup-shaped flowers are a permanent deep golden color. They are relatively large for a low bush. You can use Sun™ Hit® as a potted plant, but they are best in a bed or at the front of a border. The strikingly shiny, dark green leaves are fairly healthy.

▣ 20h 🌹🌹🌹 ☁☁

Sunset Boulevard

Sun™ Hit®

Rosa Sunshine®

(NOAson)
see *Rosa* Celina®

Rosa Sunsprite

(KORresia)
see *Rosa* Friesia®

Rosa Suntan®

(INTerbronzi) Interplant (1990)
The colors apricot, peach and light salmon-pink can

all be found on the semi-double flowers of Suntan®. The flowers bloom throughout the summer on bushes of around fifteen inches tall and wide. The shiny, dark green leaves look fresh and stay long on this dwarf rose.

🔲 15h 🌷🌷🌷 ☁

Suntan®

Rosa Super Star®

(TANorstar) Tantau (1960)
This older modern rose has a striking coral-red color, which is eye-catching and therefore difficult to combine with other colors. It may be best to plant this ever-popular large-flowered rose as a solitary, in a bed or as a cut rose. The flowers have a mild fruity fragrance. They are borne on long, sturdy stems, making it popular as a cut rose, also because the flowers stay attractive for long. The shrub has a somewhat messy, upright growth and bears glossy, gray-green leaves. The leaves are susceptible to mildew.

⚹ 45h 🌷🌷🌷 ☁☁

Super Star®

Rosa Superba

see *Rosa* Scabrosa

Rosa Supreme Cover™ Towne & Country®

(POUlor) Poulsen (1996)
The semi-double flowers of around three inches width have a very loose form. They are scentless and primarily pink in color, but show tints of red and yellow. The trusses bloom throughout the summer on a low shrub with glossy, medium green leaves.

🌸 15h 🌷🌷🌷 ☁

Supreme Cover™ Towne & Country®

Rosa Surrey

(KORlanum)
see *Rosa* Sommerwind®

Rosa Susan Ann

(Harkness)
see *Rosa* Southampton

Rosa Swany®

(MElburenac) Meilland (1978)
A shrub rose with champion qualities: an extremely rich and long-lasting flush of blooms, extremely full, white flowers and very vigorous growth, whereby the ground is completely hidden from view by the white flowers and the healthy, glossy, bronze-tinted leaves (later dark green). The bushes grow wider than they

do tall. Swany® has good resistance to mildew and black spot.
20h

Rosa Sweet Dream

(FRYminicot) Fryer (1988)
Sweet Dream is a remarkably low-growing floribunda rose with beautiful apricot-colored flowers, which often have salmon-pink hues. The flowers are two inches wide, cup-shaped and very full. They have a light, sweet rose perfume. Although the bush has attractive dark green leaves, it often looks somewhat bare. Sweet Dream is also suitable for pots and flower boxes. This rose can easily be regarded as a patio rose as well.
15h

Sweet Dream

Rosa Sweet Juliet™

(AUSleap) Austin (1989)
It is up to you how you prune English roses. Moderate pruning produces more flowers, which remain relatively small. Harder pruning, on the other hand, leads to fewer but larger flowers. This applies particularly to the vigorously upright growing Sweet Juliet™. With this rose it is also important that you prune away the thinner branches. If they remain they will inhibit the blooms. After pruning you can enjoy in late spring the rosette-shaped, full flowers. They are soft apricot which fades particularly on the edges. They have a fresh tea rose fragrance. The blooms occur in waves. If you choose to prune moderately, plant

Sweet Juliet™

it at the back of a border, where the flowers will still rise above the other plants. The lancet-shaped leaves are bronze-green when young, later turning a fresh medium green.
GB 120h

Rosa Sweet Magic

(DICmagic) Dickson (1987)
Sweet Magic is a good choice if you love orange. The semi-double flowers seem to erupt from the bush, all the more so because of the dark green foliage. The flowers quickly open out to a cup to saucer-shape. This reveals the golden color surrounding the pollen in the heart. The flowers have

Sweet Magic

a light, spicy fragrance. The bush grows equally wide as tall and bears many healthy-looking leaves.
🏵 30h ♀♀♀ ☁☁

Rosa Sweet Revelation

(HARzazz)
see *Rosa* Sue Hipkin

Rosa Sweetheart Rose

(Pernet-Ducher)
see *Rosa* Cécile Brünner

Rosa Sympathie®

(-) Kordes (1964)
This is a vigorously growing climbing rose with full, beautifully formed, intense scarlet flowers, which can withstand bad weather. They appear throughout summer on the vigorous climber that can reach seven to thirteen feet high. The climber has the tendency to go bare on the underside. Deeper pruning can help avoid this. The flowers are borne on dense trusses and have a delicious, old-fashioned rose perfume. The leaves are dark green and fairly resistant to disease. Many regard Sympathie® as one of the best red climbing roses.
🌿 80–160h ♀♀♀ ☁☁☁ ✚ ADR

Sympathie®

Rose Taboo™

(TANelorak)
see *Rosa* Barkarole®

Rosa Tango

(MACfirwal)
see *Rosa* Rock 'n' Roll

Rosa Tapis d'Orient

(Harkness)
see *Rosa* Yesterday

Rosa Tapis Rouge

(INTerop)
see *Rosa* Eyeopener®

Rosa Tapis Volant®

(LENplat) Lens (1982)
The long, light green, thorn-free branches grow outwards from the heart of the shrub, but soon bend and cover the ground within a radius of forty inches with very fresh, light green, glossy leaves. On their underside they have hooked thorns. The light pink, single flowers appear in full trusses. Within the soft pink there is a white eye that grows larger during flowering. Eventually the blooming flower is practically white. The two-inch flowers attract hover flies in particular. They are almost scentless. Black spot and mildew hardly ever affect this ground cover rose.
↔ 20h ♀♀♀ ☁ ✚

Tapis Volant®

Rosa Tea Time®

(TANetee) Tantau (1994)

The full flowers of Tea Time® display a blend of orange and copper-yellow. They are borne singly or in small numbers on sturdy, long stems and are suitable as cut rose. They emerge cylinder-shaped from tapered buds. They are practically fragrantless. The leaves are burgundy, later turning dark green in color.

⚘ 30h ❦❦❦ ☁

Tea Time®

Rosa Teasing Georgia

(AUSbaker) Austin (1998)

It may seem unfair to compare the flowers of this English rose with an egg sunny-side up, but the resemblance is striking. The very full and often

Teasing Georgia

quartered flower has an egg yolk-yellow heart with much lighter surrounding petals that curl backwards. They have a delicious tea rose fragrance. The shrub grows vigorously to over forty inches tall, but you can also use it as a climber: with the right support and tying it can reach ten feet. It is for good reason that this rose is sold also under the name *Rosa* Teasing Georgia Climbing.

❦GB/✣ 50–120h ❦❦❦ ☁☁☁

Rosa Telluride

(POUlbut)

see *Rosa* Butterflies Cover™ Towne & Country®

Rosa Tempesta di Neve

(TANmurse)

see *Rosa* Schneesturm® (TANmurse)

Rosa Tendresse

(DELtendre)

see *Rosa* Comtesse de Segur®

Rosa Tercentenary

(TANtasch)

see *Rosa* Goldschatz®

Rosa Terra Jubilee

(-) Zary (1995)

Beautifully formed buds open to reveal equally beautiful cup-shaped flowers. They are semi-double, and have an open heart with red stamens and golden pollen. Below the petals of the young flowers are golden with further hints of apricot and soft pink.

Terra Jubilee

The older flowers, which grow to four inches wide, turn pale yellow to ivory-white. This beauty with a fresh rose perfume grows on a dense, moderately-growing bush. The young leaves are initially reddish, eventually turning a dull gray-green. They are susceptible to black spot.

✹✹ 30h ❦❦❦ ◌◌

Rosa Tess of the d'Urbervilles

(AUSmove) Austin (1998)

The carmine-red flowers open cup-shaped. They eventually form loose, full, pompon-shaped flowers. They bend under their own weight on the flower stalk, increasing the decorative effect. They are borne on a profusely branching shrub that grows equally wide as tall. They can also be grown as a low climbing rose, and are then sold under the name *Rosa* Tess of the d'Urbervilles Climbing. The large leaves are dark, gray-green and go beautifully with the flowers.

❦GB/⚲ 50–80h ❦❦❦ ◌◌

Rosa Testa Rossa

(KORdiam)

see *Rosa* Holsteinperle®

Tess of the d'Urbervilles

Rosa That's Jazz™ Courtyard®

(POUlnorm) Poulsen (1999)

The beautiful flower form of the full, red rose resem-

bles that of the classic large-flowered roses. But these lightly fragrant flowers bloom on a rambler, seven to ten feet high. The glossy leaves are medium green. The rose has a shrub-like appearance and does not become bare at the base.

⚲ 100h ❦❦❦ ◌◌

That's Jazz™ Courtyard®

Rosa The Alexandra Rose

(AUSday) Austin (1992)

Both the large, dull blue-green leaves and the long branches betray this variety's origins as alba rose. The small flowers bloom as of early summer, but not continuously. They are single, pink on the outside and soft yellow towards the middle. The heart bears a prominent tuft of stamens. They have only a light musk fragrance. The stems branch out

The Alexandra Rose

to form a tall shrub, but can also be tied to form a low rambler.

◐ / ⚶ 55–80h ❦❦ ☁☁

Rosa The Conductor

(Tantau)
see *Rosa* Dirigent®

Rosa The Cottage Rose

(AUSglisten)
see *Rosa* Cottage Rose

Rosa The Countryman®

(AUSman) Austin (1987)
The Countryman normally blooms twice, first in the summer and then again in late summer or fall. Especially if you cut off the spent flowers of the first flush of blooms, you can encourage a good repeat bloom. The pink flowers are very full and rosette-shaped, making them resemble small, full peony roses. They bloom amid and above the mat, medium green foliage and have a delicious fragrance of old roses with a hint of fruit. The shrub is bushy, profusely branching, with somewhat en-tangled branches, and often grows wider than tall.

❦GB 35h ❦❦ ☁☁☁

The Countryman®

Rosa The Dark Lady

(AUSbloom) Austin (1991)
Despite its moderate growth this shrub, with a spreading habit, produces quite a few flowers. They

The Dark Lady

are velvety carmine-red, and resemble the flowers of the tree peonies often seen in Chinese prints. On opening the very full flowers are initially tapered. They later turn rosette-shaped, with the outer petals bending backwards, producing a loose form. They have the fragrance of old roses. The leaves are a mat dark green.

❦GB 35h ❦❦❦ ☁☁

Rosa The Dove

(TANamola 85)
see *Rosa* La Paloma® 85

Rosa The Fairy

(-) Bentall (1932)
This is undoubtedly one of the most popular roses due to the dense growth of the low shrub and the overwhelming blooms of semi-double, light pink flowers. They are borne in groups among the healthy, glossy, medium green foliage. The blooms begin

The Fairy

later and occur in waves, although the plant is never without flowers. It can be used in all sorts of ways: unpruned as a low shrub rose, as ground cover and as marginal plant; with regular pruning it can be used as low shrub rose and weeping tree rose. The Fairy is very resistant to mildew and is only occasionally affected by black spot.

◔ / ▦ 30h 💮💮💮 ∽ ✚ TOP

Rosa **The Herbalist**™

(AUSsemi) Austin (1991)

The cup-shaped, semi-double flowers of the Herbalist™ have a sweet yet fruity fragrance. The pink petals loosely overlap one another and expose their lighter heart. Some apricot-yellow can be seen behind the golden pollen. The flowers bloom throughout the summer on thin stems, which still manage to stay fairly upright. The shrub branches very well and bears many leaves around the base. The young leaves are light green, later turning mat, gray-green.

💮GB 45h 💮💮💮 ∽∽∽

The Herbalist™

Rosa **The Mayflower**

(AUStilly) Austin (2001)

English roses tend to have a bad reputation when it comes to resistance to rose diseases. The varieties on the mainland of Europe are particularly susceptible to mildew, black spot and rust. That's why The Mayflower is all the more out-standing. David Austin proclaims this newcomer to be a genuine breakthrough. On the experiment field

The Mayflower

the dull green leaves proved totally unaffected. And though this rose does not produce rich blooms, the very full, pink flowers last the whole summer. They have a pleasant fragrance of old roses. The shrub has bushy growth and branches profusely.

💮GB 50h 💮💮💮 ∽∽∽ ✚

Rosa **The McCartney Rose**®

(MEIzeli) Meilland (1995)

Paul McCartney can be pleased with having this large-flowered rose named after him. During special tests by the 'Allgemeine Deutsche Rosenneuheiten-prüfung' (ADR) the full, bright pink rose scored very well. In the period 1995-1998, during the stringent tests – which are carried out in various rosariums in Germany – The McCartney Rose® was shown to have good resistance to rose diseases. The beautifully formed buds open to reveal a perfect, full Hybrid Tea rose that blooms cup-shaped and has an incredibly sweet fragrance. The bush grows upright and is fairly irregularly formed. The young

The McCartney Rose®

leaves are olive green; the mature leaves are extremely large (up to 5 x 3 inches) and mat gray-green.

✳ 35h 🌹🌹🌹 ⌒⌒⌒⌒ ✛

Rosa **The New Dawn**

(Somerset Rose Nursery)
see *Rosa* New Dawn

Rosa **The Pilgrim™**

(AUSwalker) Austin (1991)
The soft colors of English roses allow you to combine them easily with other colors. Also the soft

The Pilgrim™

yellow of the very full flowers of The Pilgrim™ go well with many other colors in the border. The very full heart of densely-packed petals is soft yellow, and the outer ones even softer, almost white. The flowers have a light vanilla fragrance, making them even more attractive as a cut rose. They are so heavy that the flower stalks bend. The bush has vigorous upright growth and is usually bred as a shrub, but can also be used a low climber if trained. The Pilgrim™ is then sold under the name *Rosa* The Pilgrim Climbing. The leaves are shiny, medium green.

🌹GB/ ✀ 50–100h 🌹🌹🌹 ⌒⌒⌒

Rosa **The Queen Elizabeth Rose**

(Lammerts)
see *Rosa* Queen Elizabeth®

Rosa **The Royal Brompton Rose**

(MEIvildo)
see *Rosa* Yves Piaget®

Rosa **The Scotsman™ Paramount®**

(POUlscots) Poulsen (2001)
The mauve of the full flowers contrasts beautifully with the shiny, dark green leaves. Breeder Poulsen included this recent variety in the Paramount series, in which he grouped together low, large-flowered roses. The flowers of the Scotsman™ grow to around four inches wide. They are lightly fragrant.

✳ 30h db2 ⌒⌒

The Scotsman™ Paramount®

Rosa **The Times Rose**

(KORpeahn)
see *Rosa* Mariandel®

Rosa **The Wife of Bath**

(AUSwife)
see *Rosa* Wife of Bath

Rosa **The World**

(DieKOR)
see *Rosa* Die Welt®

Rosa **The Wyevale Rose**

(MEIbalbika)
see *Rosa* Iga®'83 München

Rosa The Yeoman

(AUSyeo) Austin (1969)

This is one of the earlier English roses. The Yeoman does not grow vigorously enough to form new flower shoots the whole summer and is sensitive to insects. The full flowers are not very heavy, but their stems still end up bending. They open light pink from their buds and fade fairly quickly to ivory-white. They have a light and fresh fragrance. The mat, medium green leaves are borne on a very upright shrub. There are now English roses with better qualities, so that The Yeoman is really 'on its way out'.

🌻GB 60h 🌸🌸 ☁☁

The Yeoman

Rosa Thornhem

(INTerway)
see *Rosa* Milky Way®

Tintinara™

Rosa Tintinara™

(DICuptight) Dickson (1999)

The semi-double flowers do not really have a refined form, but are cheerful in color, varying from bright orange to salmon-pink with all possible shades in between. They bloom singly or in small trusses on slender stems above the light green leaves. The blooms begin rich, after which flowers appear on the bush throughout the season. They are lightly fragrant.

☀ 30h 🌸🌸🌸 ☁☁

Rosa Tivoli 150™ Hybrid Tea Poulsen®

(POULduce) Poulsen (1996)

The wide-branching low bush launches trusses and single roses on long, vertical stems, which reach over forty inches tall. The full, soft yellow flowers are globular and reach around five inches wide. They have a light, typical rose perfume. The foliage is somewhat boring: initially olive-green, later turning mat, dark green.

☀ 45h 🌸🌸🌸 ☁☁

Tivoli 150™ Hybrid Tea Poulsen®

Rosa Tivoli Gardens

(POULduce)
see *Rosa* Tivoli 150™ Hybrid Tea Poulsen®

Rosa Tojo®

(-) McGredy (1978)

Tojo® is a good bedding rose if only for its dense - foliage that fills the bed beautifully. The leaves are large, and initially reddish. They later turn via yellow-green to shiny dark green. The orange-red to crimson flowers appear in rich trusses and are

Tojo®

Topkapi™ Palace®

long-lasting.
They are full, but quickly bloom cup-shaped with the petals overlapping one another. They are slightly fragrant. The relatively low bush has a wide-spreading habit and branches well.
✸✸ 30h ♀♀♀ ⌒ TOP

Rosa Top™ Hit®

(POUltop) Poulsen (1996)
Rosa Top™ Hit® is one of the popular miniatures from the Danish breeder Poulsen. The full flowers bloom wide and cup-shaped, and reach over two inches wide. They have no fragrance. Young shoots are red wine-tinged. The leaves later turn glossy, dark green with a red hue.
▣ 15h ♀♀♀ ⌒

Top™ Hit®

Rosa Topkapi™ Palace®

(POUlthe) Poulsen (1996)
The full flowers with their deep pink color have an Eastern feel. They are named after the royal Ottoman palace in Istanbul. A beautiful miniature rose

for a large pot or flower box, or for beds in smaller gardens. It has a light perfume of wild roses.
▣ 20h ♀♀♀ ⌒⌒

Rosa Tornado®

(KORtor) Kordes (1973)
Just above the fresh green foliage develop trusses of roses throughout summer and fall. They are slightly fragrant, semi-double and bright orange-red. The low, well-branching and healthy bush cleans well; once spent the flowers completely fall apart. Excellent for bedding, margins and public green areas.
✸✸ 25h ♀♀♀ ⌒ ✚ ADR

Tornado®

Rosa Toscana

(KORstesgli)
see *Rosa* Gärtnerfreude®

298

Rosa Toulouse Lautrec®

(MEIrevolt) Meilland (1994)

These large-flowered roses have the color and fragrance of lemons. The flowers have a loose, peony-like form. They are usually borne singly on a stem, which have medium green leaves. The rose forms an attractive, compact bush. Despite its informal look, Toulouse Lautrec® is a good cut rose.

�֍ 30h ♚♚♚ ☁☁☁

Toulouse Lautrec®

Rosa Toynbee Hall

(KORwonder)
see *Rosa* Bella Rosa®

Rosa Träumerei®

(KORrei) Kordes (1974)

The beautifully formed flowers have a coral-red to salmon-pink color. They are full and appear through-

Träumerei®

out summer and fall on the profusely branching bush, from which an attractive bouquet can be cut off for the vase. The flowers have a pleasant fragrance. They clean well and are weather-hardy. The leaves have a red tinge and slowly change to dark green.

�֍✖ 30h ♚♚♚ ☁☁☁

Rosa Travemünde®

(-) Kordes (1968)

The full flowers of Travemünde® have a pronounced dark red color. They appear in rich trusses above the mat, dark green leaves. The young leaves have a copper-red tinge. The bush has profuse branching and wide-spreading growth. Due to its deep red flower color, continuous blooming and good growth, this veteran floribunda rose is still being sold, despite its lack of fragrance.

✖✖ 25h ♚♚♚ ☁ ADR

Travemünde®

Rosa Traviata®

(MEllavio) Meilland (1998)

The cup-shaped, very full, red flowers of Traviata® can reach up to four inches wide. They are usually borne singly on the ends of the shoots and are lightly fragrant. The upright bush has dark green, glossy leaves. Breeder Meilland included this rose in the Fleur Romantica® series probably due to its classic flower form and color.

✖ 25h ♚♚♚ ☁☁

Traviata®

Trier 2000®

Rosa Trevor Griffiths™

(AUSold) Austin (1994)

The semi-double flowers of Trevor Griffiths™ open flat and nonchalantly, like a true old rose. They also have the fragrance of that once forgotten group, which is now again of interest to rose enthusiasts in part thanks to the work of David Austin Sr. The heart of the flower has a warm pink color, which fades towards the edges. The shrub has profuse branching growth, wider even than it grows tall, and bears dull medium green leaves.

🌷GB 35h 🌺🌺🌺 ☁☁☁

Trevor Griffiths™

Rosa Trier 2000®

(KORmetter) Kordes (1985)

The numerous awards received in various countries bear testimony to the popularity of this

floribunda rose. In summer and fall the wide-spreading, profusely branching bush is covered with relatively large, light pink flowers. The flowers are semi-double to full, have a light sweet apple perfume, and when older reveal their heart. With rain it is best to cut off the spent flowers as they clean only moderately. The low bush is covered with medium green leaves.

✹✹ 30h 🌺🌺🌺 ☁☁ TOP

Rosa Troika™ Hybrid Tea Poulsen®

(POUltroi) Poulsen (1974)

As soon as the deep orange buds open, there emerge apricot to orange-colored flowers that open cup-shaped and reach four inches wide. The heart contains red stamens and yellow pollen. They have a delicious, typical rose perfume. The bush grows upright. The leaves change from mahogany when young via olive-green to glossy, dark green.

✺ 35h 🌺🌺🌺 ☁☁☁

Troika™

Rosa Tropicana

(TANorstar)
see *Rosa* Super Star®

Rosa Trumpeter

(MACtrum) McGredy (1977)
The oval buds open to reveal bright red flowers of around three inches wide. They are full and open out cup-shaped, with the pollen usually remaining concealed behind the numerous petals. Particularly due to the extremely rich and long-lasting blooms, Trumpeter is a highly valued bedding rose that has won many awards. Although it was developed in New Zealand, the flowers are quite weather-hardy and clean well. They are very slightly fragrant.
✲✲ 25h ✿✿✿ ☁

Trumpeter

Rosa Tryfosa

(POUltry)
see *Rosa* Kronborg™ Castle®

Rosa Turbo Meidiland®

(MEIrozrug) Meilland (1994)
This shrub has the distinctive rough foliage of the ramanas rose. Descendants of these were crossed with large-flowered roses. The result is impressive: an upright, bushy shrub with very thorny stems, bearing large fuschia-pink flowers. With bad weather the flowers cannot bear the lushness of their own form: they collapse, concealing the attractive light heart and yellow stamens. Turbo Meidiland® is highly suitable for natural gardens, particularly due to its good disease-resistance.
✲ 30h ✿✿✿ ☁ ✚

Turbo Meidiland®

Rosa Turbo Rugostar®

(MEIrozrug)
see *Rosa* Turbo Meidiland®

Rosa Turbo™

(MEIrozrug)
see *Rosa* Turbo Meidiland®

Rosa Twinkle®

(INTertwink) Interplant (1989)
The full, yellow flowers of Twinkle® are relatively large. They bloom in trusses on a dwarf of ten to fifteen inches tall, which is pruned like a shrub rose. They are often sold as a tree rose. The practically

Twinkle®

scentless flowers appear throughout summer. Do not confuse Twinkle® with the rose Twinkles, because that is a white flowering dwarf rose.

⊕ 15h ♀♀♀ ☁

Rosa Twist™ Courtyard®

(POUlstri) Poulsen (2000)

This is a further variation on a theme that we also saw with another rambler of Poulsen, Calypso™. With this recent rose Twist™ the colors are even more striking: bright red, pink, apricot and cream, combined in a single striped flowers. The fragrantless flowers bloom in trusses on a shrub-like rambler with glossy, dark green leaves.

⚘ 70h ♀♀♀ ☁

Twist™

Rosa United Nations Rose

(HARbella)
see *Rosa* Peacekeeper

Rosa Valeccia

(KOReklia)
see *Rosa* Valencia®

Rosa Valencia 89

(KOReklia)
see *Rosa* Valencia®

Rosa Valencia®

(KOReklia) Kordes (1989)

The beautifully formed copper-yellow flowers of Valencia® unfold from elongated buds. Nearly all flowers are borne singly. Although they have a wonderful sweet fragrance they are not often used as cut rose as they do not last long. The bush grows vigorously with thick wood and branches well. It bears large, medium green leaves. In 1967 Kordes introduced a large-flowered, apricot to orange-colored rose under the name 'Valencia'. This is no longer available, but you may still come across it in gardens.

⚹ 30h ♀♀♀ ☁☁☁☁

Valencia®

Valiant Heart™ Floribunda Poulsen®

Rosa Valiant Heart™ Floribunda Poulsen®

(POUlcs001) Poulsen (2000)

The intense crimson flowers are cup-shaped and semi-double. They are fragrantless and grow in trusses on a well-branching bush. The leaves go well with the color of the flowers. They are initially mahogany, later changing to glossy dark green.
❋❋ 25h 🌷🌷🌷 ☁

Rosa Veilchenblau

(-) Schmidt (1909)

This is a vigorously growing rambler with practically thorn-free shoots. It is a multiflora hybrid. The young leaves are light green, later glossy medium green. In June-July this 'rambler' blooms with rich trusses of almost fragrantless, semi-double flowers of just over one inch diameter. They have a striking color of violet with white stripes. This is a tough rose, which is also suitable for a semi-shady location, although the

Veilchenblau

blooms there would be neither rich nor long-lasting.
🍃 210h 🌷 ☁ ✚

Rosa Velveteen

(MEIsoyris)
see *Rosa* Matilda

Rosa Vent d'Eté

(KORlanum)
see *Rosa* Sommerwind®

Rosa Vercors

(HARvintage)
see *Rosa* Savoy Hotel

Rosa Veronica

(KORflüg)
see *Rosa* Flamingo®

Rosa Veronika

(KORflüg)
see *Rosa* Flamingo®

Rosa Viborg™ Castle®

(POUllug) Poulsen (2000)

This is one of the new varieties from the Castle series, in which Danish breeder Poulsen includes

Viborg™ Castle®

floribunda roses that remain relatively low and are therefore considered by some to be low shrub roses. The full, deep yellow flowers have beautifully ruffled edges. They have a light wild rose perfume.
❋❋ 25h 🌷🌷🌷 ☁☁

Rosa Victor Borge™ Hybrid Tea Poulsen®

(POUlvue) Poulsen (1996)
The apricot-colored buds open to reveal beautifully

Victor Borge™ Hybrid Tea Poulsen®

formed, full flowers with a blend of soft colors: apricot, soft orange and tinges of salmon-pink. They have a light wild rose fragrance. The leaves are initially mahogany-green, changing later to dark green.
⚹ 45h ❦❦❦ ◌◌

Rosa Victor Hugo®

(MElvestal)
see *Rosa* Senator Burda®

Rosa Victorian Spice™

(HARzola)
see *Rosa* L'Aimant

Rosa Viking

(TANydor)
see *Rosa* Rody®

Violet™ Hit®

Rosa Violet Blue

(Schmidt)
see *Rosa* Veilchenblau

Rosa Violet™ Hit®

(POUltin) Poulsen (1996)
This miniature rose, with its semi-double, bright pink flowers, can also be placed in a pot or flower box. The two-inch-wide flowers are fragrantless. The leaves are glossy and dark gray-green.
▣ 15h ❦❦❦ ◌

Rosa Violette Niestlé

(HARvintage)
see *Rosa* Savoy Hotel

Violina®

Rosa Violina®

(TANanilov) Tantau (1997)
Deep red buds open to reveal the large, cup-shaped flowers. They are very full and extremely wide, and have a beautiful soft pink color. They have a mild and typical rose perfume. Most flowers are borne singly. The leaves are medium to olive-green.
⚹ 30h ❦❦❦ ◌◌

Viridiflora

Walferdange

Rosa Viridiflora

(-) unknown (1843)

This variety originates from one of the first continuous-flowering Chinese roses, *Rosa* Old Bush. Viridiflora also blooms constantly, although many people actually think that there are no flowers on the bush. This is because they are green, with subtle rose-red stripes and spots. This rose clearly shows that petals are really no more than rosettes of apical leaves in a different color to that of the normal leaves. The flowers of Viridiflora change increasingly to wine-red with age. This makes them popular with flower arrangers as filling material for bouquets. The rose is very resistant to disease.

❀ 25h ❦❦❦ ✿ ✚

are semi-double and cup-shaped, and when fully open reveal their stamens. They have a light, sweet fruity fragrance. In the summer as well as in the fall the large shrub is covered with flowers. The bright green leaves remain healthy, making the rose very suitable for parks and natural gardens.

❀ 60h ❦❦❦ ✿✿ ✚ ADR

Rosa Walferdange

(-) Lens (1990)

This is a remarkable moschata hybrid (see also *Rosa moschata*) with full flowers. The flowers are cup-shaped, with petals that overlap one another. They are yellow at the base, but give an overall pink impression. They are borne on long shoots that bend sideways. The shrub grows quickly and blooms relatively early. The large, dark green leaves

Vogelpark Walsrode®

Waltz™ Courtyard®

Rosa Vogelpark Walsrode®

(KORlomet) Kordes (1988)

The light pink flowers of this shrub rose fade with age until they appear white from a distance. They have an attractive shine.

🌱 45h 🌹🌹🌹 ☁

Rosa Waltz™ Courtyard®

(POUlkrid) Poulsen

Rich trusses of round buds open to reveal full, creamy white flowers that contrast beautifully with the glossy, dark green leaves. The shrub is included in the Courtyard series of the Danish breeder Poulsen. Here he groups together large-flowered, continuous-flowering ramblers.

🌱 70h 🌹🌹🌹 ☁☁

Warm Wishes

Rosa Warm Wishes

(FRYxotic) Fryer (1993)

Warm Wishes looks quite impressive with its very upright growing flower stalks, which can reach up to fifty inches high. They are heavily thorned, and are thick and sturdy enough to bear the trusses of full flowers, each around four inches wide. The flowers have a fruity fragrance, and are apricot to

Waterloo®

soft orange in color, later turning a little pink in the outer most petals. They clean moderately well. However, this is a rewarding rose that has won several awards. It is suitable for borders and bedding, in part because of the abundance of large, mat, dark green leaves.

✳ 45h 🌹🌹🌹 ☁

Rosa Waterloo®

(-) Lens (1996)

This moschata hybrid (see also *Rosa moschata*) is a real treat for flower arrangers. The small, full, white flowers are in dense trusses at the end of the shoots. They contrast beautifully with the red-tinged stalks and with the dark, gray-green leaves. The shrub is excellent as a solitary due to its tidy, well-rounded form, but can also be planted in a row for hedging. By cutting off trusses for the vase, you will actually encourage the formation of new flowering shoots.

🌼 50h 🌹🌹🌹 ☁

Weisse Immensee®

Rosa Weisse Immensee®

(KORweirim) Kordes (1982)

The cherry-red buds open to reveal single flowers of just over an inch wide. They are practically white, with a hint of pink. They have a light, fresh fragrance. The main flush of blooms is in early summer – after which repeat blooms will occur – on the wood of the previous year (take care therefore with pruning). The stems can reach almost seven feet. They bend and nestle on the ground, forming a green carpet with their fresh green foliage. It is

Weisse Max Graf®

resistant to mildew but susceptible to black spot. However, this ground cover rose retains its leaves well into fall.

↔ 20h 🌹🌹 ☁☁

Rosa Weisse Max Graf®

(KORgram) Kordes (1983)

The growth habit of this shrub is very similar to that of *Rosa* Rote Max Graf®: it reaches a height of up to forty inches, though it has a ground cover habit, as the around seven-feet long branches bend under the weight of the leaves and flowers. The flowers are initially creamy white, later fading somewhat. They are single, have a fruity fragrance and attract many insects.

Weisse Wolke®

You can enjoy the blooms throughout the summer, provided that you take care with pruning as the flowers appear on the wood of the previous year.

↔ 35h 🌹🌹🌹 ☁☁ ✚

Rosa Weisse Wolke®

(KORstacha) Kordes (1993)

Although the white flowers are full, they bloom cup-shaped and clearly reveal their heart with yellow pollen. They are borne in dense trusses above the strikingly glossy and decorative, grass-green leaves. The shrub branches profusely and grows equally wide as tall. Suitable as border plant, as well as low hedge.

◍ 35h 🌹🌹🌹 ☁☁

Rosa Welwyn Garden Glory

(HARzumber) Harkness (1996)

The large flowers have a strikingly scalloped edge. They are orange in the heart. The color fades towards the outside, changing via amber and apricot to deep yellow and to sometimes a light salmon-pink on the edge. They are pleasantly fragrant and bloom singly or in small trusses on an upright bush of over forty inch-

Westerland®

es tall and more than twenty inches wide. Welwyn Garden Glory is highly recommended as cut rose.

✻ 45h 🌹🌹🌹 ☁☁☁

Rosa Westerland®

(KORwest) (KORlawe) Kordes (1969)

This is a shrub with a very variable flower color: the apricot and salmon-pink tints permeate through the basic orange color. Depending on the conditions, particular colors will the get the upper hand during a certain year. The full, wonderfully fragrant, flowers have a loose structure. They appear throughout summer and fall, but never in large numbers, on a shrub that is sometimes used as a climber. The grass-green leaves are disease-resistant.

◍ ⌁ 60h 🌺🌺🌺 ☁☁☁ ✚ ADR

Whisky®

Rosa Whisky Mac

(TANky)
see *Rosa* Whisky®

Rosa Whisky®

(TANky) Tantau (1967)

Once the full amber-colored flowers have opened to a cup-shape they reveal tints of orange and salmon-pink. The basic color remains the warm yellow of whisky that has been matured in oak. The flower form is also classic: well-formed, full flowers that emerge from orange buds. They have a delightful fragrance. The young leaves begin burgundy and later change to a glossy medium green. They appear susceptible to mildew, and in cold climates the bush has to be protected against severe frost, as the wood freezes easily.

✱ 30h 🌺🌺🌺 ☁☁☁

White Bells™ Towne & Country®

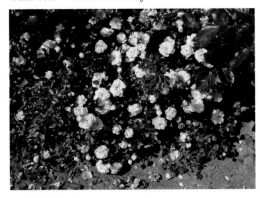

Rosa White American Beauty

(Lambert)
see *Rosa* Frau Karl Druschki

Rosa White Baby Rambler

(Lambert)
see *Rosa* Katharina Zeimet

White Cover™ Towne & Country®

Rosa White Bells™ Towne & Country®

(POUlwhite) Poulsen (1981)

The full flowers have a light yellow heart, but this color quickly fades to the extent that the name now becomes appropriate. The ground cover shrub is sometimes grouped among the miniature roses, but is really too tall for this. Trusses of small flowers

White Decumba®

White Dick Koster

bloom throughout summer. They contrast beautifully with the shiny, dark green leaves.

⚇ 45h 🌷🌷🌷 ☁

a shrub of around thirty inches wide and only ten inches tall. The shiny, dark green leaves are borne on red-tinged branches. White Decumba® belongs to the Stecktii® group of roses and is propagated through cuttings.

↔ 10h 🌷🌷🌷 ☁☁☁ ✚

Rosa White Cover™ Towne & Country®

(POUlcov) Poulsen (1991)

This is one of the most rewarding and popular low shrub roses, due to its ceaseless blooms, which continue up to frosty temperatures, as well as its excellent health and manageable size. The around two-inch-wide, semi-double flowers are cup-shaped. This reveals their heart with golden pollen, which is visited by insects. They have a light fragrance of wild roses.

⚇ 25h 🌷🌷🌷 ☁☁ ✚ TOP

White Diamond®

Rosa White Decumba®

(HANwidec) Hanekamp (1997)

This is the counterpart of Rosa Pink Decumba®. The fragrant, single flowers are pure white with a striking tuft of yellow pollen in the heart. The branches have a spreading and ground cover habit, and form

Rosa White Diamond®

(INTerdia) Interplant (1993)

The attractive, compact bush with glossy, dark green foliage launches the forty-inch flowering stems into the air. They bear trusses of round, light green buds that open out to white flowers. They are initially cup-shaped, changing later to saucer-shaped. The flowers are two-and-a-half inches

White Dream®

wide, have good resistance to bad weather and clean well. They are lightly fragrant.

✹✹ 20h 🌷🌷🌷 ☁☁

Rosa White Dick Koster

(-) Grootendorst (1946)

The green-yellow buds of this polyantha hybrid open to reveal globular flowers of over one inch width. They are white with a hint of green, and are scentless.

White Fairy

The profusely branching bush is also very suitable as tree rose. It bears many glossy, light green leaves, which turn dark green with age.
🔲 15h 🌹🌹🌹 ➷

Rosa White Dream®

(LENblank) Lens (1983)
The cream-colored buds open to reveal white, semi-double, cup-shaped flowers. They are fragrantless, but have an attractive form and remain so for long. Ideal for combining with other flowers and ornamental foliage to make a biedermeier bouquet. With a height of ten to fifteen inches this is a true miniature.
🔲 10h 🌹🌹🌹 ➷

Rosa White Fairy

(-) Sequoia Nursery (1952)
The bush forms a beautiful dome full with shiny, dark

White Fleurette®

green foliage. The twenty-inch tall dome is covered with trusses of very full, white flowers of around an inch in diameter. They are fragrantless. They sometimes revert to one of their unknown ancestors, resulting in pink flowers. However, it remains a recommended polyantha hybrid due to its extremely rich blooms and healthy foliage.
🔲 20h 🌹🌹🌹 ➷ ✚

Rosa White Fleurette®

(INTerflowi) Interplant (1987)
It is the butterfly-like, loose form of the two-inch-wide flowers that give White Fleurette® much of its charm. On opening they are creamy yellow, with sometimes some pink, but quickly turn to white. It is only slightly fragrant, but the decorative tuft of pollen in the heart of the flower is visited intensely by bees and other insects. The shrub has a loose, branching growth habit, and bears small, mat, medium green leaves. It grows equally wide as tall. Although the rose is presented as being very resis-tant to rose diseases, it appears to be very susceptible to black spot.
🌐 45h 🌹🌹🌹 ➷ TOP

White Pet

Rosa White Max Graf

(KORgram)
see *Rosa* Weisse Max Graf®

Rosa White Pavement®

(UHLensch)
see *Rosa* rugosa Schnee-Eule®

White Spray®

Rosa White Pet

(-) Henderson (1879)

One of the charms of this polyantha rose is the difference in color between the bud and flower. The buds are cherry-red and the flowers pure white. The cherry-red of the bud can still be seen on the underside of the two-inch-wide, full flower. It is fortunate that the flowers are only lightly fragrant, as the smell reminds me of Lysol. The bush reaches twenty inches tall and the upright branches bear gray-green, glossy leaves. The flowers appear throughout summer, even though White Pet originated as a sport from the once-flowering *Rosa* Félicité et Perpétue.

20h

Rosa White Spray®

(LENpaya) Lens (1980)

Do not confuse this ground cover rose with the floribunda rose of the same name from Le Grice from 1968. The White Spray® from Louis Lens is the white variant of the better known *Rosa* Pink Spray® from the same breeder. The slender, light green leaves remain on the bush until deep into fall, and with mild winters even up to spring. The single, white flowers bloom primarily in early summer, but in an exceptionally rich flush.

Cutting away the spent trusses will stimulate continued blooms. If this is not done only repeat blooms will result. The branches produce long, sidewards-growing shoots of up to five feet long. As a solitary the branches will bend and form an effective ground cover rose of over twenty inches tall. If the shoots find support they grow higher.

↔ 25h

Wife of Bath

Rosa Wife of Bath

(AUSwife) Austin (1969)

This older English rose still sells well, although breeder David Austin Sr. no longer promotes it. The full, soft pink flowers have surprisingly little fragrance for an English rose. They have a light Lysol odor. The numerous petals form a very full, cupped flower of around four inches wide, in which the golden pollen is clearly revealed in the heart. The young leaves are golden-green and change later to a dull medium green. The relatively low shrub branches well, but does not grow very vigorously and so produces only modest blooms.

GB 30h

William Lobb

William Morris

Rosa William Morris

(AUSwill) Austin (1998)

In this fairly recent English rose we can see the progress made by this group. The flower form has been perfected even further, repeat flowering can be guaranteed and the leaves have greater resistance to disease. William Morris is a clear example of this. The very full, cup-shaped flowers seem to have a very soft and sought-after color: a blend of apricot and soft rose. They also have a delightful fragrance. The shrub has vigorous upright growth, but also has branches that gracefully bend to the side. The mat, gray-green leaves seem quite resistant to disease. This rose can also be bred as a climber, whereby the branches have to be trained. In this case they are sold under the name *Rosa* William Morris Climbing.
🌷GB/🌿 50–90h 🌷🌷🌷 ☁☁☁

Rosa William Lobb

(-) Laffay (1855)

The first thing you notice about this rose are the gland-like structures on the buds and stems, which look like moss. This characteristic has given this group of roses the name moss rose. The buds open to reveal semi-double, purple flowers. The back of the petals is much lighter. The fragrant flowers appear in mid-summer. William Lobb has vigorous upright growth and does not branch much. It is therefore often planted against a rose pillar or wall with other pants in front. The stems are very thorny and covered with large, gray-green foliage.
❋ 100h 🌷 ☁☁☁

Wimi®

William Shakespeare 2000

Rosa William Shakespeare 2000

(AUSromeo) Austin (2000)

In 1987 David Austin Sr. introduced *Rosa* William Shakespeare. Three years later he replaced this rose

Rose, which is described earlier in this encyclopedia. Whilst the latter blooms pink, Winchester Cathedral produces white flowers, which is actually the only difference between the two. The shrub branches very well and forms many mat, medium green leaves, which remain healthy. The long flower stalks branch off at the top and bear red-tinged buds from which full, pure white flowers appear. They have a delightful fresh and sweet fragrance of old roses, honey and almond blossom. The flowers have a loose form and look a little untidy. The advantage is that they clean well when spent. The three-and-a-half inch flowers appear through-

with the William Shakespeare 2000. And it is best to forget the rose from 1987, as it is very susceptible to rust and mildew. However, this recent version seems quite resistant to the various rose diseases. William Shakespeare 2000 has beautifully formed, velvety, carmine-red flowers, which slowly turn purple. They also have a delightful, old-fashioned fragrance of old roses. The shrub has vigorous upright growth, branches profusely and bears large, mat, medium green leaves.
🌹GB 45h 🌹🌹🌹 ◌◌◌

Rosa Wimi®

(TANrowisa) Tantau (1983)
The bright pink of the very wide flowers blends with the silver permeating through the petals. Particularly the back of the petals have a strong silvery hue, which increasingly gets the upper hand as the cup-shaped flowers open wider. They have a delicious rose perfume. The good, constant growth helps to produce new flowers deep into fall. The attractive, regularly branching bush bears medium green leaves.
✳ 30h 🌹🌹🌹 ◌◌◌

Rosa Winchester Cathedral

(AUScat) Austin (1988)
Winchester Cathedral is a sport from *Rosa* Mary

Winschoten®

out summer and fall in large numbers. The stems are strong enough to stay upright.
🌹GB 45h 🌹🌹🌹 ◌◌◌ ➕

Rosa Windrush®

(AUSrush) Austin (1984)

Breeder David Austin Sr. no longer includes Windrush among the English roses. It does form a vigorously growing shrub, but does not bloom constantly, and considering its flower form it can best be grouped among the park and shrub roses. The flowers are single to semi-double. They are creamy white with a yellow heart and have a large tuft of stamens. They grow to almost four inches wide, have a sweet and spicy fragrance, and bloom in trusses on the ends of heavily thorned stems. The shrub branches extremely well at the base, which is also well covered in mat, dark blue-green leaves. By cutting off the spent flowers, thereby stopping the formation

Wonderland

of hips, you can stimulate a second flush of blooms.
⊚ 50h 🌹🌹 ☁☁☁

Rosa Winschoten®

(MEIafone) Meilland (2000)

Winschoten is a large-flowered rose, with full, red flowers which is still not very widely sold. It was named

Yellow Button

after the rosarium in Winschoten. Due to its wonderful fragrance, the breeder Meilland has included this rose in his Parfums de Provence® series.
✳ 30h 🌹🌹🌹 ☁☁

Rosa Wirruna White Fairy

see *Rosa* White Fairy

Rosa Wisbech Rose Fragrant Delight®

see *Rosa* Fragrant Delight®

Rosa Wonderland

(-) Dickson (1994)

The golden buds open to reveal light yellow flowers, two-and-a-half inches wide. In a short time they fade to light pink, sometimes with cherry-red parts. This bi-colored flush of blooms is quite a remarkable sight. The long shoots with full flower trusses rise above a shrub that branches well at the base and bears many shiny, dark green leaves.
⊚ 35h 🌹🌹🌹 ☁

Yellow Fairy™ Towne & Country®

Rosa Xenia

(KORpinka)
see *Rosa* Sommermärchen®

Rosa Yellow Button

(-) Austin (1975)

Yellow Button was the first yellow-flowering English rose. Considering the loose pompon flower form it is an apt name. The loose form of blooming clearly comes from its mother plant, Wife of Bath. The yellow comes from the other parent plant, the floribunda rose Chinatown, from which the low shrub has also acquired its glossy, dark green leaves. The flowers of Yellow Button are too heavy for the stems and so hang. The shrub grows equally wide as tall. Yellow Button does not grow so vigorously and is suscepti-

Yellow Fleurette®

ble to rose diseases.

♀GB 30h ♀♀ ⌒⌒

Rosa Yellow Cover

(POUlgode)
see *Rosa* Golden Cover™ Towne & Country®

Rosa Yellow Fairy™ Towne & Country®

(POUlfair) Poulsen (1989)

Semi-double, yellow flowers of two inches wide bloom in trusses on this low shrub rose.

They are only slightly fragrant, but do have an attractive open form and go well with the glossy, grass-green leaves.

☀ 25h ♀♀♀ ⌒

Yesterday

Rosa Yellow Fleurette®

(INTerwell) Interplant (1992)

This shrub from the Fleurette series of Interplant remains somewhat more compact than Fleurette® and White Fleurette®. The branches are sturdier and bear flowers of over two inches wide. The single flowers are yellow, which is an unusual color for a shrub rose. They have a light rose perfume. The shiny, olive-green leaves of this well-branching shrub remain healthy longer than those of the other Fleurettes, but are susceptible to black spot as well.

☀ 30h ♀♀♀ ⌒⌒ TOP

Yves Piaget®

Rosa Yellowstone

(POUlreb)

see *Rosa* Marselisborg™ Castle®

Rosa Yesterday

(-) Harkness (1974)

Yesterday forms a wide shrub that grows equally wide as tall, and is regarded by some as a ground cover rose. During the bloom period the slender, medium green leaves are hidden from view by the trusses of single to semi-double flowers. They are barely an inch wide, but appear in large numbers on the trusses. They have a light musk fragrance. The flower color of this polyantha rose is pink with a lighter heart. Yesterday seems strong and healthy and has received many prizes and awards. It is

Zambra®93

attractive in bedding, but is also good as a weeping tree rose or even in a pot.
@ 35h � ADR

Zéphirine Drouhin

Rosa Yves Piaget®

(MEIvildo) Meilland (1985)

The large, pink flowers have a characteristic globular form with scalloped petals. The rose is popular particularly due to its intense yet fresh lemon fragrance. It won the Bagatelle Fragrance Prize in 1992. Unfortunately, the variety is only suitable for areas with long, warm summers, in cooler and wetter climates it is disappointing.
✱ 35h 🌺🌺🌺 ◌◌◌◌

Rosa Zambra®

(MEIalfi) Meilland (1961)

This is the predecessor of *Rosa* Zambra®93. The latter is now supplied by Meilland, but is often unjustly given the earlier name. See *Rosa* Zambra®93.

Rosa Zambra®93

(MEIcurbos) Meilland (1992)

The figure 93 in the name is there for good reason. Another floribunda rose from Meilland is called Zambra® (MEIalfi) and is from 1961. The flower color, coral to salmon-pink, is almost the same, but the form of the new Zambra®93 is more tapered and the bush is less susceptible to black spot. In short, an improvement under a familiar name.
✱✱ 30h 🌺🌺🌺 ◌

Zwergkönig 78®

Rosa Zéphirine Drouhin

(-) Bizot (1868)

It's probably because you won't prick yourself on this old Bourbon rose that it is still available. The thorn-free branches of this rambler can easily be tied up in bundles. With support it can reach up to thirteen feet high. It has mat, yellow-green leaves that have a reddish tinge. On the sideshoots bloom trusses of bright pink flowers, arranged in small groups. They are semi-double, cup-shaped and have a light, fresh and sweet fragrance. Its main disadvantage is that it is very susceptible to black spot.

◉/☙ 160h ❦❦❦ ◌◌

Rosa Zonta Rose

(HARtanna)

see *Rosa* Princess Alice (HARtanna)

Rosa Zwergkönig 78®

(KORkönig) Kordes (1978)

This is the successor of the popular, carmine-red flowering miniature rose from 1957 with the name *Rosa* 'Zwergkönig'. With Zwergkönig 78® Kordes has introduced a new version to the market that grows somewhat taller. The rose is more of a patio size and has dark red flowers. The bush branches profusely, grows vigorously and is well covered in fresh green leaves. Zwergkönig 78® is also available as a tree rose.

▣ 15h ❦❦❦ ◌

5 Roses via the Internet

Although this encyclopedia features primarily the most popular roses, it may be difficult to find certain roses. After all, it is not possible for suppliers to have every rose in stock. Suppliers have to make a selection and this sometimes makes it difficult finding the rose you want to buy. The Internet provides new possibilities for finding out where you can buy a particular rose. Behind the name of each rose you will see the name of the breeder, the person who created the cultivar. Many of these breeders have their own companies, and so you can contact them directly to place an order, or you could ask the breeder as to who distributes the rose you are seeking in your country.

Below is an overview of the web sites of the rose breeders. They sometimes may only give you the address details with general information about the company. Others may give you an e-mail address with which you can contact them. But sometimes you may be able to order the roses via the Internet. If that is the case we indicate this by placing 'sales' in brackets. If there is no web site available we have simply given the telephone number of the breeder.

Beales:	www.classicroses.co.uk (information/ contact)
Cocker:	www.roses.uk.com (sales/ information/ contact)
Delbard:	www.delbard.com (sales/ information/ contact)
Fryer:	www.fryers-roses.co.uk (sales/ information/ contact)
Harkness:	www.roses.co.uk (sales/ information/ contact)
Kordes:	www.kordes-rosen.com (sales/ information/ contact)
LeGrice:	www.netl00.co.uk/pages/legrice.html (sales/ information/ contact)
Lens:	Belgium 059 267830
Meilland:	www.meilland.com (information/ contact)
Poulsen:	www.poulsenroser.dk (information/ contact)
Tantau:	www.rosen-tantau.com (sales/ information/ contact)
Verschuren:	The Netherlands 0485 313350

Contents

Photo credits

l = left, tl = top left, bl = bottom left, r = right, tr = top right, br = bottom right

Jan Spek Rozen B.V., Boskoop, the Netherlands: *65tl 95tr 101br 117r 149tr 169bl 190bl 202tr 294br 307br*
Rosen Tantau, Uetersen, Germany: 17r 40tl 40r 48bl 53r 55r 57br 58r 59l 59br 62tr 65r 77tl 79r 80bl 82br
88l 91br 105tr 107r 108l 111l 114l 131bl 140bl 142r 143bl 144l 154r 156r 162l 165tl 172bl 175l 178tl 178r
180br 188tr 191br 200tr 205l 207l 207tr 217br 219bl 220tr 221tr 229br 231tr 236br 237bl 242l 246tl 249bl
254l 255tl 255tr 264 265br 267tr 272 273bl 276l 280bl 281bl 285bl 286tr 289bl 292tl 304r 308l 312r
All other photos: Nico Vermeulen

Acknowledgements

The author and publisher would like to thank the following people and bodies for their cooperation with this publication:

David Austin Roses, Wolverhampton, England
Belle Epoque, Aalsmeer, the Netherlands
Boomkwekerij Dedemsvaart, Dedemsvaart, the Netherlands
Georges Delbard Pepinières et Roseraies, Malicome, France
Mariëtte Edelman, The Hague, the Netherlands
Groenrijk Vroom, Groningen, the Netherlands
Piet Hanekamp B.V., Scheerwolde, the Netherlands
R. Harkness & CO. Ltd, Hitchin, England
Heikie Hoeksma, Harkema, the Netherlands
Interplant B.V., Leersum, the Netherlands
Kasteeltuinen Arcen, the Netherlands
W. Kordes' Söhne, Klein Offenseth-Sparrieshoop, Germany
Boomkwekerijen Louis Lens N.V., Oudenburg, Belgium
Meilland, Le Luc en Provence, France
Moerheim Plantenwinkel, Dedemsvaart, the Netherlands
Moerheim Roses & Trading B.V., Leimuiderbrug, the Netherlands
Baum- und Rosenschule Werner Noack, Gütersloh, Germany
Klaas Noordhuis, Leens, the Netherlands
Poulsen Roser ApS, Fredensborg, Denmark
Sächsische Landesanstalt für Landwirtschaft, Dresden-Pillnitz, Germany
Mr A. van Schaik, Winschoten, the Netherlands
Jan Spek Rozen B.V., Boskoop, the Netherlands
Dr. Burkhard Spellerberg, ADR, Hannover, Germany
Rosen Tantau, Uetersen, Germany
Tuincentrum Lottum, Lottum, the Netherlands
Rozenkwekerij Van der Woning, Wagenberg, the Netherlands
Vaste Keurings Commissie (VKC) Aalsmeer, the Netherlands
Jac Verschuren-Pechtold BV, Haps, the Netherlands
Ted Verschuren, Haps, the Netherlands
Rozenkwekerij De Wilde, Bussum, the Netherlands